CREATING AND PLANNING THE CORPORATE DATA BASE SYSTEM PROJECT

CREATING AND PLANNING THE CORPORATE DATA BASE SYSTEM PROJECT

Leo J. Cohen

Q.E.D. Information Sciences, Inc.
Wellesley, Massachusetts 02181

CREATING AND PLANNING THE CORPORATE DATA BASE SYSTEM PROJECT

Printed in the United States of America

Library of Congress Catalog Card Number: 81-52903

International Standard Book Number: 0-89435-050-1

Contents

CHAPTER 1
OVERVIEW OF THE DATA BASE SYSTEM PROJECT

Consideration of the data base problem begins with drawing a distinction between the traditional file system and a generalized data base system. Although the differences are subtle, they are of fundamental importance, particularly if it is accepted that a data base system represents an extensive commitment in terms of manpower, money, computer time, and general organizational resources.

In gross terms one can say that the data base system is data oriented, while the traditional file system is function oriented. Speaking broadly, the file oriented system is a dead end in terms of the data it represents. On the other hand, the data base system is, by implication, capable of growth into new problem solutions, new data, and new applications. It offers, in fact, the potential for creating a corporate data resource.

FILE SYSTEMS

To illustrate the difference between the traditional file oriented approach and a generalized data base system, consider the problem of inventory management. As with any problem, its statement can be thought of as a set of objectives or requirements for that problem; for example, inventory relief against current orders, back ordering, raw materials and finished goods management. It is then the job of a system analyst to determine the nature of these objectives and how best to meet them. Furthermore, the analyst must express his solution to the problem in the form of a set of functions to be implemented through specified logical relationships.

These relationships are usually stated in flowchart form, which has as its objective the computer implementation of what is now considered as the solution to the problem, in this case, the inventory management problem. Thus, the problem as originally specified has derived a set of programs whose execution implements the solution to that problem. The data associated with these programs has the important property that it is arranged and organized to provide optimal performance for their execution. In other words, the arrangement of the files, their distribution over devices, and any internal organization that they may be given are all chosen with respect to achieving optimal performance in terms of the programs for which they were constructed. This means that they are organized according to the dictates of particular programs for the purpose of maximizing the program's performance efficiency, not the information use of the data content of the files.

Problem-Program-Data

Figure 1.1 illustrates this relationship between the problem, the programs, and the files for a problem. As can be seen, this is a linear relationship which implies that the problem derives the programs which in turn derive the files. Growth will only occur in terms of data volume, and will necessarily always be associated with the particular problem for which the system was organized.

It is in this sense then, that the traditional file system approach is a dead end. That is, the data in the files for a particular set of programs is generally unavailable for other problems and the programs that they may in turn derive. This is not to say that such data is unusable, but rather that in order to be effective, it may be necessary to preprocess the files of one system into a different form or format for use in a second, different system. The "spin-off" file is the usual medium for this. Consequently, common data spreads throughout the various files, leading to considerable data redundancy. In addition, each new problem must either work from its own data entirely, or provide utility programs for preprocessing data in already existing files.

File Oriented System

Figure 1.1

Program/Data Relationship

What all of this says is that there is a fixed relationship between programs and data in the file oriented system. A set of data goes with a set of programs, and vice versa. Furthermore, the set of programs is rather self-contained with respect to its data, since these programs must also include the responsibility for its management. In this sense there is an almost rigid, one-to-one relationship between programs and data. To observe this in an extreme case, look at any tape oriented system. There is little hope of severing the tape files from the programs that process the data these tapes hold.

Program/Data Dependence

Another issue to be taken up with respect to the file oriented system has to do with program/data independence. As was pointed out, the application program essentially determines the structure and organization of the files on which it operates in the file oriented system. Both the format of the data and its field structure or syntax are functionally described by the logic of application programs in terms of the operations that they carry out in order to process it. Similarly, the physical and logical organization of data in such files is known to the application program and therefore is reflected in the logic of both its writing and its execution. It follows that if any change is made in such files, there will be a direct impact on the application program itself. Consider two simple examples.

In the first case, let us suppose that a ten byte field must be expanded to fifteen bytes. If our application program has been designed to handle ten bytes, in the sense that instructions were written to carry out specified manipulations and calculations within the parameters of this field size, then a change in size would require a change in this part of the program. Furthermore, those portions of the application program which are dimension dependent will have to be changed. That is, if the application expected the next field after the one of present interest to be in a certain work space position, then that position has been shifted by five bytes so that any such explicit specification in the application program will have to be changed as well.

Now consider a second example where the format of a particular field is changed from, say, BCD to binary. Obviously this calls for a change in the application program, since its processing has presumably been written relative to the BCD format, and conversion will have to be supplied at each point where this data is employed in the application.

In both of these examples we see that the application program is very much dependent on the data and its arrangement in the file. If any change occurs to the data and its arrangement, the application program must be changed as well. Clearly this is not a serious difficulty with just one or two programs, but in a large system, any such change to a single file might involve many application programs and expensive man-hours of program maintenance.

File Oriented Utilities

If there is a one-to-one correspondence between programs and the files of data on which they operate, and if these programs are strongly dependent on the data in these files, then it follows that the management of that data, i.e., addition, deletion and update, must be accomplished by a set of programs which have specific intelligence about the data.

To put this differently, we might say that the file oriented system demands that its data management utilities be associated with specific data just as application programs are. Furthermore, these utilities will be data dependent, as the application programs are. Thus the program's dependency and its rigid relationship to a set of data in the file oriented system creates a need for dependency in the utility functions, and a similarly rigid relationship.

New Problems and Redundant Data

A proper perspective must be adopted when considering data base systems in relation to file oriented systems. We must keep in mind that the file oriented systems do indeed work -- that most payrolls, for example, are produced by these techniques. File oriented systems, furthermore, can be efficient in terms of processing capability.

A problem arises, however, when the data they contain is apparently useful in another data processing problem context. It is at this point that the limitations of the file oriented system become apparent. Common data subsets are created, redundant utilities must be developed, and the net result is redundant processing to accomplish simple data processing ends.

Common Data Subsets

As the data used in one problem area is employed for application to other problem areas, common data subsets are developed in various programming systems. For example, consider a personnel file which is used to operate a personnel information system. If a second system is designed to keep track of work station hours by employee, then there is certain data in the personnel file that would be valuable in this regard. This data consists of the employee's name, his employee number, department, and so on.

It is safe to assume that the format in which the data is carried in the employee file may not be satisfactory for application to the hours station system.

Furthermore, the data as it appears in the employee file might have been organized in a certain sequence -- for example, alphabetical order by name -- whereas in the work hours processing system we may require organization by department, and within department, by employee number. Thus, not only will the format of the data change, but its organization as well. It is for such reasons that we have common data subsets throughout the data processing environment, with the format and the organization different in each case.

Redundant Utilities

It is an observable fact of the computing industry that the cost of peripheral storage is rapidly reducing. This lessens our interest in minimizing data redundancy and moderates this as a motive for taking the data base approach. But the difficulties with the file oriented system and the redundant data it creates go well beyond this.

In the first place, if data has been abstracted from a given file and reorganized, reformatted, and merged into a second file for use by a separate application system for a new problem, then the utilities for the management of that data must be separate as well. That is, an update utility, a delete utility, a compaction utility and so on, must all reflect the specific formats and physical structures of the files on which they operate. Because such structure is intimately connected with the application programs that process the data in the files, there is no generality to the structure, and as a consequence, each application program system requires a set of management utilities for the data that it carries in its associated files.

Thus, the traditional or file oriented approach to data processing not only creates redundant data but sets up utilities to operate, organize, and generally manage that data. Because these utilities carry out essentially common functions, they represent redundant systems.

Figure 1.2 illustrates two sets of data, each associated with its individual programming systems. One of these sets, however, has had data derived from the other. This data is designated as X. Let us suppose system A was delivered first and then the development team for system B discovered that data X within system A would be of use. As we have described it thus far, that data was abstracted from the data of system A, perhaps reformatted and reorganized, and then incorporated with the data of system B. Now we have common data subsets in these two systems, attached but independent utilites for managing the data of these two systems, and a redundant execution of the utilities. To see this, consider any activity or function which updates the data of system A. Such an update process will operate on the data subset X and bring it to a current state. Of course, it is now out of synchronism with the same data X associated with system B, and it is therefore necessary to run the utilities for system B so that the common data subset X can be updated there as well.

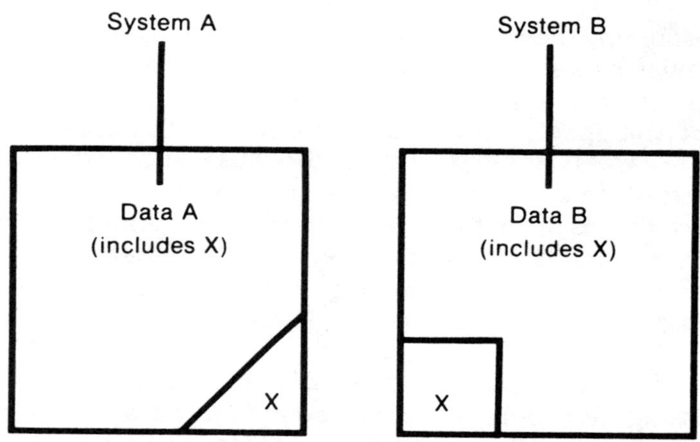

Figure 1.2/REDUNDANCY

The Currency Problem

Often file oriented systems involve sets of files where data is made purposely redundant in order to meet several objectives simultaneously. For example, the employee payroll file may carry employee names and organize all payroll records alphabetically by those names. In addition, the employee names will appear in the job assignment file which is organized by job within department. Now suppose that a female employee gets married and the payroll department changes her last name on its records. Until that change is made in the job assignment file, the two systems taken together, for all intents and purposes, identify two employees. It will, therefore, be impossible to draw reports from the data of these two files that are based on a name commonality until the name data in the two files is made concurrent.

This simple example illustrates a basic difficulty with large, file oriented systems, namely that of the currency of common data across files. Thus, reports received in one department may not agree with reports in a second department simply because those reports are based on two different files of data and synchronism in the values of common data that they employ cannot be maintained.

Integration Problems

At one time or another everybody in data processing has heard the complaint, "I know the data is down there, but they claim they can't give it to me." What this means, of course, is that the data necessary to satisfy someone's data processing interest is available, but the way in which it is available makes it unfeasible if not impossible to use. This occurs most frequently when data in two different file oriented systems must be combined to suit the information needs which the data jointly supports. Thus, in the file oriented system, where data is arranged with respect to the programs that process it, additional difficulties are raised in accomplishing any degree of integration of the data taken as a whole with respect to new problem applications.

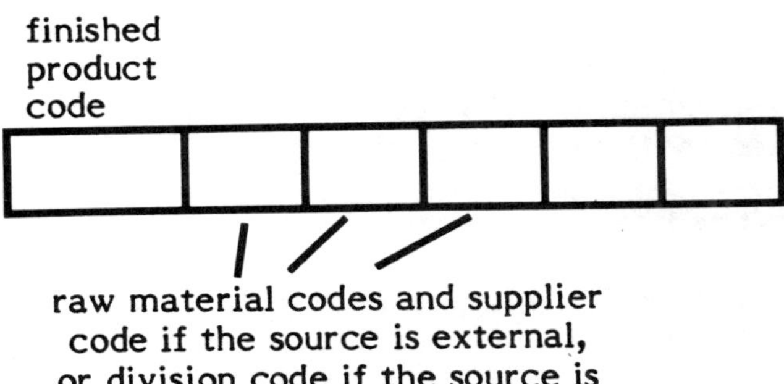

One can restate this by saying that in a file oriented system, it is difficult to consider the total data as a general resource, but rather only as a resource for the specific programming function it supports. For instance, suppose that we have an inventory of finished products but carry in its inventory coding further information about the raw materials and their source, as illustrated above. Suppose also that these records are kept in sequence by inventory code made up of all of these codes in the sequence shown.

At the same time, we have a purchasing file that provides us with data about raw material purchases by time and supplier. That data may appear in records in sequence by raw material code as follows:

Supplier code

Raw material code

Purchase code

Consider now any problem involving finished products and dates. For example, "What suppliers provided the most raw materials of type X, Y, Z for finished products A, B, C, D, E, in the time period T?" Clearly, "the data is down there," and just as clearly, a new programming system will have to be written to integrate it into a useful whole by-passing each of these files separately and sorting into corresponding sequences. Figure 1.3 illustrates an overview of the process that might be required. It also implies that programming is needed, along with testing, and human and computing resources as well.

Spin-Off Files

One method for integration in a file oriented system is the spin-off file. In this approach, a program is written which passes the data which it contains and which is of interest in system B and to its process. This pass produces the data in a separated temporary file. In all likelihood, it also reformats, and possibly reorganizes, the data to suit the needs of the system to which it will be applied. The spin-off file then becomes an input to the second process. The difficulty here is that the spin-off operation is essentially a redundant execution much like the redundant utility execution discussed above. This is a price that must frequently be paid in file oriented systems if a wider use of data is to be accomplished.

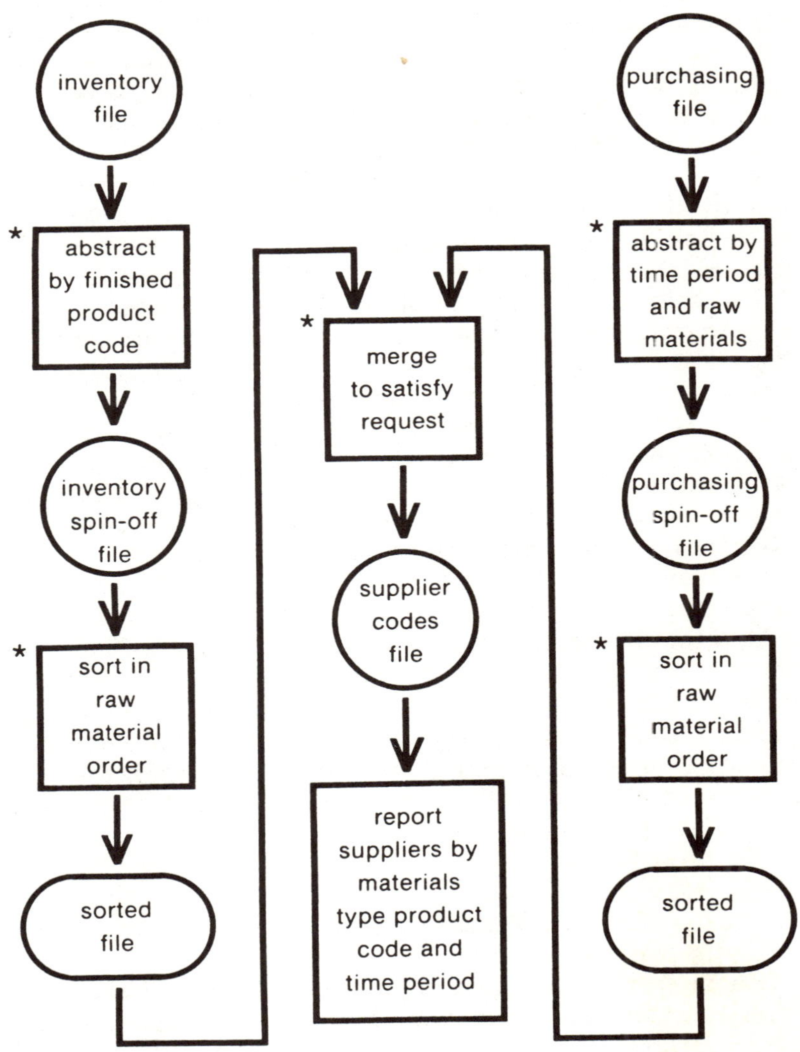

Figure 1.3/SPIN-OFF SYSTEMS

Integration by Programming

There are many circumstances in which an application program system can be written to use the data or a subset of the data in a current system A, and a second, different subset of data in a current system B in order to produce data for a second application. Full passes are made, spin-off files are created, the data required is abstracted, reformatted, possibly reorganized, and merged to suit the needs of the second application. In essence then, we have created an integration of data in these two current systems for the purposes of our second application by integrating that data via programs. In a data base system environment, we will see that by means of file relationships we can create structures that provide an integration of data within the data base itself, so that there will be no need for special programs that integrate this data. In fact, the major difficulty with integrating data by programming is that the integrating program is not part of the problem being solved, but rather a means of circumventing the limitations of the data processing environment. In the example of Figure 1.3 this is illustrated by the processes marked with an asterisk. Thus, the skill levels required of the designers and the programming staff go well beyond that required for solution of the problems of interest to the organization. As a consequence, the organization discovers that a rather significant part of both its data processing development and execution is associated with this essentially unproductive activity of non-problem solving data processing.

DATA BASE SYSTEMS

Looked at in the strongest light, virtually all of the difficulties that we have cited with the file oriented system stem from the way in which we have thought about our data processing problems. That is, the problem has derived the programs which in turn derive the files on which these programs will operate. This means that there is a fixed relationship between the files and the program, which in turn creates the utilities problem, the redundancy problem, the synchronization problem and all of the other difficulties noted in the foregoing discussions. We turn now to some of the properties of a data base system, and the qualities and characteristics that it exhibits with respect to our thinking in data processing terms.

Problem-Data-Programs

Where the file oriented system is essentially program oriented, the data base system is oriented toward its data base. This view of the data base system is represented schematically in Figure 1.4. There again a particular problem is the starting point for a data base system.

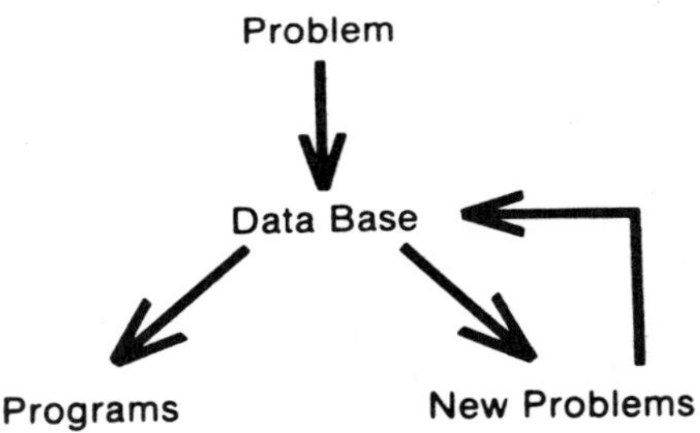

Figure 1.4/DATA BASE SYSTEM VIEW

This problem may be thought of as a set of "problems" which are jointly under consideration for implementation via the data base approach. Notice, however, that the data base problem does not derive a set of programs, but rather a data base which is designed to contain all data elements necessary for any implementation and solution of the given problems, without specification of just what those solutions might be in their programmatic form. To put this somewhat differently, the data base is designed for generality -- for flexibility and extensibility -- both in the various record designs that it encompasses and in the several files that it may include. As the figure suggests, once that data base is established, the next step is to design and implement those programs that will operate on the data base in order to provide solutions to the original set of problems.

Thus the structural relationship between the problem, the program and the data is much different in the data base system environment. That is, we begin with the problem, proceed to the data base and its data, and from there write programs that will satisfy the needs of the problem. This difference in procedure in the data base system is its fundamental philosophical difference in comparison with the file oriented system.

The Data Base as a Generalized Resource

Far more important, however, is the generality of the data base and its organization. The vastly expanded availability of data will suggest new problems over and above the original problem set that initiated the data base system in the first place. That is, the data base or "data bank" is a resource to be drawn upon by the community of users in the system's environment. As an example, the data base necessary to inventory management may in large part also be necessary to other operations such as order management, where orders are drawn against available and backlog inventory, and cause the relieving of that inventory. It follows that with a data base available for inventory management, the order management problem may then be suggested.

Program/Data Independence

It should be clear from the foregoing that one quality a data base system achieves is the centralization of the data and its treatment as a community resource. This implies that the programs necessary for managing and manipulating the data as a physical entity may be centralized as well, obviating the requirement for individual file utilities that the traditional approach to data processing dictates, because the necessary data management activities can be carried out on this centralized community of data.

This centralization will also allow for standardization of format specification, syntax, and general data base architecture. Consequently, the utilities for managing the data base can include programs for satisfying the requirements of any data base user. Furthermore, the actual architecture of the data base can be made transparent to the users. Application programs may then be several steps removed from direct dependence on the architecture of the files on which they operator. This is clearly in the direction of program/data independence.

Currency and Redundancy

The problem of currency in the data base still remains. That is, there is no guarantee, and in many cases not even a necessity for, a minimum of redundancy in the data. As a consequence, currency issues will arise where two elements of the data base may be identical in semantics and therefore redundant, but at once resident in different files of the data base. Data base systems still require that the application program environment assume resonsibility for currency (where such redundancy exists). The minimization of redundancy is, however, indeed far simpler to achieve in a data base system environment where centralized control of the management of data is available.

Because so much of file oriented data processing has to do with physically sequenced files there is usually a significant time lag in achieving currency via the spin-off method. In a data base it is not necessary that the records be sequenced physically but rather only logically. This is accomplished by file organization so that arbitrary sequences can be structured in the data for sequential processing without the need to abstract, reproduce, reorganize, and merge. This means that both a reduction of data redundancy and the elimination of sorting to produce new physical arrangements for sequential processing can be achieved, thereby vastly shrinking the currency time lag.

Data Bases and Data Base Systems

All of us in data processing have been operating for years on data bases. That is, any collection of information formulated to be operated in a computing system environment may indeed be thought of as a data base. Thus, card files, tape files, discs and drums are individually data bases, and jointly form a data base. The difficulty is that there is no integrative, organizational quality to this data base other than that defined by the specific programs which operate on the individual units of data in their respective files. Obviously, what is needed in such data bases is some form of systematization providing an organization of the data that results in a community data resource designed to support a community of users.

The Encyclopedia in a Barrel

It is quite simple to illustrate with an everyday example of a data base what the difference is between a data base and a data base system. Consider the encyclopedia on the shelf at home. If we cut each article out of the encyclopedia and throw it into a barrel, mixing up the pages as we go, it is clear that the information content of the encyclopedia has not been lost. That is, the original encyclopedia data base is in fact still contained in our encyclopedia in the barrel.

What has been lost, of course, is any kind of systematization, and as a consequence we do not have an encyclopedia data base system. Now if we want to find information on the actions of the British government during the great Irish potato famine it would be necessary to go through the barrel article by article looking for key words in each of the titles. This is clearly the brute force method, and is indeed applicable to the searching of any file in a computing system whether it is imbedded in a data base system environment or not. Of course it is not satisfactory from the point of view of the user, since it can take a good deal of time, and even less satisfactory from the point of view of the owners of the system because it is extremely expensive in terms of utilization of the system's resources.

Encyclopedia on the Shelf

Now let's put the encyclopedia back together in its more usual form. If we started with the materials in our barrel then we would have to choose a key word in each of the titles, sort all of the articles by those key words, and then segregate the articles into books based on groups of key words in alphabetical sequence. If we wish to find something about Ireland we would look for the "I" book on our shelf, and then within the "I" book search alphabetically for a title containing the word "Ireland" in it.

In addition to this sequential order by key word in the title, the encyclopedia also provides us with a second mechanism for entry to its data base. This mechanism is the index usually carried at the back of the encyclopedia which provides a set of prominent words in the articles themselves that are key for finding articles containing those words. Thus in the index we could look up the word "Ireland" and there find a list of pages in which the term "Ireland" appears in the content of the associated articles. As an interesting aside, it should be noted that in order to determine the articles in which there is information concerning the role of Britain in the great Irish potato famine, we might go to the index, look up "Britain" and get the list of page numbers in which such a reference occurs, then look up "Ireland" and get a list of page references for this subject as well. If "famine" were listed in our index as a topic, then the page numbers associated with it could also be abstracted, so that finally by merging together all of the page numbers for "Britain," "Ireland" and "famine," we would end up with the set of page numbers that are common to all three terms. Obviously the articles on these pages are about these three topics.

There is a proper data processing file organizational term for the type of indexing just described. At this point, however, it is only important to recognize that the file organization itself is associated with, and in part derives from, the organization of the data in the data base into some structured arrangement. Thus the data in our encyclopedia data base is much different from the data in our barrel data base in that it has organization and structure, and therefore we can apply systematic methods for making reference to and use of the data that it contains.

Growth Potential

Figure 1.4 shows that the data base both suggests and derives new problems for inclusion in the data base system. These new problems will draw on the existing data base for their design and ultimate implementation. The figure also suggests that the completion of new problems will cause additional data to be gathered and incorporated into the already existing data base. That is, the existence of the data base suggests new problems, which in turn may add additional data to the data base. This data addition is the growth potential that is a basic motive for the data base approach. As a consequence, as more data of varied type becomes available within the data base, problems of ever widening organizational interest become possible for implementation.

The Bowling League Data Base System

Suppose that we would like to structure a data base system for managing the data and general information of the bowling league in our company. The first question according to the discussions we have had so far is what data must be present in the data base to support a bowling league data base system. The answer clearly would go something as follows:

BOWLER'S NAME
HOME ADDRESS
HOME TELEPHONE NUMBER
JOB TELEPHONE NUMBER
TEAM NAME
HANDICAP
CURRENT AVERAGE
etc.

Given this sort of information and a mechanism for entering new data as it is created during the team play, it should be evident that we have a data base against which we may calculate the current standings of the teams in the league and the individual performance of each of the bowlers.

Now consider the following scene on one of the league nights. The personnel director belongs to one of the teams and has just finished his turn in a match. Our bowling analyst, who has designed and implemented the bowling league data base system, is operating a terminal borrowed from the company which he has plugged into the computer via telephone connection. As each bowler rolls, his scores are entered by our bowling analyst, and we therefore have an immediate summary of the status of the matches. Our personnel director observes all this and on inquiry discovers that the number of bowling employees represents approximately 45% of the total number of employees of the company, and therefore by adding the names, addresses, home telephone numbers, and work telephone numbers of the remaining employees he will have that information for everybody. If he then in addition, adds the department code, job description, experience, wage, etc., for all employees, our personnel director will allow the data base to grow from its current application for personnel management.

The Growth Performance Problem

The foregoing illustrates the growth potential of the data base system environment. It derives from the fact that the data itself is considered as a resource and is generally available, up to privacy constraints, and by arbitrary methods of reference, to any user of the data base system environment. The problem which the growth potential raises, however, can be significant, namely maintenance of performance in the face of growth.

To put this differently, consider the case where it is necessary that our bowling league data base system provide a complete analysis of the current standings of the teams in the league within one minute. If the system is designed for this purpose and implemented successfully, then indeed this requirement will be satisfied and those people interested in the bowling league data base system, namely the bowlers, will see the system as a success.

Now let's assume that the personnel department gets its data base system up. The data base system to support personnel needs to share a significant portion of its data resource with the bowling league data base system. As a consequence, there may well be a degree of interference between these two systems in their run time utilization of this data. The example here is extreme since we bowl in the evening and do our personnel analysis during the day, but the point is made that since data is a shared common resource in a data base system environment, then new applications of that data must be carefully understood, analyzed and developed so as to preserve the performance achieved in the already extant data base and the systems it supports.

DATA BASED DATA PROCESSING

Halfway through the 1960's it probably would have been possible to coin a term such as "computer based data processing." The intention of such a term would be to imply that while all organizations process data in order to manage their affairs, only some of those organizations use computers. If we think in terms of "computer based data processing" as meaning a situation in which an organization carries out virtually all of its data processing activities via the computer, then we can see some parallel sense to the term "data based data processing."

The notion of data based data processing is one in which an organization carries out its data processing activities in the context of a data base system environment. That is to say, the data processing activities largely rely on a common data resource, referred to as the data base, and this resource supports virtually all data processing activities of interest to the organization. In this sense, data based data processing might be thought of as the long term objective for an organization getting into the data base approach. This long term objective is designed to suit the needs of three broad classes of data processing users, classified as the end user, organizational management and systems development. Each of these not only has a stake in data processing, but potentially can reap certain benefits from the data based data management environment.

Outlet	Merchandise Class 1	2	3	4	5
Meridian	11306	12192	5041	7861	1428
Platt	9424	14177	3491	8650	1559
Hopefield	11700	10146	8946	8700	2142
28th St	9006	8090	4989	5800	768

Figure 1.5/REPORT AS A DATA BASE

End Users

The end user of a computing system, whether he approaches it via a card punch machine, an RJE terminal, or an intelligent terminal is generally restrained in the activities that he can carry out by the degree of data processing support provided. This is not to say that the user cannot think for himself, but rather that there are limits to what he can do.

To make a simple example, consider a retail buyer who receives a weekly report, a portion of which is shown in Figure 1.5, on current sales by outlet location and merchandise class. This report in effect represents a data base with but a single key, namely, outlet location. That is, the buyer can specify a given outlet location, find the corresponding line entry in the report, and read off current sales in each of the merchandise classes. The buyer may sometimes wonder which outlets have current sales in the range of $8,000 to $10,000 for a particular merchandise class, but in order to determine this, he would have to scan the entire column of the report for that merchandise class. This is admittedly not a trivial task if the reoprt has any volume, even though the query, in data base terms, is a simple one. But here is another query that would render the manual task all but impossible: What outlets have lower sales in merchandise class 3 than in class 4, and have class 1 sales greater than $10,000, or class 5 sales less than $1,000? Faced with the manual processing involved, it is likely that our buyer would go immediately to other things.

Consider now a data base system environment which, instead of producing the report on paper, stores it in the data base as part of the data base system. This makes all of the access methods of the data base package available for referencing the report, but more importantly, all elements of the report can now be considered as potential keys and the query capabilities of the data base system may be employed to investigate questions such as those posed above, and a broad spectrum of arbitrary inquiries that go well beyond them.

It is this aspect of data base which can expand the user's thinking about the job that he does. By making data and its derivative information available in arbitrary, easy to specify form, the thinking that he would devote to the process of manufacturing the information can now be expended in exploring some of the horizons that such information makes available. Thus the advent of data based data processing support may indeed radically modify the way in which he envisions his function, plans for its operation, and finally carries it out.

Organizational Management

It has been said that a successful data base system that achieves a high degree of data based data processing must necessarily become a model of the organization itself.

That is, an organization's activities at present and as projectable into the future are to a very large degree dependent on the ways in which information flows through the organization and interacts with the organizational elements that process, manipulate and employ it.

A data based data processing environment, in which a significant amount of the information processing of an organization is supported by data base, is therefore a mirror of this information flow and, as such, forms a model of the organization's activities. In this context then, where information flows throughout the organization, the mode of organizational management becomes one of monitoring performance at critical points of interest, and synthesizing the information thus gathered into tactical and strategic planning. This represents the true function of organizational management.

Thus the data base system environment not only provides the model of the organization in the sense described above, but because of the access that it offers to the data base, which in turn is part of the data base system environment, it is clear that the monitoring of information flow in the organization is the equivalent of inquiring into the data base system. Obviously, any data base system that incorporates services to support organizational management is one that is prepared to offer that management new latitudes of flexibility. In fact, in terms of management functions this may well represent new dimensions of organizational control. It is the accuracy, responsiveness, and timeliness of information about the organization and its operation that gives this dimension meaning and ultimately makes it one of the most powerful motives for considering the data base approach.

Systems Development

The third strong motive for considering the data base approach has to do with the development of new application systems. As pointed out earlier, the file oriented approach looks at each problem separately. We specify a problem, derive algorithms for its implementation, and directly associate programs with data in files. This implies that the data has essentially one functional application, so that any subsequent use of the data demands that it be abstracted from the file, reorganized to suit the needs of the new application and replicated for that purpose. The data is redundant, but furthermore a new application also requires the development of additional programs to prepare, present and maintain the data.

In the data base system environment one of the major virtues is that the data base provides data as a community resource for its community of users. This means that data that is present in the data base is available to all current users (up to privacy and security considerations) and therefore becomes a major building block -- already constructed -- in the planning and implementation of new systems development. This also implies that if the data base grows, this resource of already developed data modules grows as well, and one consequence has to be that system design and implementation schedules are ultimately foreshortened, since new systems build primarily on what currently exists.

This point becomes more forceful when one considers that application programs in a data base system environment are effectively I/O free. That is, all I/O activity that leads to data presented to an application program in a data base system environment is carried out on behalf of the application program by the data base management package. This is achieved in the application by means of a subprogram CALL. Thus there is no direct I/O application program. As a consequence, the application program itself is less complex, easier to write, debug and document, smaller in the execution environment and achievable in greatly contracted schedule time. It also follows that because the I/O dimension has been removed from the application program environment, no longer is it necessary to provide file maintenance programs with each application. And finally, this apprach to application program development offers an unparalleled opportunity for standardization and documentation.

Cost Trend Qualities

We can identify three major cost areas in the general development of data processing. These are design, implementation, and ongoing maintenance of systems. The data base systems environment offers excellent opportunities for achieving significant reductions in cost associated with these. Because of its properties, it follows that in a growing data base resource the subsequent design problems for new application systems that build on the extant data base and the data base system environment must steadily reduce in magnitude as the life of the data base system extends. This is particularly evident in view of the fact that such design efforts no longer need consider the complexities of file construction, operation, and maintenance since these are handled and controlled by the data base management package in the context of the overall data base system environment.

Similarly, implementation for a specific system design should observe a significant reduction in cost. In fact, this should be an absolute reduction so that the cost to implement on a per-line-of-code basis should indeed go down. This occurs because the data base is an extant resource, so that little or no implementation effort with regard to the data is required. It also results from the fact that application program implementations free the programmer from I/O considerations, and the standardization opportunities offered by data base provide a coincident opportunity for true modular program development. This last means that already developed program modules may be considered as a library of available functions that subsequent system development may employ as "black box" elements with an input-output specification. In data base system environments where this approach has been adopted as a specific application programming standard, the impact on implementation costs is dramatic.

Finally, as already pointed out, the maintenance of data is the centralized responsibility of the data base management package. No longer do application programs develop their own utilities for file management and file maintenance on an individual basis, but rather provide only the necessary specifications via the data base management package for having those maintenance activities carried out. Thus we may envision the costs of data to be maintained rather than a non-linearly increasing function of the number of redundant presentations of what would otherwise be common data.

Cost Trend Graph

Figure 1.6 expresses these ideas in graphical form, presenting costs as a function of time in each of the design, implementation and maintenance areas. The time scale for this representation is large, with units in months, or perhaps even quarters. In this context then, the graph represents a situation that presumes the introduction, development, and significant extension of a data base and its data base system environment.

Design Curve

With this in mind, let us look first at the design curve. this begins near the onset of the data base project initiation and rises rather rapidly as the first phase of the data base system project is designed for implementation. It can be seen that the broken line graph for implementation suggests that implementation follows the design, and at this early point in the data base project has a cost which parallels that of the design effort. Note, however, that as time progresses and data base success is recorded, the succeeding stages of the overall data base system project will rely more and more heavily for their design on the existence of the already developed data base.

Looked at in the roughest sense, design for a data base system environment requires design and installation of a data base, plus design of the application programs which will operate on the data base. However, this first element of the design problem is gradually reduced as time continues and the data base grows, so that the design problem for data base ultimately reduces to the problem of application program design for a data base that already exists. Thus

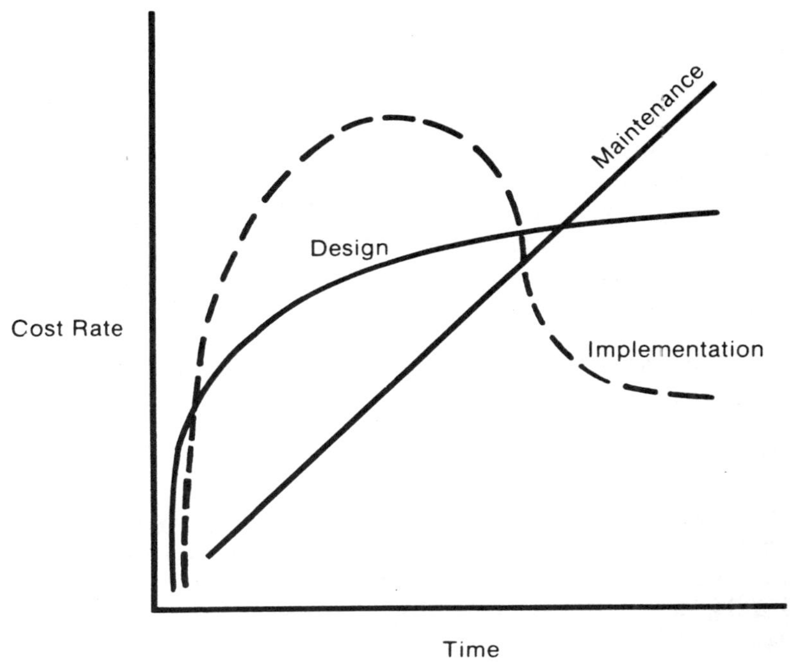

Figure 1.6/COST TREND QUALITIES OF DATA BASE

one would expect the design cost curve to flatten out with time at a level that represents the average rate of new systems development within the organization.

Implementation Curve

The broken curve for implementation cost as a function of time rises rapidly with the design cost, as noted above, hits a maximum and then, as time progresses, falls off dramatically to a greatly reduced cost level. As put forward in the earlier discussions, this is the expected quality of implementation cost performance over time because the data base system environment provides the opportunity for building I/O free programs using modular concepts so that each new development can depend on the data base that already exists and the library of modular elements that have already been developed. Thus there is a threshold area on the time axis, corresponding to maximum implementation cost, throughout which the modular library reaches a point where it has accumulated a significant number of highly useful modules and the data in the data base is supportive of the information needs of a significant proportion of the total end-user population. From this point on then, subsequent implementation can largely rely on these available modules and data resources. It follows, therefore, that their individual implementation costs should drop significantly to a point that represents the cost of maintaining an average rate of new application program implementation.

Maintenance Curve

Maintenance costs for a computing system may be roughly described as dependent upon the numbers of files of data to be maintained. Such files need update, reorganization and purging runs, and therefore a degree of maintenance activity. Hence, maintenance costs for computer operations must be associated with the number of such maintenance activities that must be carried out. It therefore follows that, in a data base system environment which consolidates data by obviating the need to replicate it in order to satisfy the requirements of a new application program system, the number of files, and as a consequence the number of maintenance activities, will be cut back. This suggests that in a data base system environment the cost of maintenance for the data base is directly proportional to the volume of data to be maintained, and on the assumption that this volume grows linearly with time, we expect total maintenance costs to grow in the straight line fashion indicated in the figure.

General Remarks

The data base system approach is high in cost and high in risk. It represents an expensive and long term project that can derive its value only from the payoffs that are available. It must be remembered that as with any large undertaking, the risk of failure is not only in the development costs that may be lost, but in the time costs as well. For most organizations, data processing is an ongoing development, and the diversion of this development mainstream into the data base channel will delay for a time this progress forward. But once data base has become the established method of data processing, development progress can be expected to accelerate with a coincident dramatic reduction in the observed unit costs.

Staged Development

The achievement of data based data processing clearly has a scope that can be considered as company wide. In this context it is not unreasonable to state that it is literally impossible to consider the achievement of data based data processing in one single development step. Therefore it is necessary to conceive of a data base system project as a succession of steps or stages which lead to this overall, long term, large scale objective that we have referred to as data based data processing.

Implementation/Integration

If there is to be a staged development of data based data processing, there must be identifiable, discrete project events which occur, and which in each case deliver a portion of the data base that will support data based data processing and the associated data base system. What this means is that the completion of a stage delivers data based data processing to a portion of our organization. The next stage builds on the data base already extant, and on its completion delivers data based data processing to yet another part of the organization.

Thus we have a process of implementation of new data bases, and the data base systems that they support, and their integration with the already extant data base and its data base system environment. This, in fact, is completely characteristic of data base system development because there is an ongoing cycle of implementation followed by integration, stage by stage, until a significant portion of all data processing activities is encompassed in the data base context. Once we reach this point we might say that we have achieved a staged development of data based data processing in our organization.

Data Base Extension

The implementation/integration process clearly implies that the creation of data based data processing evolves from an extention of the data base at every point of its staged development. This means that there is an incremental development of the data base that ultimately supports data based data processing for our organization overall, and the increments of this development are the project stages. Figure 1.7 is an illustration of a staged development in terms of the growth of the data base itself. In this figure, project stage A is the first effort, and it results in the data base represented by a circle. Project stage B follows A and requires the data in the rectangle for its support. Roughly 70% of this data, however, is already in the data base because of project stage A, and only the data of the shaded area, representing data of a new type, must be added to the already extant data base. Thus the data base grows by virtue of project stage B following project stage A. In the same way, the data represented by the triangle for stage C, and by the hexagon for stage D, are incremental developments of the overall data base for the organization.

The 80% Objective

The power of the data base technique is in its potential for providing a data processing resource that is commonly available to its users as described above. Furthermore, that power, particularly in the context of development, derives from the fact that a significant part of the data required for a project stage should already be available in the data base as the result of earlier stages. This has been suggested in Figure 1.7.

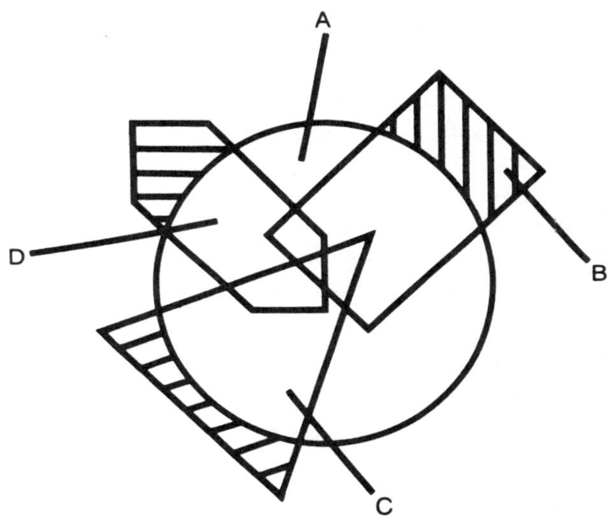

Figure 1.7/DATA BASE GROWTH

If we assume that we have organized our project staging so that each successive stage needs to contribute a progressively smaller fraction to the total data base, then there is a point at which we will discover that virtually all data needed for new project development is in the data base already. As described earlier, this means that its design has been completed, the modes and methods of reference are established, and only the problem of application programming remains.

This is an important watershed point for the data base project, as it represents a level of data requirement after which the data base portion of our effort for any new projects is essentially completed. It is probably reasonable to assume that this occurs when about 80% of our data base requirements have been developed and installed in the data base system environment.

Distributed Data Base Systems

The development of data base and data based data processing seems to have proceeded in parallel with the rapid development of the mini-computer systems. The significance of this is a strong resurgent interest in the notion of distributed processing, and consequently in the concept of distributed data based data processing. This is made possible because the cost of the minicomputer has plummeted while its capabilities and capacities have grown beyond our strongest imaginings. As a consequence, the mini is cheap in absolute terms, and it is very frequently cost/effective to seriously consider distribution of our data processing from a central source, or in combination with a centralized system, to the outlying points of data processing activity. This data processing activity may incorporate data gathering, data manipulation, message switching and any of the other data processing functions with which we are today familiar.

Distributed Processing

The point of distributed processing in this context is that the processing capability for the execution of specific functional activities is moved out from a central site to the functional activity itself. In effect, the hardware is being distributed, as well as some of the software and the responsibility for the processing of certain functional activities. In the general distributed processing context we expect to see a network of computers, a joint load over the network which is distributed to best suit the momentary capacity of the system, and generally a complex communications protocol for moving data, programs and results around the network between the sources and sinks involved.

Distributed Data Base

The problem of distributed data base, and data based data processing in a distributed computing network, is a good deal simpler than the general problems of distributed processing. The reason for this is that we can consider the total network as containing a total data base, with portions of that data base distributed to various nodes of the system. We expect this data base to remain geographically fixed so that there is no movement of data base blocks across the general data base network. The elements of the distribution then consist of the hardware, the data base management package (in terms of functions that may be carried out at various nodes of the overall data base system environment), the data dictionary which describes what part of the data base is associated with which machine of the network and the properties of the data in that machine, and finally the data base itself.

In a well structured distributed data base system, local data bases will be used to mainly support local users. There will then be an approximate hierarchical requirement that is generally related to references made from higher levels of the network by other "foreign" users of this local data. The objective here is to make the data available throughout the network without creating a data transmission overload both in terms of computing capacity and communications costs.

Distributed data base is a fascinating new area of data based data processing and deserves attention by organizations which are seriously considering the distribution of their data processing capability from a central source to the peripheral elements of the organization. It is, however, a subject that is directly dependent on the basic precepts and concepts of data base in general, and data based data processing in particular. In essence then, we may say that a prerequisite for any serious consideration of distributed data based data processing is a solid appreciation and understanding of the centralized data base system.

SEVEN STEPS OF A DATA BASE SYSTEM PROJECT

We have described data bases and data base systems, and have used the term data base system project. It is to this term, with data base set in a project context, that we now turn our attention. There is a good deal of cautionary intention in this since in some organizations such a term might seem rather grandiose, because the data base package itself is viewed as yet another programming language. Thus the responsibility for data base is put into the individual hands of the application system designers and programmers for their respective projects. In such organizations applications are implemented function by function, the package is employed as an access method, and in overall quality the data processing result is a replica of the old file oriented systems, only with more keys available and a larger amount of computing resources consumed.

What is lacking in this unplanned approach to data base is a centralized control over the problem and its implications for the data base system project. By its very nature, as a community of data for a community of users, data base demands a centralized description of the problem environment and the data that supports it, and centralized control of the design, implementation and maintenance of the architectural structures that make the data base system usable and operable by the community of users. All of this clearly suggests some centralized planning with respect to those segments of the organization that will have a vested interest in data base.

To state it succinctly, the data base system problem environment must be defined, and a cost/benefit project environment must be designed. It is therefore our purpose to introduce a formal approach to the development of the data base system project. This centers around seven primary steps, which are:

DATA BASE SURVEY
SERVICE ANALYSIS
DATA DICTIONARY
DATA BASE ARCHITECTURE
PACKAGE SELECTION
COST/BENEFIT ANALYSIS
IMPLEMENTATION SPECIFICATION

Each of these is an essential step in the direction of a

successful data base system project, and each has a specific objective in itself, while at the same time preparing the project for the next steps to follow. That is to say, there is a dependency in the steps and therefore the sequence is important and should be observed.

Data Base Survey

We have mentioned in previous discussions that it is virtually impossible to undertake the achievement of data based data processing in one single stage. This implies that a sequence of steps or stages must be developed which build data bases toward the final data base that will support the data based data processing environment. Therefore, it is necessary to understand what stages are available. It is required of the data base system project that it start somewhere, and prior to the selection of an organizational area in which to initiate the effort, it is necessary to know what areas are available. The achievement of this is the purpose of the data base survey. It is designed to survey the current status of data processing to determine best potential candidates for consideration in the data base system project. These candidates are assessed in terms of risk, benefit and other factors, and then ranked from best choice to least. The data base survey seeks to provide an initial ordering of the stages for the data base system project. This ordering involves not only the major functions which must be supported in the organization, but those functions which are crucial as well.

The data base survey is also concerned with assessing the available resources for the data base system project. This in fact is one of the criteria for the ordering of the candidates. Manpower and skill levels, training history and organizational attitude toward training maintenance are considered. Computer resources are, of course, a central issue, and the organizational structure within which the data base system project will operate must be taken into account. In this last regard the initial issues for the structure and placement of a data base administration facility must be considered.

After the data base survey effort has been completed, the project team has available to it a list of best candidates ranked in preferred order of execution. This is the data base project plan, which is an essential step in the structuring of a formal requirement analysis for the data base system effort.

Service Analysis

It is one thing to know what area of the organization will be supported by a data base system as a result of the project's efforts, and quite another to have a formal description of what that support should be. Since it is clearly impossible to accomplish data based data processing for the entire organization in a single stage, we must break the overall project into successive stages. This suggests that we will accomplish our formal requirement definition stage by stage as well.

The purpose of the data base survey is, among other things, to identify the first stage (at the beginning of the project effort) and the successive stages (as the project progresses) to be tackled in achieving data based data processing. As a result, we are able to turn our attention to some particular area of the organization as the subject of the next project stage in order to define and formally structure a requirement statement for its data base and the data base system environment. This is referred to as the service analysis.

The notion of a service is quite simply any activity that supports the functional responsibilities of an organizational element via the data base. A formal definition would involve certain primitive actions in the data base, but at this stage it is sufficient to say that a service is broadly descriptive of a number of computing events which will result in a particular action that satisfies the needs of individuals in an organizational entity. It is not enough, however, to merely state a data base service without a set of parameters which will make the delivery of the service satisfactory. That is, a service creates action and has delivery constraints.

These are the essential ingredients of a requirement statement for the data base, and serve to fully define a particular service. These service delivery constraints have to do with the frequency of use of the service, the data elements that must be present somewhere in the data base to support the execution and delivery of the service, the computing function applied to those data elements in order to arrive at the results of the service, and the turnaround time performance demands by the users of the service.

These are the primary parameters or constraints on the delivery of a service. Secondary constraints concern the maintenance of the data quality in the data base, establishment of security and privacy, and the requirement for recovery in the face of data base failure and subsequent restart of the data base system environment. It is these two sets of delivery constraints which not only define services but provide the data base system project with a formal requirement statement for the data base and its system environment in meeting the needs of the users supported by these services.

The net result of a formal service analysis therefore is a structure, formatted statement of data base and data base system requirements. This is an essential element in the chain of project activities that leads to a suitable data base architecture and data base system design. Without a formal requirement statement, the users are not heard from, and the designers are isolated from the users and therefore tend to concentrate more on data processing niceties than on service delivery realities. As a consequence, any delivered data base system will in all likelihood satisfy no one. In this context, the formal requirement statement is an absolute must in the project, stage by stage. This formal statement, executed as a service analysis effort, is the keystone second step of the data base system project.

Data Dictionary Development

A data base consists of data occurrences of particular data

element types. A payroll number may be a data element type and the various instances of payroll numbers then represent data occurrences for that data element type. A data base is made up of a collection of data element types and the occurrences of data for each of the data element types. The purpose of the data dictionary is to provide a formal mechanism for associating information about a data element type with information about the data occurrences for that element of the data base. When we do this for all data base elements, we then say we have a data dictionary and can sum up its function by stating that the purpose of the data dictionary is to provide information about the data in the data base.

One objective of the service analysis is to determine what data elements are necessary to support the services that will be delivered by a particular project stage. These data elements will of course appear somewhere in the data base of the associated data base system. Thus, each stage of the project has data elements, those data elements have characteristics and descriptions, and therefore we must have a data dictionary for them. Development of the data dictionary for the next stage of a data base system project will logically follow the requirement definition for that stage since the necessary information is contained in the requirement statement itself.

It should be stressed here that not all of the information is in the requirement statement since only that part of it that has to do with services can be gathered at this point. However, the data dictionary that has been developed at this time is essential to the next step, namely the architectural design of the new data base. On completion of this architectural design effort, the second portion of the data dictionary information can be filled out. This information has to do with both the physical and logical disposition of each data element, certain relationship characteristics that they have in the data base, and such detailed issues as format, syntax and semantics.

With the data dictionary for a given stage completed, the information can be added to the data dictionary for the already extant data base. This of course presupposes that the stage with which we are dealing is some stage subsequent to the first stage of our project. If indeed this is the first project stage, then in formulating our data dictionary we have inaugurated the whole process of data dictionary development in the data base system project. The result of the data dictionary effort is a formal statement of the characteristics of required data elements, and is essential to the next step of the data base system project.

Data Base Architectural Design

The problem of data base design is essentially that of determining where to place the data elements that are specified by the data dictionary. These data elements have "location" in the data base in the sense that they are associated with other data elements to form records, and these records structure files. Then there is relationship, or logical placement, in that data element A in one physical location is logically located relative to data element B in a second physical location. Therefore the problem of data base architectural design is to determine where the data elements, as defined by the data dictionary, are to be located in the data base. The second requirement is to determine what the formats for these data elements will be and how they will be handled in the data base in order to satisfy the service delivery constraints defined by the data base service analysis. In fact all of the necessary information comes from the service analysis, either directly in the information that results from that effort, or indirectly from the service analysis by way of the data dictionary.

It should be recognized that the purpose of the data base and its architecture is to interface users with data. These users reference the data base via the services that support their functional activities. The mechanism of reference is the application program which is written to take advantage of the architecture of the data base in order to provide these services to the users within the delivery constraints, and with a suitable degree of computing system efficiency. However, the problem of architectural design does not stop at the data base itself, but is equally concerned with the overall system environment. The design step in the data base system project therefore uses the results of the service analysis and data dictionary efforts to develop a suitable architecture for the data base that will support effective application programming in the development of the data base system.

DBMS Evaluation and Selection

Generally speaking there is a set of computer functions in the context of the data base system which need to be written one time only. These functions carry out the indexing which map keys into positions in the data base, execute file organizations structured in the data base, provide data conversions, and so on. In fact, we may say that this standard set of routines forms a fixed utility group for the manipulation of the files of the data base. Such a system, though loosely defined here, is already familiar to the reader as a data base management system, or DBMS.

There are a number of commercial DBMS available today. They are not all alike and no one of them is better than all the others. Rather, there is a best choice of DBMS package for a given organization and its problem class. This choice is dictated by the quality of its data processing in general, and the nature of its data processing as represented in a particular current system. Thus the data base survey is instrumental in establishing criteria for determining the type of DBMS package best suited to the organization. However, more specific data in terms of technical issues is available from the service analysis and the data base architectural design step. In fact, with a completed design we can map it into each of the packages of interest to the organization. Thus the issue is what criteria are to be used in deciding which package is best.

There is always some set of potential package features which are of lesser interest to a particular organization. Other features are of extreme importance, and it is necessary for the organization to therefore isolate those features potentially available with a particular DBMS which are of maximum importance to the data processing style of the organization and its data based data processing plans. Thus there is a package selection effort which must be included in the data base system project. The evaluation process is concerned with determining the qualities that the package should have in order to best meet organizational needs, and the selection process is essentially the establishment of formal recommendation data so that the selected package is completely defensible by the data base project team.

Cost/Benefit Analysis

The development of data based data processing is a long term, high risk, large expense project. It needs a justification in the first place, and positive measures of performance and control in the second. The issue of justifying the data base system project on the basis of its cost/benefit performance is essential in any project which will ultimately be identified as well managed. A cost/benefit analysis demands the collection of data regarding both costs and benefits in terms of the effort to provide the services of the data base system, the costs to maintain these services and the supporting data bases, and the benefits accrued as a consequence. The largest part of this type of information is centered on the user of the data base system and the services that support these organizational activities. Therefore, cost/benefit information is best acquired during the service analysis effort leading to the formal requirement statement for the data base.

This type of effort must again be carried out stage by stage. It is necessary to make best estimates at the outset of the project so that a cost/benefit performance prediction can be constructed in order to provide upper management with a large scale picture of the expectations for the project in terms of overall costs and cost rates, expected benefits, and a payroll date in terms of a favorable cost/-benefit ratio. As the project progresses and actual data regarding both costs and benefit is accrued, this cost/benefit statement can be revamped to provide not only accuracy in its predictions of project performance, but in addition to provide controls for the schedule of costs and benefit accruals. Where the schedules observed do not match the schedules planned, project management must institute the necessary investigations.

Implementation Specification

In a data base system project there are three aspects to the problem of implementation. These involve the physical data base description, the application programs for operating on the data base, and the creation and installation of the data in the data base itself.

In the earlier description of the development of an architecture for data base, it was implied that the DBMS to be employed for the implementation was not important to the data base architecture process. That is, the architecture developed for the data base is accomplished independently of any given DBMS. This results in a specification of all the required parametric characteristics of each of the files of the data base.

These characteristics include field specifications and definitions, aggregation of fields into records, record design, physical record distribution, indexing techniques and file organizations. If all this is carried out independently of the DBMS, then one step in the data base system project obviously must be to state this architecture in terms of the DBMS itself. This is sometimes referred to as mapping of the logical data base architecture into the specific physical structures of the given DBMS. The form which it ultimately takes is as a collectin of statements in the data description language of the package. That is, this step of the implementation specification process results in a formal description of the data base in terms of the DBMS.

Operations on the data base itself are invoked by application programs. These application programs may be run as jobs in the jobstream or may operate on transactions received from a communications interface. Whatever the source of activity, it is the application program which executes some logically constructed sequence of call statements on the DBMS. Each of these calls makes the required reference to the data base and accomplishes this in the context of the particular data base architecture and for the specific DBMS. Thus, IMS calls employ segment search arguments and PCB names, while TOTAL calls employ data element lists and linkage path names. Overall the semantics of such call statements are essentially the same for all packages, although the syntax for each of these calls may be different. What is specifically different, however, is the logic of referencing the data base as represented in the application program. That is, the application program will contain some intelligence about the architecture of the data base and will reflect this in the flow chart structure of the program itself. These programs will differ depending on the selected DBMS because of the way in which an individual DBMS describes its data base. In all events, application programs for making reference to the data base must be designed and implemented, and this is the second part of the implementation specification function. It should be noted in addition that the application program portion for making calculations and computations based on data delivered from the data base referencing portions must also be designed and implemented. This is not considered, in the present discussion, to be part of the data base system problem, but rather as belonging to the MIS problem.

Finally, the data base itself must be created. This means that whatever its source, the actual data to be installed in the data base must be aggregated, each of the field values must be formatted according to the definitions given to the DBMS, and then fields of data must be arranged into record occurrences according to the record descriptions for the DBMS. The DBMS prescribes a loading order for record occurrences, and other information regarding designation of specific data as keys, and so on. It is up to the implementation stage of the effort to design and build the necessary data processing programs which will aggregate and organize the data according to the needs of the DBMS in general, and more specifically according to those needs as designed into the particular physical data base architecture as described by the DBMS. This data must then be loaded into the system as files in the data base, and the wise data base administrator will furthermore plan to verify that the proper data is in the proper location of the data base once the loading is complete.

PERSONNEL ROLES

The data base system project will involve a number of people playing a diversity of roles in its execution. Each of these roles can be defined and broadly described in terms of the tasks that are to be executed. These tasks are in turn directy related to the seven steps of the project itself. Therefore, the definition of these project roles will be in terms of the expectation for skills to be achieved and exercised in the completion of the data base system project effort.

General Data Processing Management

General data processing management is ultimately responsible to the upper management of the organization for the progress and overall success of the data base system project. With such responsibility, it is therefore incumbent upon general data processing management to be aware of the nature of the data base system project, and more specifically of activities in certain portions of it. The role for the general data processing manager is to generally understand the methods employed, the analyses that lead to the selection of potential data base system candidates, and the service analysis mechanism that produces the formal requirement statement for the data base system project. The project will develop a data dictionary and from this derive an architecture for the data base that is associated with the initial project stages to be implemented. An awareness of the methods used in the first place, and their application to the data base system project in the second, is important for the role of general data processing management. A central issue at the outset of the project is the selection of a DBMS. Responsibility for making the final decision on the package selection based on information developed by the data base project team rests with general data processing management. This person must also have insight into sources of costs and benefits in the data base system approach. In particular, the cost/benefit models should be of interest, as well as the project controls that can be developed from it.

Technical Data Processing Management

The technical data processing manager who is associated with the data base system project will have technical responsibilities both as supervisor and participant. In addition, it is expected that he will participate in certain decision making responsibilities with the data base administrator in support of final decisions to be made by general data processing management. His roles and responsibilities are with respect to the initial analyses leading to the selection of potential data base candidates, the structuring and conduct of the service analysis, and the formalization of overall data base requirements. He must be aware of the significance of the data dictionary and its content with respect to the data base systems to be implemented, and therefore must understand not only the concept of the data dictionary, but its line of development as well.

In addition, the data dictionary information that arises as a consequence of the data base system project must be analyzed in order to understand the way in which the various data elements are used. The technical DP manager should also participate in the effort required to produce an optimized data base architecture, and to assure that all details of this design are completed. Furthermore, where a package is to be selected, a significant aspect of the role for technical DP management is observed. Here he must participate in the various activities necessary for the structuring of a formal and solidly based package recommendation. The technical manager also has a role to play in the development of a cost/benefit model of the data base system project and its subsequent optimization. The implementation effort will largely be done under the technical supervision of technical management. Therefore he must be aware of the requirements for standards, documentation and modular specification of the overall data base system implementation.

Data Base Administrator

The data base administration responsibilities in a well structured data base system project are both managerial and technical. The data base administrator has responsibility for seeing that various activities and action items of the project are carried out to satisfactory completion in a timely fashion, and he is responsible for the technical quality of the various designs and implementations that result. We can also describe to the DBA certain user oriented functions that have to do with maintaining the quality of the data base and its associated data base system. In this context we might say that the data base administrator has a diplomatic role to play as well. The nature of an operating data base system is such that virtually all performance issues are centralized around the data base, the DBMS, and the application programs. The nature of the data base system project therefore demands that performance be a DBA responsibility.

The Business System Analyst

The business system analyst in the data base system project serves as a guide for the technical personnel in the project with respect to the business activities that the data base system developments will support. It is assumed that the business system analyst acts somewhat as a translator of the data processing department to those functional areas of the organization which data processing serves. In the data base system project the business system analyst will participate in many of those activities which are directly associated with the initial analyses and requirements development. He must be aware of the meaning of the data dictionary and its application to the data base system project in the context of the functional users of the project's results. He will participate in the cost/benefits, and should add his understanding of the organization's methods of operation to the DBMS package selection effort.

Data Base System Designer

The general responsibility for the technical design of the data base system falls on the shoulders of the data base designer. In order to be able to assume that responsibility it is necessary that he understand the methods of analysis employed in the development of the candidates selected for the data base system project, and the service analysis process which results in the formal requirements for the data base system. This is necessary in order to participate directly in the development of the data dictionary and an optimal architecture for the data base. In addition, the data base system designer will play a significant technical role in the evaluation and selection of the DBMS.

Application System Analyst

The application system analyst is responsible for expressing the functional support requirements for the data base system's users in implementable terms. In order to fulfill this role in the data base system project it is therefore mandatory that the application system analyst participate in various aspects of the project development. In particular, he will have a role to play in both the data base survey and the service analysis. These requirements are expressed in the form of services and it is these services for which the application system analyst will have to develop support systems operating in the context of data base. His major obligation, however, is with respect to the development of implementation specifications for the data base system to be delivered. As a consequence, it is necessary for him to be aware of the concepts of the data dictionary and the architectural structure of the data base system itself. Furthermore, the applications system analyst will have to be familiar with the technical aspects of the DBMS that is selected, and in fact may be very close to, if not a participant in, the evaluation and selection effort itself.

Programmer

The programmer has the responsibility for carrying out the actual implementation. It must be remembered, however, that data base system implementations have much larger data processing objectives than the file oriented systems they replace. This demands that the programmer therefore know something more than the set of invocable commands that the DBMS makes available. He must understand the general architectural intent of the data base design, be thoroughly familiar with the data dictionary, and have complete knowledge of the DBMS package characteristics that impact programming and program performance.

Role/Task Matrix

The roles described in the preceding section will participate in various data base system project activities. These activities are listed in matrix form in Figure 1.8 for the individual roles. The activity codes employed are:

NI - not involved
TP - technical participation
TS - technical supervision
MP - managerial participation
MS - managerial supervision
DP - decision participation
DR - decision responsibility
OB - observer

DATA BASE ACTIVITIES CHART

Every data base system project is essentially the same in the sense that they must all accomplish in some degree the major steps of any data base system project. From a more detailed point of view, however, we can identify a set of activities which it is likely every data base system project will execute. These activities can be placed in the context of a chart of actions to be taken leading to the final integrative steps of adding the finished data base system

	General data processing management	Technical data processing management	DBA	Business systems analyst	DB systems designers	Application systems analysts	Programmers
Data Base Survey							
analysis of current DP activities	NI	TS, TP	TP, MS	TP	OB	TP	NI
assess potential for DB	DR	TP, TS	TP, MS	TP	OB	TP	NI
select best DB candidates	NI	TP, TS, DP	TP, DR	OB	NI	OB	NI
Service Analysis							
determine SA size & scope	NI	MP, TP, DP	TS, MS, DR	NI	NI	NI	NI
structure interview sequence	OB	TP	MS, DR	NI	NI	NI	NI
select interview teams	NI	MP, DP	MS, DR	NI	NI	NI	NI
execute interviews	NI	TP, TS	TP, MS	TP	TP	T	TP
manage SA process	OB	MP, DR	MS, DR	NI	NI	NI	NI
Data Dictionary							
create inaugural DD	NI	TP, TS	MS	OB	TP	OB	OB
data element usage analysis	NI	TS	MS	TP	TP	OB	OB
Data Base Architecture Design							
initial data element distribution	NI	TS, TP	MS, TP	TP	TP	TP	OB
testing against services	NI	TS, TP	MS, TP	TP	TP	TP	OB
architecture optimization	NI	TS, DP	MS, DR	TP	TP	OB	OB
DBMS Package Selection							
create weighted requirements list	OB	TS, TP, DP	MS, DR	TP	TP	TP	OB
feature matrix construction	NI	TP, DP	TP, TS, MS	TP	TP	TP	OB
feature matrix analysis	NI	OB	TP, DR	NI	OB	NI	NI
package recommendation	DR	TP, TS, DP	TP, MS, DR	NI	NI	NI	NI
Cost/Benefit Analysis							
data gathering	DOB	TP, TS	TP, MS	TP	NI	NI	NI
structuring the model	NI	DP, TP	TP, DR	OB	NI	NI	NI
project optimization	OB	TP, DP	TP, DR	T	NI	NI	NI
Implementation Specification							
standards development	NI	TP, DP, MP	TP, MS, DP	NI	NI	TP	TP
modular specification	NI	TP, TS, MP	MS	NI	NI	TP	TP

Figure 1.8/ROLES AND TASKS

project for the current stage to the already extant data base and its data base system environment. The data base activities chart shown in Figure 1.9 is designed to illustrate these general data base activities and the order in which they will occur.

The project begins with initial interest in data base, usually with respect to a specific data processing problem area. This means that an important function in the organization is not adequately supported by data processing and it becomes apparent that there may possibly be significant payoffs in adopting the data base approach. Of course, it should be recognized at the outset that a single data processing problem area does not warrant the development of an entire project to achieve data based data processing for the organization overall. But assuming that the prompting of this problem area lead to a wider investigation which suggests an initial rationale for data base, then the project would be initiated with the next two activities shown in Figure 1.9 proceeding in parallel.

The first of these is the data base survey designed to elaborate all organizational areas that can be viewed as potential candidates for treatment in the data base context. Simultaneously, we should be able to investigate data administration in our organization as it stands today and data base administration as a potential organizational entity. Our interest here is in the first draft of data base administration functions in terms of the roles that the DBA will play in the data base system project.

The direct result of the data base survey is a data base system project plan. This plan will establish the proposed sequence of the staged development of the data base toward the 80% objective. One of these stages will be first, and therefore the data base survey effort should conclude with a detailed plan for execution of the service analysis in this initial area.

With a service analysis plan in hand we are then able to simultaneously execute the service analysis and develop the associated data assurance requirements, while at the same time security, privacy and restart requirements are being established. These together make up the service analysis effort and result in a formal requirement statement for the data base system project stage. We therefore have sufficient information to inaugurate our data dictionary so as to use it to develop the architecture of the data base for this project stage.

If this is indeed the first project stage of a data base system effort, it is at this point that it is necessary to evaluate and select a DBMS package. This is done in the context of the needs of the first project stage, with, of course, the data processing requirements as elicited by the data base survey as additional background information. Once a package evaluation and selection has been completed we can then begin our general design of application program systems on the data base, the general designs for both the data base itself in the context of the package, and any data communications with which our data base system stage will be associated.

As these efforts are completed we should be in a position to structure a cost/benefit analysis which takes into account the impact of the package that has been selected for the design and implementation of the data base system, stage by stage. The cost/benefit analysis should result in a cost/benefit model followed by the development of implementation standards and documentation structures suited to the needs of the data base be developed for the organization.

With standards and documentation requirements laid down we then should be able to initiate data base system specification for the design and implementation of the application programs that will operate on the data base itself, and for the conversion and installation of the data of the data base. This requires test planning and quality control development so that we can be assured of the quality of the initial data base on its installation.

At some point, the resultant data base system is ready for

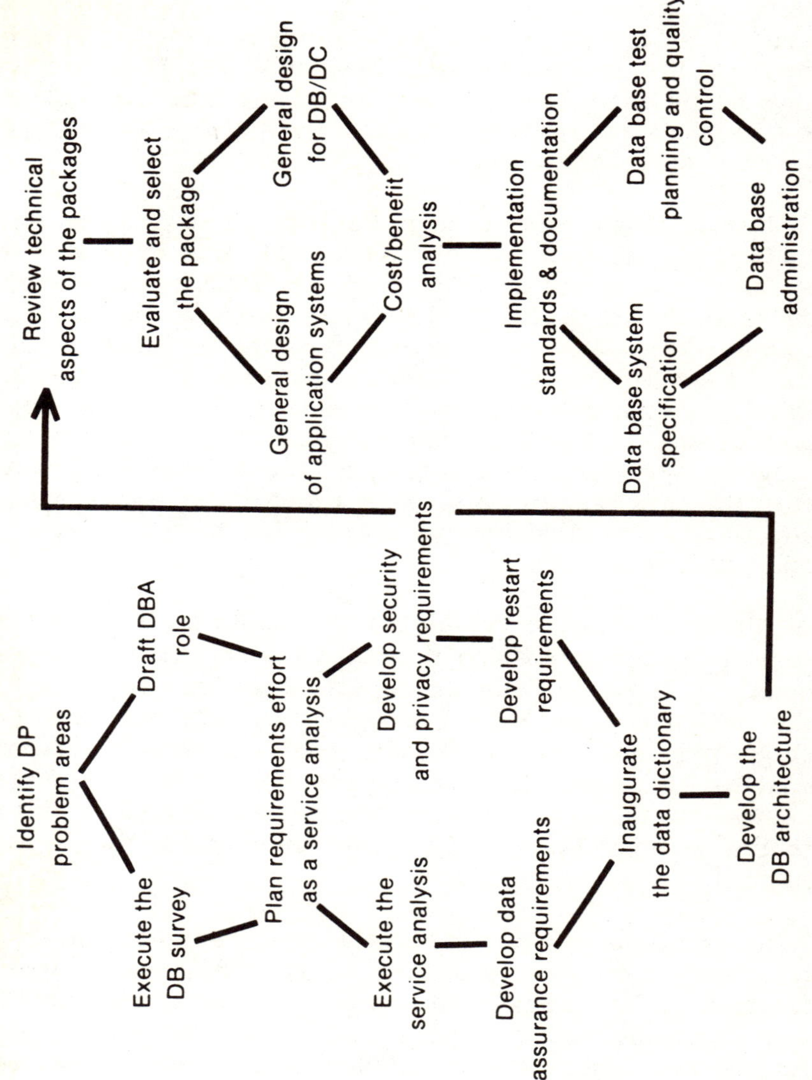

Figure 1.9/DB ACTIVITIES CHART

testing. Data base administration has, of course, been active throughout all of the steps for the data base system project, and it is here that its responsibilities culminate in overseeing the testing, installation and integration of the completed data base system project stage.

DATA BASE APPLICATION PACKAGES

All of the discussions of this chapter surely have the potential of suggesting that the data base approach is charged with complexity and risk. At the same time it may be apparent that data processing in the organization is not working as well as it should; that the payback for the cost of DP does not seem significant. There is the feeling that something should be done, but that more of the same isn't it. It is at this point that buying a "turnkey" package for a specific application area begins to be attractive. These are often built on a particular DBMS and it seems as if two birds can be got with a single stone.

Packaged Applications

The vendor of a data base application program package starts out by identifying an industry and within that industry, an application area for which a worthwhile market seems to exist. The vendor then develops a system that satisfies a statement of requirements for the particular application area across that industry in general.

Since, however, the breadth of the market is of paramount importance to the vendor, the requirements statement on which the system is built is often strong on generality, but weak on detail. The vendor tries to hide the complexity of the problem environment by covering it with a basketful of DP gimmickry: on-line this and on-line that; interactive, open-ended, user-friendly everything; plus complete data base organization and support.

After all, the application "problem" as defined by the vendor does not account for problems that the prospective purchaser may have in other areas. For example, there can be little or no planning for interfaces to other systems. In other words, the data base architecture prepared by the vendor as his solution to the requirements of the application will be relatively inaccessible to the non-data base systems of the client's environment should those systems be interested in the data base held by the package system.

The vendor does, of course, face the legitimate problem of maximizing performance in the general application system being built. Experience has clearly taught that much of the performance of data base systems depends on architectural structuring. As a consequence, the vendor's architecture is suited to performance achievement in the application problem as he has perceived it. Furthermore, the vendor structures his application programs so that they use the data base in an optimal manner. But this is where we run into problems, because the application programs are heavily vested with architecture of the data base. This means that even light tinkering with the data base architecture by the client's DP organization can have quake-like effects throughout the vendor's application system. This is wholly unacceptable for a variety of reasons, not the least of which is that packaged software is supposed to be maintenance free, at least for the client DP organization.

In any case, the result of the vendor's efforts is to produce a stand alone application system. Its data base does not interface readily with anything outside of it, meaning that the data it contains is relatively inaccessible. Since we dare not change the architecture, the only way to access the data is by brute force spin-off. The packaged system becomes a stand alone system not in the best sense but, rather, in the worst.

This message often gets hammered home when the client authorizes an enhancement in the purchased data base system. Because of the architectural dependence of the application programs, such operations often cause serious project delays.

Building Your Own

Just as the purchase of the data base interfaced application program package for some particular business area of the organization might seem at first glance to be straightforward, logical and above all efficient, the building of an in-house application system for the particular functional area might seem, in contrast, to be difficult, expensive and above all, dangerous. Managers often perceive immense risks associated with the in-house route, and the translation into potentially deadly personal possibilities does not escape them.

Unfortunately, many such managers have never been down the road of package acquisition, installation, operation and maintenance. They see the dangers of the in-house route looming large and inevitable. What they don't realize is that the lack of a complete requirements statement from the end user -- what the in-house route can offer and what the vendor does not have in building his package -- is an even larger risk.

All the choices that the designer makes for a data base architecture come from one of two places -- his imagination or an end user requirement statement. The former we can dismiss, since we know it to have a dismal track record in implementing effective systems.

How then can the latter be carried out by the head man in DP? Such an effort requires not only the energies of the people in DP, but those of the managers and staff of the end user departments as well. In the service analysis approach, we adopt the position that DP creates the requirement statement in participation with the users. We identify services and associate them with frequencies, availabilities, information elements, keys, target data, sequences, volumes, security, privacy conditions and so on. Because each of these items has an intrinsic role to play in the architectural question, we insist that the information come from the users. Although the effort is necessarily large, the rewards are large as well. The key ingredient is that the users' voice has been heard. That's what is often ultimately missing in the packaged data base application systems.

Industry Dissimilarities

The basic premise of the data based application package industry is that primary business functions in a particular industry are essentially standard, or if not, then subject to standardization through EDP measures. Indeed it is certainly the case, for example, that all banks have common major functions. After all, all banks operate savings, mortgage, small loans, etc.

In this basic functional sense, one can certainly allow that "a bank is a bank." In fact, one could go further and predict that the source data types for these major functions across different banks are probably for the most part the same. This also holds true for many other industries, including railroading, mining, investment management, manufacturing and so on.

But how deep does this similarity really go? Two points of variance can be easily spotted. First, when we decompose the allegedly "common" functions into detailed subfunctions, we will inevitably find significant variance between any two given corporate environments. In other words, the specific roles and responsibilities defined by the functional details for, say, mortgage loans in one bank will show significant variation in its detailed definition from the supposedly common function "mortgage loans" in a second bank.

Secondly, the organizational structure within which the so-called common functions and their procedures are embedded will be inevitably different. Since the detailed decomposition of functions map onto the organization chart in any definition of how procedures are carried out in a given organization, this second source of divergence has a multiplicative effect -- rather than simply an additive one -- in increasing the functional variation between two companies of the same industry. In other words, at the detailed level, "a bank is not a bank is not a bank."

What are the implications for DP? For some time now it has been well known that the pillars of a requirements statement for a data base system are information, organization and function. (Function defines what is done; organization defines who does it; and information defines what data types are needed to accomplish it.) Now if a major function of a given enterprise is done differently in its detailed subfunctions across each company that pursues that "common" enterprise, and if each company has its own particular organizational structure to carry out those subfunctions, then even though the data types in the requirement statement for the enterprise might be the same for each company, the rest of the requirement statement for each company will be very different.

What this really says is that the requirement statement for a data base system is a direct reflection of the nature, personality and working efficiencies (or lack thereof) of the organization out of which the statement arises. Like it or not, the requirement statement that is produced by the vendor of a data based application package has small chance of coming close to what the statement should look like for a particular company.

Purchase Simplicity

The strongest attraction of the package approach is that it seems so easy. Installation is merely a matter of writing a check: the vendor provides training and lead time is next to zero.

Invariably, the outputs and services that anybody's DP system delivers must be modified. No system is perfect and, if we indulge ourselves a little, even if it were perfect, users still wouldn't be completely satisfied.

So we must change a system that we either build or buy. If we're the ones who built it, then certainly we know how to change it. If we bought it, we must learn how to change it so as to avoid disastrous consequences. As already mentioned, besides the fact that venturing into vendor software is a peril-laden and essentially illogical action, there is the unavoidable fact that if we do try to change it, the architectural inertia of the system will place formidable barriers in our path.

But there is also another factor often overlooked. For some reason, the installation of data into the data base of the purchased package is almost always a painful process. It's always more work, and more time-consuming, than anybody anticipated in the beginning. This is especially true if the package was to be a quick means of getting something on the air for a user who has virtually no prior data processing experience.

So the big question in installations for this type of user becomes finding data to put into the system in the first place. The data will not be in existing systems, but rather somewhere out in the "field," wherever that is. Anyone who has dealt with this problem before knows what an immensely difficult and painful task it can be.

This is the area of largest risk in an undertaking of this sort. Failing to note and avoid this risk violates all fundamental managerial principles that we know to govern successful practices for initiating data base in an organization.

SUMMARY

Slowly, but surely, corporate managers have begun to recognize that data base offers a long term road to the revamping of the way in which the corporation goes about its data processing. The health and success of data processing, now a vital corporate function, is really endangered by the traditional helter skelter approach to systems development, because it pays little attention to either end user requirements or the concept of information as a resource. This is also a fact that is registering with increasing clarity for those managers who make it their business to know what really works in the corporate data processing world.

There is no doubt that the successful data base system project three years down the road makes the DP shop look as if a revolution had occurred. A data resource will have been created; new systems will have been built out of it; expansion of these systems will take place naturally and painlessly; the data dictionary will provide a focal point for definition and control; and perhaps most importantly, the new systems that emerge from all this will have a homogeneous and standardized structure that makes them understandable, maintainable, and above all usable.

These, unfortunately, are results that cannot be purchased. One can't buy the experience, teamwork and sensitivity necessary to produce such ends in an application package the vendor wants to sell.

CHAPTER 2
THE DATA RESOURCE

In the discussion of the several subjects of Chapter 1, reference was made to "data treated as a resource." This means that the operational problems of the maintenance of data in terms of its application currency, quality, privacy and security are carried out independently of the uses to which the data is put. These uses for the data are, of course, created by application programs, and in essence we may say that a data resource has the property that all users of the data (programs) can make reference to all of the data, all at once, all of the time, up to the privacy controls. Thus a data base can be viewed as a stand alone entity supporting its community of application program users via its associated DBMS. The objective for an effective data base system is to achieve the data resource property for all such programs, all the time, all at once, as described above.

The issue at hand, however, is not concerned with whether the data resource characteristic can be achieved via data base. This is a technical problem and if the requirements for the data base, in the context of the services that it will support and deliver to its users, are well defined, then there is no serious question as to the solvability of such technical problems. This suggests that the crucial issue is the definition of the requirements. If, however, we accept that the whole data base system project cannot be undertaken in one single step, then some piecing together of the project must be accomplished. It is the data resource concept that provides the motive for this piecing -- or staging -- of the project, and it is the objective of this chapter to develop a specific technique for accomplishing this.

THE DATA RESOURCE CONCEPT

Any file in the data processing system consists of three kinds of data. These are content, index data and structure data. Content is the data put into the file by the system's users and is the reason for the existence of the file. Thus a personnel file holds names, ID's, job locations, and so on, for the employees, and such data represents the content of that file. Index data is data in the file that is used to discriminate between records. Hence an employee ID may be used as index data since a given employee ID number will identify the records for that employee. However, not all index data uniquely identifies individual records. For example, a job type may be employed as index data. In this case, a job such as "welder" may define a set of employee records rather than a single, unique record. Index data may be used jointly to discriminate records, such as welders in department 31. In fact, index data is the stuff out of which data base queries are made. If certain index data is employed to enter the file and establish a physical location in that file, then it is referred to as a key. Thus the employee ID may be a key, and some mechanism external to the file uses the given employee number to locate a position in the file at which either the employee record is located, or the beginning of file organization which leads to that employee record.

The third type of data is structure data, and it is the means by which file organization is created. Simple sequenced files usually have no structure data. ISAM files have minimal structure data, and chain files quite a lot. Thus the structure data is the set of pointers in one record designating one or more other records as being in some association.

Many files have only content and neither keys nor structure data. These files are suited only to sequential processing that supports application programs having no needs for any more direct access for fewer than all of the records of the complete file.

Data Integration

Integrating data means interrelating it. To illustrate this, we repeat the work hours example of Chapter 1. Here, combining work hours information with personnel information integrates these two kinds of data into the requisite data for the creating of a payroll. The question for data integration is when and how is this interrelationship accomplished? In most data processing environments such integration occurs at run time and is achieved by an application program. The program passes records in one file and uses selected members of that file in a second processing context with respect to some other associated file. This selects the data to be integrated and the application program completes the integrating process. This was demonstrated in Figure 1.3 of Chapter 1. As a result, each payroll record becomes an integration of data from two separate files, and this integration is accomplished at run time by an application program. In the personnel and work hours case, the process abstracts personnel identification data from the personnel file, work hours data from the work hours file, and records this combined data in what might be referred to as the payroll history file. Thus the integration process has turned two files into three, and in the course of the process created the redundant personnel and work hours data.

Frequently, the data in a specific file exists in that file in a form and structure that is suited to some particular application programming system, which was the original cause for the creation of the file itself. Data integration often occurs as an afterthought in the construction of additional systems, tending not only to proliferate versions of data, but to create a certain circular dependency as well.

This is a situation that is represented in generalized form in Figure 2.1. This example illustrates five systems, A through E, and their associated files. The dashed lines with their arrows indicate spin-off processes that make abstracts from one file and deliver it to the indicated second file. Thus the processing for system C requires

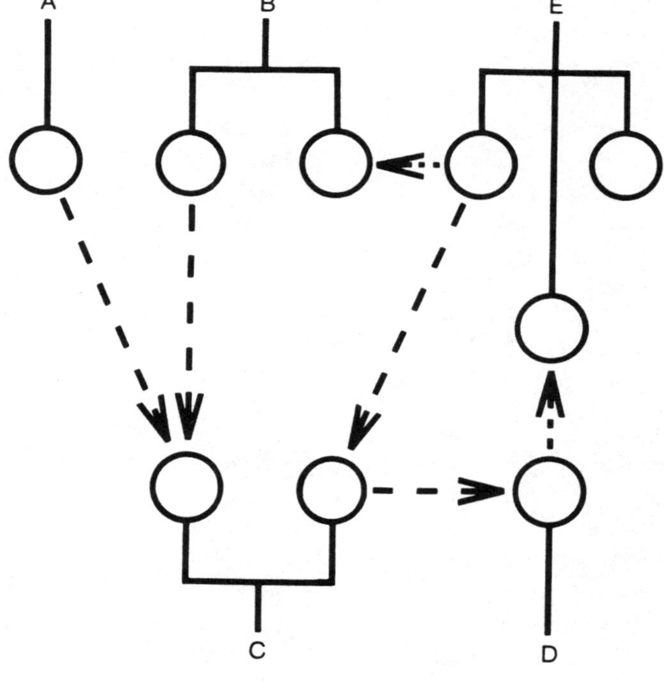

Figure 2.1/"DATA INTEGRATION" VIA SPIN-OFF FILES

that spin-offs be made from files associated with systems A, B and E. Furthermore, there is a certain degree of circularity implied for one of the files for system C in that it in turn is a source of data for system D, which supplies data to a file of system E, and it is this system whose files must support system C. Clearly there is an issue of currency in time that has to be considered as well. It becomes evident then, that data integration via application programs at run time implies a complex intersystem timing problem which dictates a sequence for system execution if the results of the various integration processes are to be valid.

This is certainly a familiar issue to operators in the computer room. Their run books are thick with processing sequences, files to be mounted and demounted, systems to be loaded and run, and so on. And the development group in the data processing department is most frequently huddled over the bugs and performance problems that this form of integration, with its elaborate run time relationships, must necessarily create. In fact, in most data processing shops it is probably true that a large majority of the total design and programming staff is engaged in the maintenance and "enhancement" of current systems, as opposed to the development of new systems. To put this another way, in all likelihood the largest fraction of the programming and execution effort of data processing is devoted to creating data integration, and the smaller proportion of such manpower and computer resources is devoted to producing the finished products from these data processing activities.

The Data Resource View

The difficulties created in the usual data processing system by the methods of integration that are traditionally employed essentially derive from the time at which integration occurs and the means by which it is accomplished. That is, integration occurs at execution time via spin-off systems and is achieved by application programs. In the data resource concept, the time of the integration is prior to execution and the point of integration is prior to execution and the point of integration is within the data base itself, and not in the application program. To put this differently, the integration of data is achieved in the data base as an intrinsic part of the data base. This is designed into the data base architecture in advance of the employment of that data by application programs.

Thus the personnel data, the work hours data, and any payroll data stored as a consequence of these two data collections, are all retained jointly in the data base. Furthermore, the portions of the payroll data that would otherwise be a reproduction of personnel and work hours data need not be redundant in this data base. This view is expressed more generally in Figure 2.2. Here data processing system A requires the set of data in the circular area. Program system B requires the set of data in the rectangle and they share between them the cross-hatched data. That data is then available not only to systems A and B, but to any future systems which may need to employ it. Similarly, data for system C shares some portion of data with that for A and B as do systems D and E. By looking back at Figure 1.7, it can be seen that this view of the data resource is entirely compatible with the growth of the data base. In Figure 1.7, the point was made that each stage of the project contributes to the growth of the data base. In the present discussion, the focus is on the applicability of the extant data resource to subsequent data base project stages. From these two viewpoints then, it is clear that the growing data base creates the data resource, which in turn supports not only the next stages of the data base system project, but the further growth of the data resource as well.

The data resource provides a means for centralizing the availability of data, and achieves this by structuring the data itself with a data base architecture. This means that the individual data elements that define the data base in its totality are themselves defined as to format and content; data elements are grouped into record types which define various files of the data base, and the data occurrences or values for these record types, making up the actual content of the data base, are then distributed

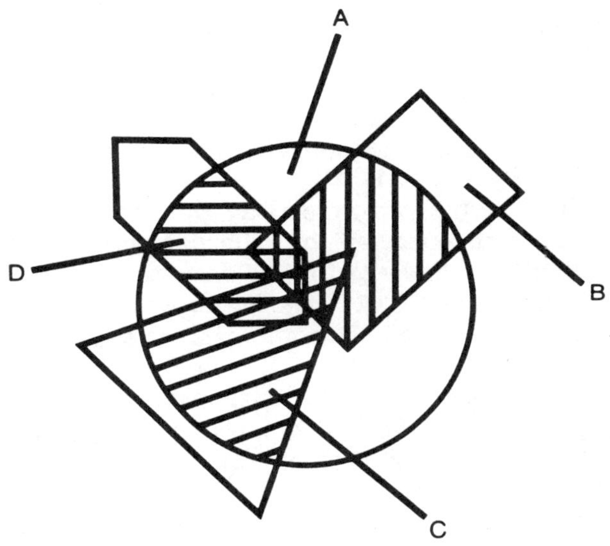

Figure 2.2/THE DATA RESOURCE VIEW

into allocated data spaces in the storage environment. Structure data provides inter-file and intra-file relationships among the content and keys, and the indexing methods complete the architecture by providing mechanisms to enter the physical data spaces in which the data occurrences are stored as records. Thus an application program user of the data resource employs keys to describe the conditions for reference to the data of interest. The data base management system translates the given key values for these keys into a specific position in the data space assigned to a particular file of the data base. In all probability, the data wanted is not actually at this location; rather, this is an initial point for file organization. The file organization process is then exercised to arrive at the set of data being referenced.

It follows that in a data base with an architecture suited to its treatment as a data resource, there will be no spin-off files and minimal redundant data content. There will be little or no redundant processing to create currency, and more importantly, the lack of redundancy will literally obviate the currency issue. Looked at from this general point of view, the data resource concept seems to suggest that the data base exists as an entity in its own right. In more succinct terms, we might say that the intention for a successful data resource is that the data base it represents be maintained and managed in its data quality, privacy and security, independently of the uses to which the data itself is put by the application programs that it supports.

Of course, the content of the data base is independent of these programs. In fact, these programs might, on first consideration, be thought to establish the context for the data base. This is traditional data processing thinking in which the payroll system, for example, is thought to associate with a certain identified collection of data. While this is indeed true, the notion of a particular system defining a particular set of data is specific to the file oriented view. The actuality is that programs deliver results to their end users. In more precise terms we would say that programs create the services to be delivered to the users from the data base system. These services satisfy user needs and functions in the organizational environment which indeed are the true contexts for the data base. To put this in sharper focus, a given set of services supporting the end user community will by themselves formally define the required data resource. Specific application programs are then merely the service delivery mechanisms. Therefore we may say, as a result of this point of view, that the data resource is the content of the end user service requirement context, and that the data base system objective is to provide an architecture for this resource so that this content may be managed and maintained independently of the application program uses to which that data is put within the end user context.

Growth of the Data Resource

From what has been said, it would seem that if a data base design to support the whole organization were to be created all at once, then necessarily the entire service context for that organization would have to be available for investigation and analysis. However, the identification of services is a necessarily detailed activity, and can only be accomplished in a reasonable period of time if it is executed relative to small portions of the organization. In the previous chapter we have referred to this as a project stage, and to the creation of a project plan as a mechanism by means of which each project stage contributes to the overall data base growth and its support of subsequent stages.

This is the "small is good" philosophy that is clearly in direct opposition to the "one giant step" approach. The difficulty with the latter is that a far larger number of human resources is required, a much longer development time is demanded over which the services to be delivered must remain stable in the user community, and there is an all or nothing characteristic to the finished data base system product. That is, if after two-and-one-half years of development the data base system project has produced only marginal results, the expense has been enormous and the loss comparable. In small project stages, however, each increment of the overall project delivers a result. The time is short, the requirements remain stable, the man power resources employed small, and any failures that may occur should have minimum impact and might even go unnoticed outside of the immediate data base system project community.

There is a price to be paid for this staged approach which has to do with the possibility that a later stage may demand some reorganization of the current architecture of the data base in order to satisfy the end user needs provided by the services that this later stage will deliver. Such reorganization may affect the performance of programs for earlier stages, and may indeed possibly call for a degree of rewriting. This growth of the data resource and the potential problems of the stages approach to the development of data based data processing is illustrated in Figure 2.3. Here, program system A, providing some organizational unit with data processing services, is supported by the indicated data base. This data base contains, among others, data segments X and Y. Similarly, B has a data base which among its content contains data X, but in a reorganized and reformatted form here indicated as X1. If program system A results from the first stage of the second stage, producing program system B, the result is the conjoined data bases of the two as illustrated. This contains the data Y for the first stage and the new data Z for the second. In addition, there is the data X whose architecture in the data base has been designed to best support the data needs X of stage A and the similar data needs X1 of stage B.

It may well be that the form X for the first stage data is satisfactory to support the form X1 of the second stage data. In this case, no modification of the stage A data base would have to be made in order to support stage B. The execution of the next stage, however, may not only introduce new data to the data resource, but as shown in the figure, might also make some new demands for changing the architecture of the data base that resulted from the completion of the first two stages.

Clearly if each such architectural change called for the reworking of the entire application program systems of the preceding stages, the staging approach would be virtually useless. In practice, however, this is very far from the actuality. The reason for this is a direct consequence of certain important characteristics of the data base and the means employed by users for making reference to it.

DATA RESOURCE STRUCTURE

The data elements of a data base identify the specific types or kinds of data that are present in the data base. For example, if there is a PAYROLL data element, then the data base contains a field for holding whatever data is defined as "payroll data." To be more exact, we say that the data base is made up of data elements and occurrence values for these data elements. Thus, a data base may have, say, 300 elements, but the actual data content of the data base may run to millions of occurrence values for these data elements.

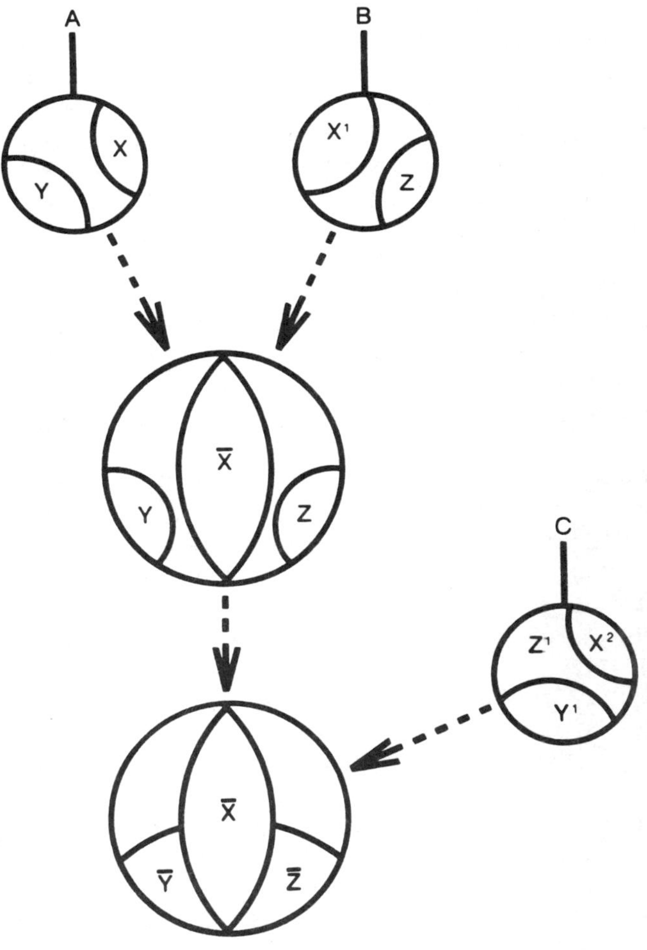

Figure 2.3/GROWTH OF THE DATA RESOURCE

All of this suggests that when we speak of redundancy we must consider two types. First, there is the familiar redundancy of the data itself; for example, an employee number value that occurs two or more times in the data base in two or more different places. In this case, we have redundant data values, and any modifications made to one of these values demands that similar modifications be made to this same value wherever else it appears redundantly in the data base. It follows that the usage of the same data in two different places in a data base will call for either two different data elements, or two versions of the same data element. Take the case of an employee identification number, which we will refer to as the data element EID. Suppose that EID occurs in a work hours file and EID also occurs in a payroll file. In this case, the data element EID occurs in two different files of the data base, and in each of its data occurrences in these files there is redundancy of the actual employee identification number. But in order to speak of the data element EID unambiguously, it is clear that a qualification regarding the particular EID must be made. This qualification is, of course, with respect to the file of interest at the moment.

The second type of redundancy is with respect to data elements in the context of the using environment. We say that if EID is jointly employed by the assembly department and the payroll department, then there is a redundancy of usage by data element type. This says nothing about data redundancy as we have discussed it above, but rather relates only to the redundancy of usage of the data, however it may appear in the data base. This second type of redundancy is important to the data base system project because without it there is virtually no meaning to the concept of the data resource since there will be no broad community of users interested in a concentrated set of common data types. Thus in the using environment for our proposed data base system project we expect to find some degree of redundancy of data usage by data element type. Indeed, a very high degree of redundant data usage is very often the case.

Experience indicates that the total number of unique data

elements to support a broad spectrum of operational activities in an organization is generally rather small. However, there is no surprise in this when one recognizes that since data elements define the kinds of data that are of interest, they must in turn reflect the kinds of data that are of interest to the business of the organization. To put this in a different way, the business of the organization is effectively summed up in its data element types, and for the purposes of establishing a data resource view, it is entirely valid to think of the data elements necessary for an organization as defining the data base usage context for that organization. The content of the data base is then described completely by this context.

Creating the Data Resource

If indeed the business of the organization is characterized by the collection of data elements necessary for its data base, then there is clearly an upperlimit to the number of such data elements. Furthermore, it was suggested in the preceding section that this number is generally somewhat smaller than one might suspect. The importance of the limit to this number cannot be overstressed, however, particularly in the context of a data resource view and the creation of that data resource. This importance derives from the fact that if we build a data resource as the consequence of the staged development of data based data processing, then each stage will use the data resource resulting from the preceding stage and will in addition contribute to its growth. This growth is in the form of data element types and data content volume. If the data element types expand, then the scope of the data base expands as well. It follows from the notion that there is a limit to the number of data element types of interest to the organization as a whole, that at some point the problem of defining new data elements is complete.

This view is expressed in Figure 2.4. The graph shows the growth of the number of data element types in the data base as a function of the data base system project stages. The first stage will be supported by a certain data base, and as a consequence will call for the definition of a certain set of data elements. The second stage will employ these data elements and perhaps the data values put in for stage A, and will define some new data elements for the data base. The next stage and those that follow repeat the process until the upper limit of the total number of data elements required to define the usage context for the organization as a whole has been reached.

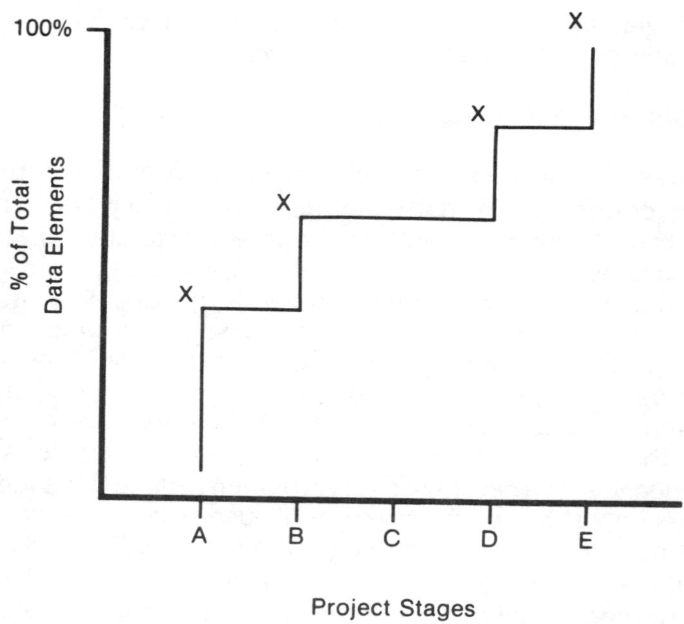

Figure 2.4/CREATING THE DATA RESOURCE

At some point in the data base system project then, the data resource is effectively defined. If there is also some point at which all possible data values of interest to any user whatsoever have been included in the data base, then the data resource is complete; it will also be static and unchanging. The actuality, of course, is that though the data element types may be exhaustively defined and the data resource from that point of view is complete, data values change, are deleted and new ones are added as the users employ the data resource. Thus it is the definition of the data resource that reaches the limit, from which point forward all current systems and new systems are able to use the data resource in common as defined, employing it for their individual data value purposes.

Data Element Classes

From the foregoing, we conclude that the construction of the data resource is a result of the data base system project. For this to work, we must be able to define the data base system project stages so that they accomplish the creation of the data resource. To do this, it is necessary to identify both the data types to be used by the organization and who uses them. That is, the data base system project stage will support user groups in the organization and as a consequence will require data elements to be present in the data base that these users need. This suggests that stages be defined based on a separation of the offices of the organization into groups or sets, with each such set of users being characterized by a certain collection of the data elements in the data resource.

In order to be able to make such an identification of users with data elements, it is necessary to think in terms of three data element types or classes. These are source, operational and managerial data elements. Each is given discussion in the sections that follow.

Source Data Elements

The existence of an office in an organization is based on the need to accomplish some functional activity relative to demands made on the organization as a whole. For example, a credit evaluation unit in the organization chart exists because credit must be evaluated in order to suit the needs and objectives of the overall business activity. Thus the motive for a particular office being present in the overall organizational structure derives essentially from sources outside of that organizational element, and in general we may say that the overall impetus for the organization taken as a whole is from outside the organization itself. To put this in more simplified terms, outsiders create actions and activities to which the organization has been designed to respond and react. As an explicit example, the customer desiring to order a particular product is the reason why the company makes the product; and is organized to receive the order, evaluate it, process it, ship it, guarantee it, service it, and so on. Each of these functional activities is, of course, accomplished by organizational units in the overall structure, and these organizational units come into play because an order has been placed.

It is important to recognize that actions in an organization, particularly those that are created from outside of the organization, always create some record of the activity. Thus an order creates a recording of the order -- perhaps in a computer system, or merely on paper -- but in either case there is indeed a recording. What is important here is that the order can be thought of as an entity of interest to both the organization as a whole and to a particular office or operating structure within it. Furthermore, this entity -- in this case the order -- has certain characteristics or attributes which distinguish or define it. For example, there is the customer's name, the shipping address, the billing address, order date, items in the order, and so on. The property of interest to us here is that these attributes of an order entity may be thought of as data elements of specific use to the organizational office dealing with orders. Because these data elements have their data values supplied from outside of the organization, we will say that they are source data elements.

A source data element -- computerized or otherwise -- is one for which the data values are provided from outside of the organizational unit or the organization as a whole. We extend this to data derived from inside the organization which is designed for use by individuals outside of the organization. In general, we will find many such data entities consisting of a collection of data elements which are of interest to various offices in the organizational structure. If these entities are made up of source data elements, they are referred to as source data entities. The order might be considered as a source data entity, for example, and the waybill for shipment verification by the customer might also be considered as a source data entity. Source data entities and their associated source data elements may well turn out to be of interest to not only some one office in the organization, but more broadly to several such offices. We will make a distinction between source data elements and data elements containing data values derived from them because it is expected that source data elements have a broad spectrum of use in the organization over its various offices. However, though we have been definitional in the notion of a source data element, suggesting that it is directly associated with activities and functions of the customers of the business, i.e., those outside of the organization, there is no need to be rigid about this. Any data element or data element set forming a processing entity of interest which has a broad spectrum of application use in the organization can be thought of as a source data element or source data entity.

One rather important quality that we can asociate with source data entities and their data elements is that they tend to characterize the nature of the business or some major portion of it. That is, source data entities tend to characterize the objectives of our business activities. It is in this sense that customers, orders, items in an inventory shipping, suppliers, reordering, and so on, might very well belong to the class of source data elements in our data base.

Derived Data Elements

The major distinction between source data elements and the other two types is that these latter are derived from the soruce data. It is very important to make this distinction because without the source data, the derived data and the associated data element types have little meaning. We identify two types of derived data. These are operational data elements and managerial data elements. Although they share the common quality that their values are derived from source data, they each have certain characteristics which are of fundamental importance to the data resource concept and to the overall planning of a data base system project.

Operational Data Elements

An operational data element associates directly with a particular office in the organizational structure. The purpose of an operational data element is to represent a specific activity, or the data associated with a specific activity for that office. In effect then, an operational data element characterizes operational activity for a particular office, and we might say that a collection of operational data elements for an office defines its functional activities relative to the rest of the organization in the context of the available source data.

At the same time, operational data elements are derived from source data. This derivation may have been accomplished by the organizational office of interest, or by some other organizational unit making the operational data available. In this case, both organizational offices have the operational data and the operational data element in common. The general expectation, however, is that operational data elements are more local in use and definition, particularly with respect to the source data elements. It is this last characteristic that is indeed most important. As we will see, a data base system project will be structured so as to create a data resource and deliver data base systems that provide services supporting the operations of individual offices in the organization. This requires that the data resource be built up as a combination of source data entities and their data elements for a broad spectrum of users. A data base system project stage will entail the addition and incorporation of operational data elements for specific offices. These together will provide the necessary data element types and data values for the delivery of services to support these offices in the context of the overall data resource.

Managerial Data Elements

The third and final type of data base data element of interest is the managerial data element. These too are used to support certain operational activities of the organization, and in all likelihood are centered in their use on one or several offices. The difference of interest is that managerial data elements tend to be summaries of source data elements, summaries of operational data elements, and combined summaries of both. To put this in simpler terms, we might say that operational data elements are for the tactical, moment by moment daily operation of specific offices relative to the source data element business of the organization as a whole. Managerial data elements, on the other hand, might be thought of as larger in scope and more as strategic information suited to the long term, large scale guidance of the organization overall.

It is necessary to remember here that we do not have to deal with the entire corporation in these discussions. We can just as easily deal with organizational subsets of the corporation. Strategic management is carried out at this level, as well as specific operational activities. Both of them rely on source data elements and their associated source data values for their respective content.

Summary Comments on Data Elements

Source data elements have broad scope and general applicability over the many offices of an organization. They reflect the relationship of the organization to its external environment and are characteristic of the business of the organization itself. One might say that until the nature of the business changes, the set of source data elements will remain constant.

As opposed to this, operational data element values are derived from the source data element values. They provide the data and consequent informational wherewithal for operating individual offices of the organization. Generally speaking we may say that operational data elements provide the tactical basis for business procedures and define the business functions of a given office in the organization. The scope of operational data elements is usually limited with respect to various organizational units, even though several offices may share operational data elements. The scope is definitely limited with respect to the scope associated with source data elements.

Finally, managerial data elements have overview characteristics. They too are derived from source data elements, and may also be based on operational data elements. They represent managerial mechanisms for observing the business activities (source data elements) and its progress (operational data elements). This scope is generally broad in that strategic information is desired, and therefore may cover a multitude of activities and multiplicity of organizational offices and business functions.

As we will see below, we can also associate data element types with unit position in an organization chart, but for the moment we need only consider that there are these three general types that are of interest to our development of a data resource and in the structure of a data base system project. Again, most important is the notion that source data elements are the basis on which operational and managerial data elements are derived. It follows that any data base system project seeking to develop a data resource must plan to create a data base containing source data elements. Individual data base system project stages will then incorporate operational data elements and selected managerial data elements in order to support specific offices and their functions in the organization.

Figure 2.5 is a composite illustration of these three data element types. This might be the first of several displayed screens used by the credit evaluation group in reviewing a customer order. Note here that customer name, customer ID, date of last order, and the amount of last order are all considered in this example to be source data elements. That is, these data values are created externally to the organization by the existence and presence of a customer. On the other hand, the credit evaluation function is dependent on an operational data element, here identified as current credit line, and may make certain determinations associated with back ordering priorities. Finally, managerial data elements associated with order value for the customer and account aging may also enter into the consideration.

It is important that flexibility be incorporated into the view the project team takes of the data element types. The purpose here is to associate source data elements with the general spectrum of use of data by organizational offices. Operational data elements are used to characterize particular offices, office groups or functional activities. Managerial data elements play a role in reviewing the activities of a number of such offices and have strategic as opposed to tactical values. True, the data base system project will not fail simply because something that might have been considered source in one context is viewed as operational and/or managerial in another. The data base system project may indeed fail, however, if scope of usage and source of data is generally not observed or is seriously violated.

Customer name	(S)	ID	(S)
Date last order	(S)	Amount last order	(S)
Order volume YTD	(M)	Current credit line	(O)
Backorder priority	(O)	Account ageing	(M)

S - Source O - Operational M - Managerial

Figure 2.5/DATA ELEMENT CLASSES

PROJECT STAGING

Quite frequently one hears that data processing is "putting up the payroll under data base," or that the "accounts payable system is being done under data base." Such systems will generally involve source, operational and managerial data and will cut a cross section through the organization chart. No concern is expressed in this approach with the broad applicability of the source data types, the specific meaning to a particular office of the operational data types, or the strategic importance of the managerial data types. Rather, a general business function involving some identified group of offices in the organizational structure is tagged for implementation. Of secondary interest is the data it will employ, and there is clearly no data resource view. All the data necessary to support the processing defined by the functional activity, i.e., accounts receivable, must be incorporated into the system. Therefore, files are built for all of the data and contain source, operational and managerial data. No larger view is taken of the data resource, and as a consequence we often find that the net result is yet another file oriented system, with the DBMS acting as an access method and providing a "programming language" for referencing data in the application programs.

Without a data resource, the purposes of data base are foiled. A DBMS is an ineffective access method and certainly represents a less than satisfactory programming language. Thus the concept of developing a functional system "under data base" is directly opposed to the data resource notion and it is just this approach to data base in the organizational structure that leads to so many of the unnecessary failures that have been recorded in the data processing industry with respect to the development of data base systems.

One might say in fact that the data resources view is the only reason for building a data based data processing system. Indeed, to put this more strongly, the interest in a data resource should be taken as primary, and we should look at the data based data processing technology as the best possible data processing technique available at the moment for realizing the data resource in terms of its implementation, maintenance and ongoing management.

Data Resource Growth by Data Element Class

Let us return now to this issue of the growth of the data resource. From the foregoing discussions the data resource will at any point consist of a collection of source data entities and associated source data element types. We will of course incorporate source data element values and will include both operational data elements and managerial data elements with their associated derived data values. In all probability, the data base in terms of total number of data element types will be limited. Specifically, source data elements are reflective of the nature of the business and the limit is clearly defined in terms of the source data elements needed for these business activities. Similarly, if each office of the business has a certain collection of operational data elements that define the way it goes about executing its functional responsibilities, then there must be a limit on operational data elements as well. In actuality, it may be that there is no final upper limit on the total number of data elements in a data base for an organization. If this is the case, it is likely because managerial data elements tend to change, albeit slowly, over time. Clearly, a management perogative, given the responsibility for strategic observation, review and control of the organization, is to modify the nature of the information on which such decisions are based. This may call for a rearrangement, revamping and redefinition of the managerial data elements. As a consequence, the managerial data elements may indeed not be limited. In view of this, we might conclude that there is a constant growth potential in terms of data elements in any data base system. The reality is, however, that managerial data elements tend to vary relatively slowly. Thus at any point we can say that there is an approximate limit to the number of data elements in the data base, and most importantly, the source and operational data elements tend to be fixed. It might be of interest to restate here that the source data elements will in general change if and only if the nature of the business changes; operational data elements will change only when an individual organizational unit changes a procedure or operational responsibility; managerial data elements, of course, change as management seeks to modify the ways in which it monitors the overall business activity of the organization.

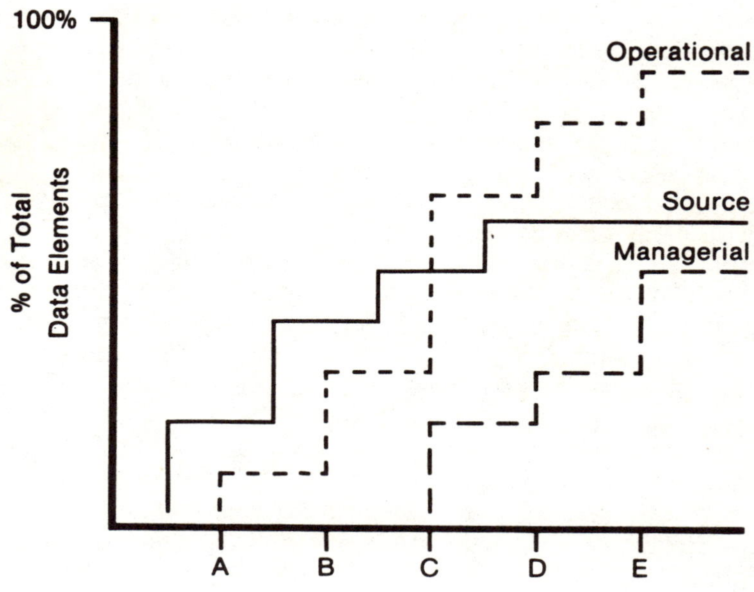

Figure 2.6/DATA RESOURCE GROWTH BY DATA ELEMENT CLASS

All of this is reflected in the chart of Figure 2.6. Again, the various project stages are shown relative to available data elements of the data base. The assumption is made that these total data elements will become essentially fixed. The source data elements grow with each stage of the project. We have an upper limit because there is a point at which finally all source data element types of interest to all operating activities in the organization have been incorporated into the data base. Operational data elements on the other hand, will grow stage by stage. Here the concept of data base system project staging begins to be evident, since it is our intention to design the implementation of data based data processing for offices of the organization and their business function responsibilities. Therefore, these offices will require that certain source data elements be present and that their specific operational data elements be incorporated into the data base. Finally, the growth of the data resource in terms of data elements is completed by the managerial data elements. These are incorporated as offices using these data elements and are included in the data base system project effort. Later stages of the project therefore will provide services to these areas which employ managerial data elements, and as a consequence, stages of the project development will add managerial data elements as well as source and operational data elements. Again, if there is an approximate upper limit to the number of managerial data elements that can be considered to be of interest to the organization as a whole, there is finally an upper limit to the total number of data elements present in the data base.

Data Resource Growth Sequence

The simplest data base system project stage will necessarily include source data elements. Each project stage will also always include some operational data elements. That is, the concept of the data base system project stage is that of the creation of a data base system set of services based on the current data resource, and the delivery of such services to a particular office or offices of the organization. As described above, this will demand the presence of certain operational data elements. The data base system project may also want to include certain managerial activities. These might take the form of reports or particular screens delivered to managerial units of the organization so that they may observe, assess, and ultimately manage the activities of the various offices in the organization. Thus, a data base system project can be characterized in terms of the sequencing of organizational units and their business functions relative to source, operational and managerial data elements.

It is essential that this idea be appreciated, since it is at the very heart of data base system project planning based on the data resource concept. Figure 2.7 expresses this concept. Here we have a collection of source data entities and their data elements which support the functional activities of two different operational offices in the organization. Each of these offices employs the particular source data shown. A data base system project stage could therefore be structured such that it would develop data element types, the associated data base architecture, and the loading of the data values for the required source data. Then operational data elements could be defined along with the mechanisms or programs for their computation developed for office number one. The data base system project stage at this point would then consist of the source data elements, the specific operational data elements for office 1 and, if elected, associated managerial data elements to suit the particular project phase. In the figure, this stage would incorporate development of the architecture for the source data entity (S) and the offices using operational data elements 01 and managerial data elements M1.

The second project stage might then be based on the same source data elements. Assuming that there are offices in the organization which need only these source data elements, their operational data elements need definition (02), and perhaps associated managerial data elements (M2). Some later stage of the data base system project might then consolidate the operational and managerial data element values into a third level of managerial data elements and their associated values (M3), to provide the strategic managerial facilities required at this level.

The data resource has obviously grown with each of these stages. The initial development was for the source data

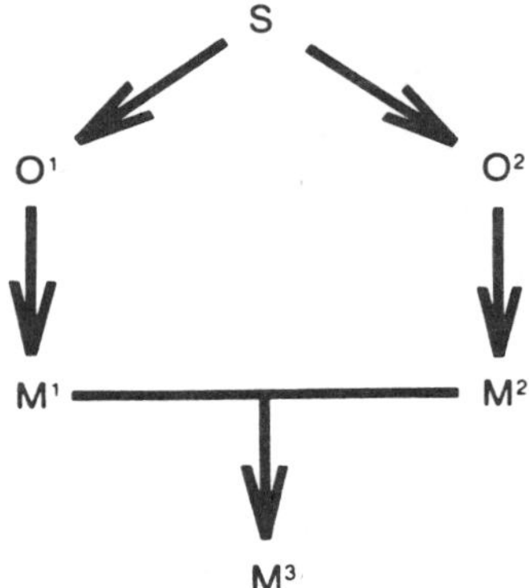

Figure 2.7/DATA RESOURCE GROWTH SEQUENCE

elements. The first project stage produced operational data elements and managerial data elements to satisify the needs of the identified associated offices. The second project stage provided the additional operational and managerial data elements indicated in the figure, and the third project stage then capitalized on these and added its data elements to the data base.

Referring back to Figure 2.6, the data base has immediately grown in scope on the basis of the source data elements, again in scope because of the first and second sets of operational data elements, and potentially in scope (since there may or may not be a broad interest in certain managerial data elements) because of the addition of managerial data element types.

In summary then, this represents the philosophy to be pursued. The data resource is to be developed stage by stage, and each stage is to contribute to that data resource. The contribution is in terms of data elements, and that contribution must first incorporate to that data resource. The contribution is in terms of data elements, and that contribution must first incorporate source data elements. Source data elements are the basis for operational and managerial data elements. Therefore project stages will be defined in terms of offices in the organization chart, and the operational and managerial data elements which they individually require relative to the source data elements that a project stage has made available in addition to those already available in the data base system architecture at this point due to earlier project stages.

Project Stages

This project staging concept and coincident development of the data resource is at the heart of the approach to the data base system project that is being offered here. It is important that this be understood since the usual data processing system project that creates a data processing implementation for functional activities, is essentially opposed to this view. Explicitly, the data base system project plan will have identified source data entities and their associated source data elements, offices employing these source data elements in their functional activities, and their associated operational data elements, and other offices providing managerial functions and their associated managerial data elements. Stage by stage, each project development will contribute to the data resource in terms of data elements types, thus expanding both the scope and data value volume. Data element types and the associated data values are then available to all organizational entities up to the established privacy controls in the organization.

This notion of a potential project staging based on the development of a data resource is illustrated in Figure 2.8. Here the figure shows that there are in fact two source data entity types of interest. These are labeled S1 and S2. Without assessing the scope of their interest, let us suppose that the data entity S1 is of interest and use to two offices whose operational data entities O1 and O2 will indeed define a particular data base system project stage. Furthermore, a third office has a set of operational data base O1. This will provide a collection of services to the associated operational offices based on their requirement statement. Next, source data S1 and operational data O2 in combination with managerial data M2: this stage will provide an additional data resource involving S1, and adding data elements for O2 and M2. The next stage will provide services that involve managerial data elements M1 and M3. Clearly, these are data elements and functional activities that are based on the preceding stages. Now consider the implementation of a fourth data base system project stage. This calls for the definition, architectural structuring and data incorporation for source data S2 in order to satisfy the requirements for operational data elements O3 and managerial data elements M4. This can then be followed by a fifth data base system project stage which will provide managerial services based on the specified set of managerial data elements M5, which in turn depend on the existence and availability of managerial data elements M3 and M4.

From all this we may conclude that if we can identify the source data elements, we are then in a position to identify operational offices in the organization chart and their associated operational data elements. Given this, we can then identify managerial offices with associated data elements, and as a consequence can structure a project having origins in source data.

The Organizational Pyramid

The purpose of an organization chart is to structure the authority responsibilities of various organizational elements and the individuals within them. The overall objective of this structuring is to operate the business activities, generally at the lower end of the chart, and to observe the operation of these business activities and control them, generally at the upper end of the chart. In terms of the discussions that have been made concerning types of data in the data base, we may say that the bottom of the organizational pyramid is where source data entities and the associated source data elements first make their appearance. This is where the orders are taken, bills of lading are filled out, registrations are validated, and so on. In short, this is where the income producing, stated purpose of the business is realized.

The organizational levels above these operating levels are supervisory and managerial. At the supervisory levels, they represent observation and immediate reaction to the tactical issues of the day. The structuring, review and

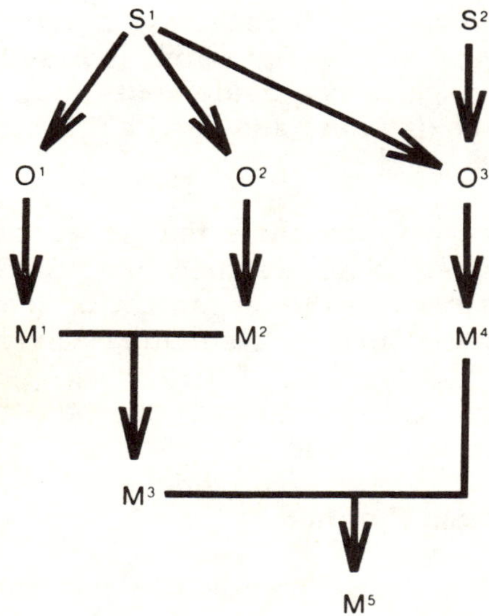

Potential project stages: S^1 O^1; S^1 O^2 M^2; M^1 M^3; S^2 O^3 M^4; M^5

Figure 2.8/PROJECT STAGES

enforcement of procedures that have been established for business operation are part of the supervisory level. This is the source of what has been referred to as the operational data elements.

Higher in the chart is the strategic interest of management in the spectrum of supervisory activities and operational actions that they control. This management concern is reflected in the managerial data elements that appear in the data base.

Thus, the organizational structure with its pyramid-like qualities indeed reflects the relationship between source, operational and managerial data elements. In the structuring of the data base system project, our primary concern is with determining those offices in the organizational pyramid which can be brought together into a data base system project stage. The specific objective of the project stage view, to repeat, is to contribute to the growth of the data resource. Thus, we are looking for some segment or portion of the organizational pyramid and the focal point of interest in our data base system project stage. The overall planning effort for the data base system project is aimed at assigning each of the organizational offices to specific office groups, where each group has the property that the services they need in terms of data processing support are based on either the data resource as currently developed as a consequence of earlier data base system project stages -- or as a result of those portions of the data resource that will be developed in order to support the current project stage.

Thus in the development of the data base system project plan we should be able to detail the overall organization in terms of its organizational units, and then be able to assign these organizational units to data base system project stages.

Data Resource vs. Application System

The traditional approach to data processing has always been to identify a business function or general operational activity of the organization and then to provide an implementation for that function in computing terms. The application system that resulted would involve source data which was more often than not brought in from other systems via spin-off files and interfacing systems of programs. Specific programs would be included in the application system so as to support the functional activities of users and their offices. These programs would involve the necessary operational data elements for those organizational elements. Finally, these application systems would include reports whose managerial data elements supported management responsibilities in the organization with respect to functional activities implemented by these application systems.

Clearly, the application system as structured in the more traditional approach to data processing, does indeed involve all of the types of data to be found in a data resource. However, this ends up being a profile of data selected specifically for the particular application system. As we have already discussed, part of the difficulty with this approach may well be that the source data required for the application system was the same source data required for other application systems supporting the organization, and that the nature of the functional or file oriented approach to data processing is such that the tendency is to reproduce this source data type - usually a number of times - with the attendant difficulties.

Another way of viewing this is from the vantage point of the discussions of this chapter with regard to the structuring of a data base system project relative to the data resource concept. In that view the organizational structure was segmented to identify those organizational units or offices having source data elements in common. This is an approach that is not dependent on data processing functional activity, but rather on organizational functional activity defined strictly in terms of data resource requirement. The view here has been that the activities of an office in an organization are essentially defined by the source data element that it requires.

In Figure 2.9 the organizational pyramid is shown with a recommended data base system project stage enclosed in the triangle of dashed lines. Each of the circles in the figure represents an office in the organization, and the six offices identified numerically represent organizational elements with a specific organization-wide functional activity in common. For the purposes of example, let us suppose that the traditional data processing approach has implemented a pay system whose functions support these six offices. They have been linked in the figure by a heavy line to indicate that all six are associated by the pay system function, and the first three of these offices are in our initial data system project. Offices four through six are not, even though they must operate with data processing support for certain pay system functions.

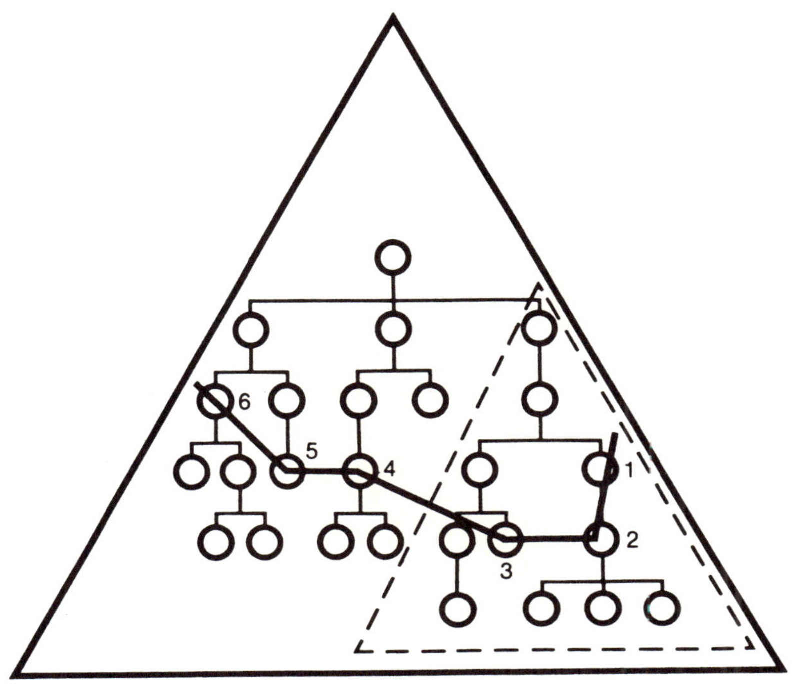

Figure 2.9/THE ORGANIZATIONAL PYRAMID

Thus, the functional approach to data processing will link together a number of different offices in the organization, and from the data resource point of view for planning a data base system project, will cross data base system project boundaries. Let us now consider two cases. First, suppose that in identifying source data required for the offices in our proposed data base system project stage, we found that offices 1, 2, and 3 required a third source data type different from the source data elements required by the other offices in the firt project stage. This situation is illustrated in Figure 2.10 showing that portion of the chart involving only offices 1 and 2.

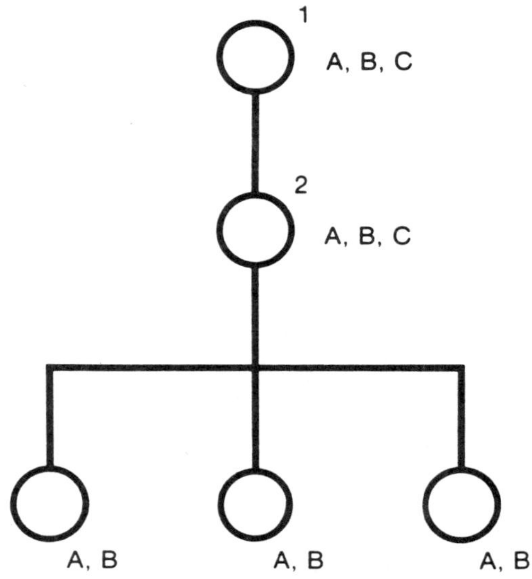

Figure 2.10/FUNCTIONAL SEPARATION

This example illustrates that the source data common to all of the offices shown, and to most of the offices in the proposed project stage are entities A and B. The third data entity, here labeled C, is for the support of the pay system functional activities of offices 1 and 2. This means that we can associate the services to be delivered from the data base system project stage with, first, two data entities A and B together, and then secondly with data entity C. This second set of services will provide the pay services required by offices 1 and 2 and, in another portion of the project stage, office 3. This suggests that offices 1 and 2 can be divided into two parts with regard to this data base system project stage. The first part will be associated with those requirements that are dependent on the source data entities A and B. The second part will be associated with the source data entity C, and may be separated from this data base system project stage. Under these circumstances, offices 1 and 2 will be supported in those services requiring data entities A and B and will continue to receive support for the pay system functions via the current pay system.

The second case is that which assumes that the services to support the pay system functions for offices 1 and 2 are to be provided by the data base system project stage, even though these services will reproduce those already received from the current pay system involving the other offices outside of this project stage. This means that the current pay system will continue even after the data base system stage is completed, and therefore redundant pay system services will be provided to offices 1, 2 and 3 -- requiring some form of integration. This, in turn, provides two alternatives. For the first, data that arrives in the current pay system may be abstracted to formulate the source data of type C needed for the offices using that data and requiring pay system functions within the data base system project stage. The second alternative would have the data base system project stage structure its services to provide the source data of type C initially in the data base system, and then provide a set of temporary data base system services which abstract this data from the data base and deliver it to the current pay system.

The second alternative makes the best sense where the offices in the data base system project are in fact responsible for the initiation of data entity C. That is, data is gathered, reviewed, validated, and installed in these offices. Under these circumstances, it is very likely that the completion of the data base system project stage will replace little more than spin-off files and associated application program integration functions in the current pay system.

Thus, the data resource approach to the structuring of data based data processing for an organization has little to do with the replacement of current systems "under data base." The replacement of a current system "under data base" will involve the delivery of data base services to offices that cross common data resource boundaries, and as a consequence will not result in the orderly development of a growing data resource.

The data resource view for a data base system project concentrates first on the data resource and its growth, and via proper project planning relative to this data resource growth and associated operational and managerial data elements, structures the delivery of services that support organizational units in the organization chart. It follows then, that the delivery of all services for a particular office will include those services which are covered under functionally oriented systems. Thus, if all organizational units using the current pay system are finally treated in some stage of the data base system project's development, then the result will be that in the course of the creation of a data resource via these successive project stages, the pay system structured according to the traditional application programming system approach, has indeed been replaced. More generally, the successive stages of the data base system project will ultimately encompass all current data processing systems, and will replace them with systems structured around the data resource supporting all of the functional requirements of the offices in the organizational structure.

CHAPTER 3
CREATING THE DATA BASE SYSTEM PROJECT

THE DATA BASE SURVEY

The fundamental motivating objective for a data base system project and the development of data based data processing in an organization is to ultimately create a data resource. This means that source, operational, and managerial data types, and the associated data values on which organizational activities are founded, are available for immediate and arbitrary support of all associated data processing activities. Given the scope of the organization's activities it follows that the data resource is itself rather broad in terms of data content. Obviously the data resource cannot be constructed overnight and, in fact, is best developed in stages so that each successive stage supports the further development of the data resource by stages to follow.

The project stage concept was established in the previous chapter. The intention is to create a data base system project so that the data resource grows, and to structure that growth so that as the project develops it supports the organizational structure. In that chapter we also looked at the relationship between the data resource and the organizational structure. Source, operational, and managerial data elements were defined and their usage throughout the organization described. Source data entities were discussed and the concept of the data base system project staging plan as related to source data entities was developed. It is the purpose of this chapter to carry these ideas forward into the pragmatic details for determining source data entities, relationships to organizational units, and the structuring of a data base system project plan. Such planning requires additional information in terms of availability of manpower and skills, computing capacity, data base administration, and so on.

All of these topics and general guidelines for creating a data base system project plan are the central subjects of discussion in what follows. Up to this point, in all of our discussions we have talked about "data," "data elements," and "data entities." However, the planning efforts of a data base system project are more intimately connected with the users, business functions, and the corporate organization. We are, therefore, more interested at this point in "information," "information elements," and "information entities." The distinction is significant.

Information and Data

The computer system carries and operates on data that is explicitly characterized by the fact that the direct definition of the data is usually not available in the data processing system itself. With the advent of data dictionary methods, however, such information about data can be made available, but in other, unrelated portions of the system. One also might argue that the definition of data must necessarily be understood by an application program and that from this point of view the program itself could be said to be a definition of that data. This is in part the case in a COBOL data definition section, but falls far short of what we usually think of as the definition or description of data in detail, particularly with regard to its semantics.

Information, on the other hand, is the interpretation of data into immediately readable and applicable external forms. Information generally appears with its definition, if not overtly, then in the mind of its user. All of which is to say that data is in the province of data processing, while information is in the province of the end users, a difference that is significant in terms of any data base system project. Users use information to carry out their business functions and job responsibilities. Data processing manipulates data via programs, and controls its security, privacy, and integrity through its systems.

The scoping phase of the data base system development process is concerned with information and the end users.

The design phase is engaged with data and the architecture of the data base system. In between links, the requirements phase forms a bridge between information and data, providing the means by which the specified information can be identified in terms of the needed data elements.

To make the point about the distinction between data and information, consider a data base element whose name is STKITMTODT and an example of one of its data values, 80036. Compare this to the information value 5 FEB 80 under a report heading TURNOVER DATES on a stock item report. In this example, February 5th is the 36th day of the year 1980, and the compressed format (probably compressed numeric format) is a convenient way to carry it in the data base. What appears on the report is obviously self explanatory.

Another and more telling example of the difference between information and data is a date, such as an accounts receivable date, whose year, month, and day values are of interest to one user, while the year value only is of interest to a second user, and the month and day value is of interest to a third user. All of these information element types would derive their information values from the same common data element type; call it ACCTREC DT, with the data value carried in some specific format convenient for data processing. Here the information content for two of these applications requires only a portion of the whole data element value.

The examples can get more complicated, however. Let's suppose that an information requirement of an end user's data processing product is for the total accounts receivable value for a given customer over a year to data interval. But suppose, in addition, that in the data base we carry only the individual account receivable values. Then in order to produce this information for the end user, it is necessary to select all of the individual account receivable values by customer, sum them, and present them in the required information format. This example points out that not only is there very likely not a direct one-to-one relationship between information elements in the end user community and data elements in the data base, but that, further, there is some intermediary data processing entity which must be used to complete the transformation from data elements to information elements, and data element values to information element values.

There is neither mystery in this nor anything new; the transformation medium is the application program and the computational fields it employs. It is such a program that will call for all of the supporting data element values from the data base, accumulate them into some assigned program field, and report in the proper format resultant data values as information in the end user's DP product. Therefore we can say that if our requirement statement defines the information elements we need to satisfy the end user, then it is these information elements which determine the data elements that are required in the data base. It is the transformation process between data elements and information elements which then determines the data fields that must be present in an application program.

Information Elements

We could characterize information elements in the end user domain by three primary attributes. The attributes have to do with business function, organizational unit, and the relationship between business function and organizational unit.

In the first place a business function, such as materials management, has a detailed breakdown or functional decomposition into its most atomic functional units. Using materials management as an example, such a detailed function at the lowest level might be "write an item issue slip." It is important to recognize that at this level of detail such business functions are overtly associated with information elements by means of specific forms (the issue slip) and/or data processing input and output media (preprinted key punch forms, entry and retrieval screens and reports). When it is recognized that data processing development actually implements specific business functions that accomodate this level of functional detail, it is clear that such implementation must involve the explicit information elements that associate with and support that business function.

Secondly, a business function may be thought of as a part of the job description or job responsibility of the individual who must carry that function out. That person resides at some point of the organization chart in an organizational unit. That is, an individual with a responsibility for the preparation of an issue slip executes that business function and deals with the information values of the elements that associate immediately with the business function. It is in this context that information elements are employed by users in organizational units.

It is also in this sense that the third attribute of information becomes apparent, for it is the information element which provides the bridging relationship between business function and organizational unit. In fact, once we have detailed our business functions we should be able to map them onto the organizational units, and, as will be suggested later, then be able to identify sequences for implementing functions for the data base system that will efficiently create a growing data resource.

DATA BASE SURVEY INITIATION—VERTICALITY

We will refer to the overall activity of establishing a data base system project plan as the data base survey. The primary activities in the data base survey are to identify both data processing and non-data processing information carrying media, from these to make estimates of the required information entities, and finally to associate these information entities with organizational units and business functions. This requires examining forms employed by the organization to determine the non-data processing information entities that are employed in common by organizational units. It also requires looking at data processing products received by these units, and possibly systems that produce them as well, so as to determine commonality of information types as used by the organization.

Thus far, however, nothing has been said about the overall scope of the investigation. Quite clearly, to look at the DP and non-DP information carrying media for an entire organization would require time and manpower resources that would be excessive. Therefore a special procedure is employed to cut the workload down to manageable proportions. This is referred to as vertical analysis.

The principle of verticality in the structuring of a data base system project is based on the definition of a vertical organizational segment. Such a segment is defined in an organization chart as the collection of all dependent offices from a given office in the chart. Thus the set of all organizational offices in the chart that are dependent from the credit department forms a vertical segment within the organization. In a similar fashion, a division vice-president defines a major vertical segment throughout the organization chart which includes many other vertical segments entirely within it. In fact, if we step one level down the chart from its pinnacle, the chief executive officer, or presidential position, then at the next level the major vertical segments of the organization are defined. At this level there is an interesting differentiation in terms of data type utilization. This differentiation is in terms of source data. That is, if we look at the boundaries between two such vertical segments depending on this presidential level, in all probability we would find that there is little, if any, source data commonality. Indeed there should be almost no operational data commonality, and only among the upper echelon offices in the respective vertical segments will we be likely to find any kind of managerial data commonality. That is, between such organizational segments for the most part, there is an information flow based mainly on summarized managerial data, usually of the financial type.

Figure 3.1 is a generic organization chart which illustrates the meaning of this vertical separation in an organizational structure. Each upper level office provides a vertical segment (A, B, C). The segment D is contained in the segment C. In all probability the source data types for segments A, B, C will be independent, while those for C and D will show a high degree of commonality. The reason for this separation in source data terms is generally due to the fact that organizations are structured at this top level to make clear-cut distinctions between business activities which in all probability have only derived data relationships of the managerial data type in common.

Suppose that two vertical segments of the organization at the vice presidential level are defined such that there is literally no common source data types between them. It therefore follows that a data base system built for one will have virtually no impact on the implementation of a data base system for the second. It is, of course, likely that each of the two data base systems for their respective vertical segments will indeed place requirements on the other in terms of derived data of managerial type, but this will have no impact on the architectural structure of the source data bases designed to support them individually.

This then is the genesis of the verticality concept in structuring a data base system project. That is, we will seek to define a vertical segment of the organization whose source data base can be considered for the most part as separate from all other source data bases supporting other vertical organizational segments. If we are able to do this, then it follows that the data base system development for such a vertical segment of the organization will be essentially independent of, and not impacted by, later data base developments for subsequent vertical segments.

However, our problem is also associated with size. After all, a data base system project is ultimately limited by the manpower and skills available in the data processing organization. It is unreasonable and infeasible to plan a project that requires manpower and skill levels that simply are not available, and as a consequence we must continue the verticality process until we reach a level of the organization where the verticality principle regarding source data independence applies to the largest possible extent and the expected size of the data base system project is within the

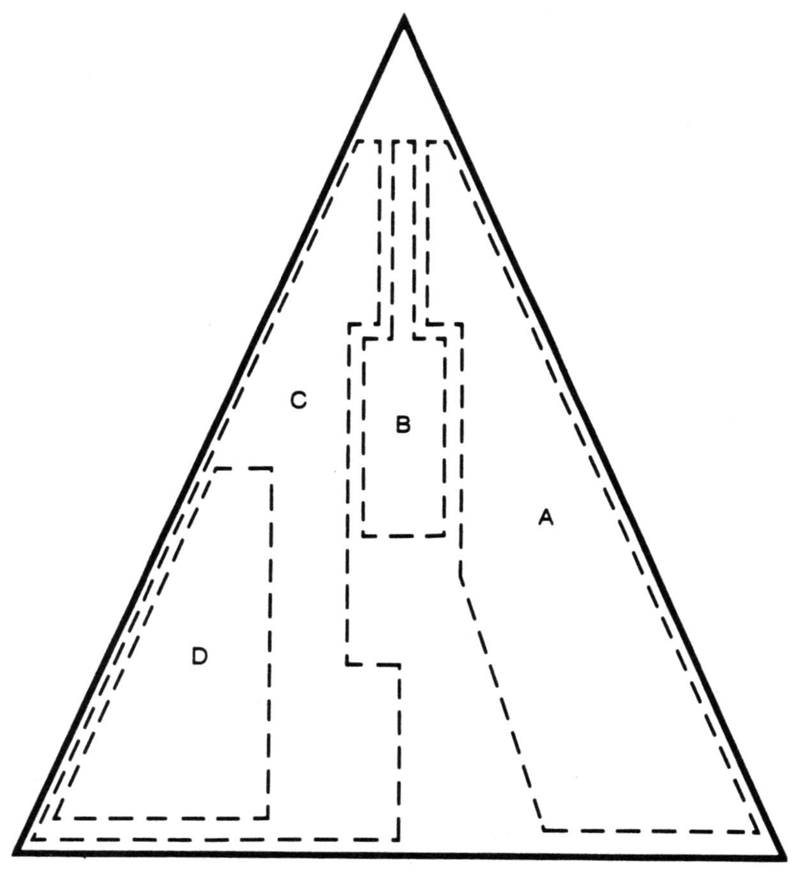

Figure 3.1/VERTICAL SEPARATION

delivery means and capabilities of the data processing organization. Therefore the vice presidential level, in all probability, creates vertical segments that are too large to satisfy our needs, and so we will go down to the next level and look at the result vertical segments in exactly the same light.

Selection Criteria

At every stage of the verticality process we are presented with choices of options for selection. It is necessary to have some criteria for selecting the vertical segment within the next step will be accommodated. That is, a vertical segment of the organization contains the vertical segments for next consideration, and therefore the criteria for making the selection must be an ever narrowing set of conditions so that we can approximate the vertical restriction on source data while at the same time having a consistent algorithm for selecting the next smaller vertical segment. The approach described below is based on minimizing risk in the creation of the data base system project stage, its implementation and its resultant data base system products.

The first step in the selection algorithm is to eliminate any vertical segment under consideration for which there is little or no current data processing support. The lack of current data processing support means that virtually no data exists in computer machineable form for this vertical segment of the organization. Therefore if a data base system project were to be structured for such a vertical segment, it would be necessary to locate that data in its orginal sources, that is, as information on non-data processing media, (such as paper forms), prepare it for insertion into the data processing environment, verify the data values after conversion, organize and distribute them into the data base, and then verify their integrity once present in the data base. This is a very difficult task and may well become the dominant activity in the overall data base system project. However, this activity has little to do with data base, and in such a circumstance the data base system project would be tied up with non-data base problems. This indeed would maximize the risk of successfully delivering data based data processing products to end users. For this reason those vertical segments of the organization at the current level of consideration which have little or no data processing available should be eliminated from further immediate consideration in the overall selection process.

For the remaining vertical segments we can then apply a second elimination criteria. This presupposes the existence of current data processing support in these vertical segments, and makes an evaluation of the general quality of the data. Such vertical segments will have data available in their current data processing systems and the data base system project will use that data as a basic source. If, however, the data quality is poor, then a large segment of the data base project activity will be devoted to cleaning up these data values. This again would represent a larger risk in the success of the overall data base project stage completion. Such areas should also be eliminated and the remaining vertical segments of the organization at the present level of consideration then examined further for selection.

If after vertical segments having little or no data processing support, or segments with data processing support but poor quality data are eliminated, there remain vertical segment alternatives, then there is one further qualification for vertical segment elimination. This has to do with the likelihood of user support of data processing in the development of a formal and exhaustive requirement statement. Many data processing organizations have arrived at a position where their difficulties with certain groups of end users make it likely that further detailed efforts on the part of end users to support a requirement gathering effort would not be forthcoming. Therefore the third criteria for elimination of a vertical segment is based on the expectation that user support can be counted on.

At any given level of the organization chart in the execution of a vertical analysis these three criteria can be used to select the alternative vertical segments which will be given further consideration in the next round of analysis. That next round should repeat the analysis until either a level in the organization is reached where it no longer can be said that the alternatives maintain a suitable degree of source data independence from one another, or a sufficient degree of source data independence remains but the criteria do not satisfactorily select a next alternative vertical segment. At this point two further considerations can be taken into account. These are an examination of the greatest needs for data processing support according to the users, as opposed to the greatest need for data processing support according to data processing. In order to validate these needs from the user's point of view it will be necessary to go to the heads of the organizational units in the alternative vertical segments to get their opinion. Data processing should, of course, be able to provide its own opinion. If there is agreement in these two opinions then the vertical segment corresponding to this conjunction should be selected. If there is no agreement it is recommended that the vertical segment corresponding to the user's preceived needs be selected.

A General Example

The methodology described above as the verticality principle has as its objective the selection of a data base system project stage based on minimizing the size of the organizational vertical segment that is planned to be treated as a data base system development stage. The technique is fundamentally structured on minimum risk in the achievement of that stage. Note, however, that the technique starts from the top of the organization and works its way down. Therefore, it always involves the bottom of the organization chart. As described in the last chapter, this is where source data makes its appearance and has its major impact. All data base activities above such source data levels are structured on derived data, operational and managerial in type, and consequently the verticality principle assures that the data base system project stage to be selected will involve the bottom of the organization and the necessary source data types.

Figure 3.2 illustrates a verticality process in terms of eight source data entity types. Here four vertical segments are shown with segments A, B, C at the top level, and segment D contained in segment C. The source data requirements for segment A consists of S6, S7, S8, while that for C is S1 through S5. Therefore source data bases for these two vertical segments can be structured independently. This is not the case for vertical segments C and D, however, since they have significant source data in common. In this example we can see that each vertical segment has an identification with a source data base, with the exception of vertical segment B. This apparently has no direct utilization of the source data but rather operates only on derived data. As described in the last chapter such a vertical segment, its offices and its end users, evidently cannot be supported with data base system services until the necessary source data bases have been implemented and suitable relationships structured on the derived data have been developed.

The verticality principle stands as a large scale mechanism designed to provide an initial segmenting of the overall organization for the purposes of scoping the data base system project. However, we have yet to say anything about the identification of the source data entities involved. In the foregoing, the description has been accomplished as if the source data entities were known. In fact, one purpose of a data base survey is to identify information entities so that we can estimate these source data entities. Therefore it will be necessary to carry out the foregoing analysis based on educated guesses concerning source data entity dependence. This can best be accomplished by data processing. It is clea, however, that these estimates can be rough since the data base survey will further refine them and the following service analysis will detail them to their fine points. As a consequence, the result of the vertical analysis should be an initial representation for the successive, staged units of the overall data base system project, designed in the long run to cover the entire organization and to satisfy its needs through the delivery of data based data processing services and support. In addition, and perhaps more importantly, the vertical analysis should suggest specific areas within which the data base survey can then focus and concentrate its activities.

Major and Crucial Functions

Simply stated, the basic objective of any data processing organization should be the provision of computational tools and support for the business functions of the organization as a whole. In data base, and in particular for the data base survey, we are interested in these business functions and the information entities they employ. However, if the data base survey reviewed each and every business function, even though restricted to the narrower confines resulting from the vertical analysis, the effort and the time required would be excessive in light of the level of information desired at this point in the project.

In order to dramatically reduce the effort involved without sacrificing the sought for level of detail, we introduce the concept of major and crucial functions. There are the business activities of an organization which are either extensive in their costs and utilization of resources, or are of primary and fundamental importance, or both. Each organizational unit will usually have just one major/crucial function, and we will discover that this function involves virtually all of the source data, and therefore source data entity types, of interest.

Major Functions

The major activities or functions of an organizational entity are best judged in terms of the resources required to carry them out. For example, customer services may provide a telephone answering capability with terminal access to certain data by means of which customer questions are answered and complaints resolved. It is very difficult, of course, to put either a dollar value on such a service function, or to estimate the dollar loss due to a reduction in the service. Whatever answers might be developed for such questions, however, the service is provided and requires a significant number of people, and

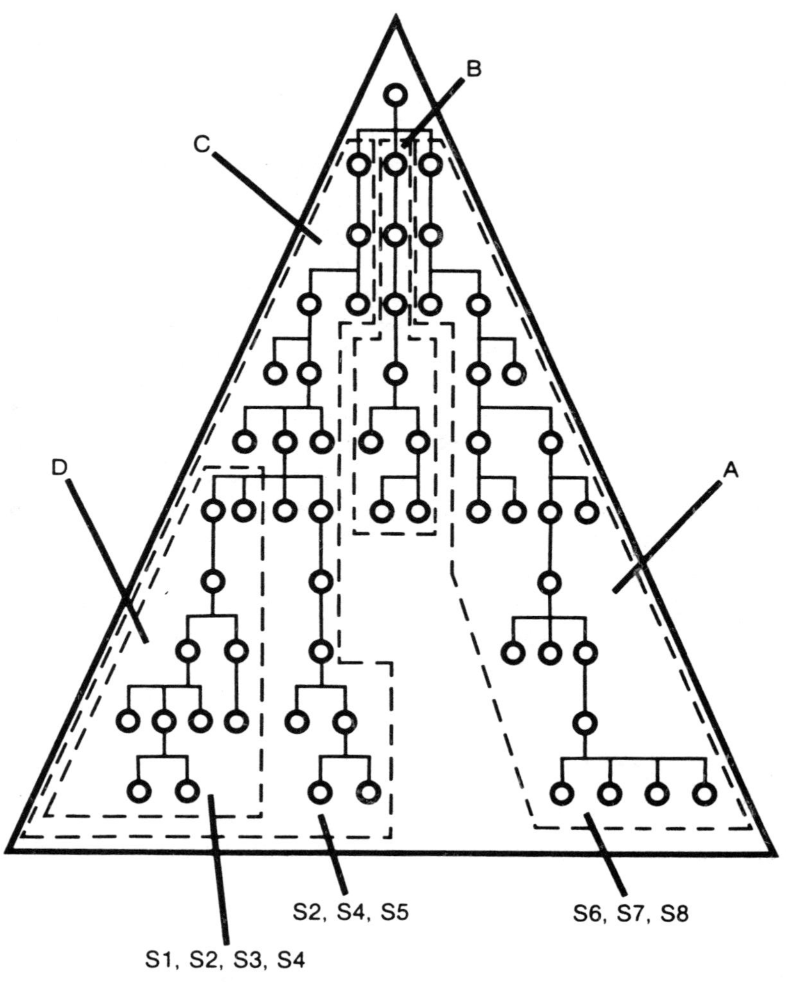

Figure 3.2/SOURCE DATA SEPARATION

telephone and computing resources to provide it. In that sense then, the current data processing support for such a function must be considered as a major contributor to the total load on the computing system.

It is in this context that major organizational functions, and therefore the data processing that supports them should be identified. It is probably completely reasonable to expect, in virtually all such major function cases, that they will be continued into the data base environment unless the advent of data base makes some significant change in procedures. Furthermore, it should be pointed out that such major business functions very often are involved with the customers of the organization and hence source data, and therefore do not change easily. That is, the external structure of the organization with respect to data processing is generally arranged to suit the needs of its business activities, and as such will not change rapidly, and certainly not simply because data processing has changed its own styles and methods by adopting data base.

In general, then, we can say that major functions identify supporting data processing systems. In terms of a particular major function identified with an organizational unit, interest will focus on the data processing support necessary to operate that major function. It is from this point of view that we can then associate major functions with reports and other data processing products.

Crucial Functions

In every organization there are a number of functions which are crucial to its success and well being. Sales, of course, will think that selling is the crucial function, and accounting will have similar feelings. Assembly operations will no doubt want to be heard on this score, and inventory management will lay its claim. The point here is that the issue of crucial functions cannot be decided in any democratic way, but rather must be related to economic well being in as specific a form as is sensible. Furthermore, no demand is made here that a formal analysis to define the most crucial function, next most crucial function, and so on, is necessary. Rather, it is important to recognize crucial functions when they turn up in the context of the data base survey analysis.

We may think of crucial functions as those which associate directly with the customer in terms of dollar volume of activity, or which indirectly impact the dollar performance of the business, or which provide internal measures of business performance that are essential to management decision making. The current statement of condition of a bank, produced daily in order to inform bank management of the actual amount of funds available for investment and lending commitment is essential and therefore crucial to the bank's performance.

Function, Organization, Information

The process of vertical analysis is primarily concerned with organization. Based on organization and the ways in which we estimate that it separates source data types, the object of the vertical analysis is to divide the overall organization into a collection of ever more numerous but successively smaller potential data base system projects. In this discussion there was a brief allusion to business function. At this point, however, the role of business function must become dominant.

The purpose of a data processing system is to produce data processing products. These products are in the form of output reports, screens for input and output of information and preprinted forms to be filled in for data entry. Indeed, it is these data processing products which are the primary view the end user has of data processing itself. It is these products that record, convey, and transfer the information on which the end user activities are based. However, it is important to recognize that while the user employs the information made available in his job, it always is needed to execute some business function that is his job or responsibility. That is, the user executes functions and employs information to accomplish that execution. From the data processing point of view it is, therefore, proper to say that data processing systems implement or support the execution of function, the user in his organizational unit carries out, or is responsible for that business function, and information is the basis on which the function is executed under the user's control.

In many respects we might expect that a commonly employed and well known business function such as inventory stock count will probably have both the same general structure and the same information types in different companies. However, the ways in which the function is executed within a given company may be decidedly different. In this user dimension, usage attributes such as the frequency of execution of the function, required turn-around time, information volume, keys, security and privacy conditions will in all likelihood vary widely from company to company. Thus a function is what needs to be implemented. Organizational units determine the attributes of the use of that function and therefore its implementation, and both the function and its usage depend on the associated information.

From this consideration it follows that in order to know what to implement we must have a clear picture of the functions for which data processing products need to be provided. This will be accomplished by the functional decomposition discussed in the next section. These decomposed functions which detail to the lowest level the definition of business function are mapped onto the organizational units that have responsibility for their execution. This is then employed in a process that determines the associated information needs for that user and thereby for the functions he executes. Based on this structured view of function, organization and information, we can then ascertain possibilities for the data base system project in terms of growth of the data resource.

Functional Decomposition

The word "decomposition" implies the breakdown of an object of interest into the set of its constituent parts. A lawn chair, for example, is usually delivered in a flat box with half a dozen pieces and a small package of nuts, bolts and screws for putting it together. These are the basic components of the lawn chair and represent, after it has been put together, it's decomposition. However, the lawn chair in the box is only one level of decomposition. Certain parts of it, for example the seat, may come out of the box as a frame made up of four pieces bolted together at the factory with metal strips that have been riveted to the frame. Thus there was an earlier and more detailed decomposition of the chair seat itself, forming in its assembly the seat as it appears in the box. And, of course, there is an even further decomposition at the factory, since the metal strips, when they arrived at the riveter or the riveting machine originally were in the more rudimentary form of strip rolls which earlier had been cut to size and properly drilled for the rivets. Prior to that, the strip rolls were metal billets in a steel mill, and back far enough were ore in the earth.

The picture puzzle is an interesting example of a different dimension of decomposition. The picture has, as its most fundamental components, thousands of individual pieces presented when the box is opened and spilled out on the table. Any two pieces that we are able to put together at the outset represent a first level in composing the picture. Any three pieces, four pieces, five pieces and so on are all other levels in that composition so that there are seemingly endless levels of composition, and therefore decomposition, for picture puzzles. However, both the lawn chair and the picture puzzle represent objects for which we can say there exists a decomposition into primary elements. For the picture puzzle there are an unlimited number of composition routes to the finished product, while for the lawn chair there is only one route from the finished product at one level to the finished product at the next level. That is, at the factory, given strips on a roll and all the other raw materials for the lawn chair, specific things must be done and certain events must occur in a specific order to result in the finished product which can go into the box. Given the box, specific events must occur (tab A into slot B) in order to result in a lawn chair, once the box gets home.

A business function is an object that can be decomposed as well. An example might be the business function "Manufacture Lawn Chairs." The most immediate level in the decomposition of this function includes the subfunctions:

Control Materials Inventory
Schedule Equipment Maintenance
Distribute Finished Products
Manage Personnel
etc.

Each of these subfunctions, in turn, has a further decomposition, down to some level of detail that we can then associate with a full definition of all the constituent elements of the business function "Manufacture Lawn Chairs."

We can identify certain characteristics of a functional decomposition. In the first place, each unit of a decomposition will represent a subfunction of the overall function itself. The unit is described with a verb ("manufacture") and a noun ("lawn chairs"). Sometimes the subfunction description will include an adjective to provide a further qualification. For example, if the primary function is "Manufacture Chairs," then two subfunctions might be "Manufacture Lawn Chairs" and "Manufacture Dining Room Chairs."

Presenting the Decomposition

The term "levels of the decomposition" has been used in this discussion. This means that a function at a given level has a further decomposition represented by functions "below" it, and is a member of the decomposition for some function "above" it. This in turn suggests that there is a hierarchical relationship between functions and their respective subfunctions, and that a hierarchical structure would be an effective means of presenting a particular business function decomposition.

Figure 3.3 is an example of a functional decomposition for the business function "Operate Parts Return" within a materials management environment. In the first place, this business function is a subfunction in some larger decomposition. It, in turn, has the decomposition shown in the figure. Its first subfunction level consists of two decomposition elements, "Receive Returns" and "Determine Routing," each of which might be accompanied by a paragraph or two describing the function in full definitional detail. However, The next level down from "Receive Returns" shows three subfunctions whose respective definitions should jointly define the function "Receive Returns." Thus, the hierarchical presentation of the functional decomposition is, in effect, a definition of each level of the decomposition up to primary function at the top of the hierarchical chart.

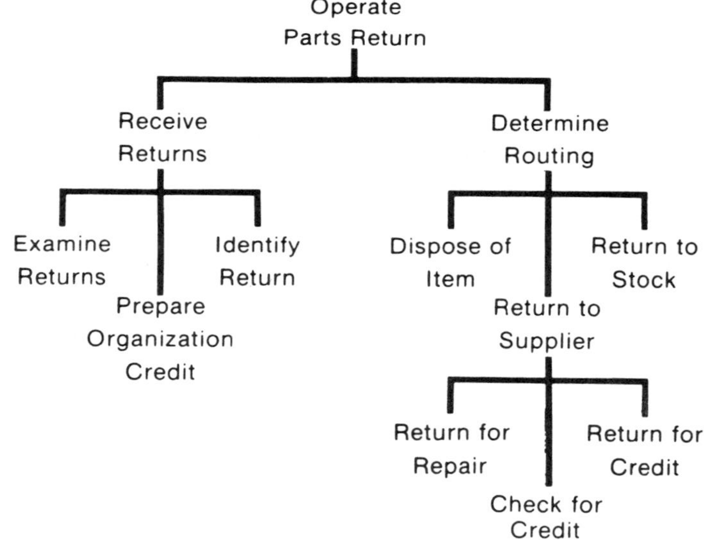

Figure 3.3/RETURNS FUNCTIONAL DECOMPOSITION

Note that each subfunction description consists of a verb and a noun. Furthermore, there is no implied order for the reading of subfunctions of a given level. In other words, the hierarchical presentation of a functional decomposition does not read from left to right, or in any other direction, in order to imply the sequence in which the functions are carried out. That is to say, the functional decomposition is a format for presenting the description of the function, not how the function is executed.

It was pointed out earlier that the decomposition can be carried out to an extreme of detail. In the example of the lawn chairs we managed to include the ore for the metal that went into the strip rolls for the seats of the lawn chair. For the buyer of the lawn chair that level of detail has little significance. In fact, for the manufacturer of the lawn chair, there is probably not much value in that level of detail either. For the maker of the steel strips, that level of detail may, indeed, be important. Thus, the degree of detail required for the functional decomposition evidently depends on the purposes to which it is to be put, and for data base, that level of detail can be rather well defined.

The data processing system delivers data processing products and these products serve to implement business functions. Thus the level of detail that is of interest in a functional decomposition is that which identifies specific actions that must be carried out and events that occur with which we can associate information and information carrying media. Such information carrying media come come in two forms. One of these is the very familiar paper form containing fields defined for information to be entered. The paper form is moved from point to point in the organization, and since these organizational points carry out the actions of specific business functions, it is this information which supports those business functions. The second information media is in data processing products. These prodoucts are used to acquire information in the computer system at one point in the organization and to deliver that information or its derivatives to other points of the organization as reports and screens. Therefore the level of detail suitable for a functional decomposition to support the needs of data base is that which allows us to identify actions and events with information carrying media and the information that these media carry.

Figure 3.4 continues the decomposition for "Operate Parts

Return" by providing the detail for the subfunction "Examine Returns." The figure indicates that there are two major actions taken in the examination of returns. One of these is "Prepare Damage Report" and this in turn involves two actions "Estimate Repairs" and "Issue Damage Slip." At this level, we can easily imagine that there is a form to be filled out or, if the system exists, data to be entered into the computer. We can readily verify this by determining whether or not these functions indeed are identified with such information carrying media. If so, we may well be done with this part of the decomposition, or we may decide that the media suggests several actions and that there is yet one more level to be added to the hierarchy. Ideally, the most atomic level of a functional decomposition associates with a single information carrying unit; i.e., form or DP product.

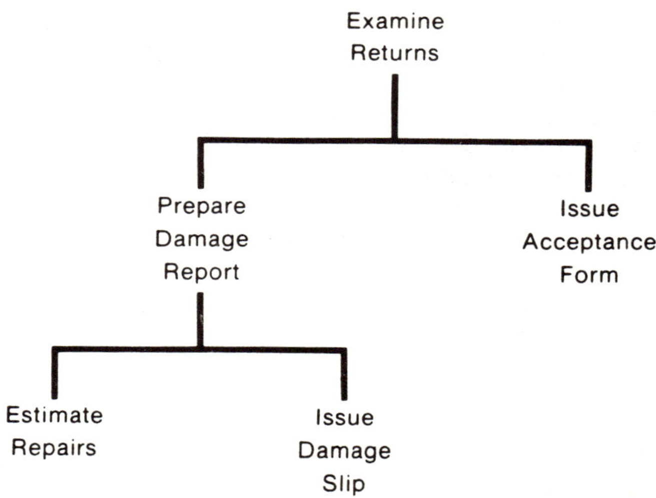

Figure 3.4/"EXAMINE RETURNS" DECOMPOSITION DETAIL

Function/Organization Sharing

Business functions and their detailed subfunctions are carried out by people who reside in organizational units.

That is, they are executed by people who have positions or locations in the organization chart. Since every element of the functional decomposition at the lowest level represents an action to be taken, this action must be taken by someone, and that someone must be placed in the organizational chart.

Moreover, since every functional description contains a verb, it indicates that some action is implied and this in turn demands that there be someone identified with that action. As a consequence, we can say that the functional decomposition should map into the organization chart. This means that each element in the functional decomposition hierarchy must correspond to at least one point in the organization chart where someone is responsible for the execution of that function. It may be that a given function is accomplished at more than one point in the organization chart, but it is clearly necessary that it associate with at least one organization chart location.

Figure 3.5 is an example of an organizational structure for the management of parts return. There are six offices identified in this chart and the example assigns organizational identification to each (manager returns: 42001). The business functions in the decomposition of Figure 3.3 are executed by the individuals in this organization, and Figure 3.6 is a matrix which displays the relationship between business function and organizational unit. This is referred to as a function-organization sharing matrix. It lists the six organizational units of Figure 3.5 and the twelve business functions of Figure 3.3. For the sake of simplicity, these have not been augmented by the detailed functions of Figure 3.4. This matrix then shows which organizational units are responsible for particular business functions. Thus the organizational unit, "Receiving Clerk" is responsible for the business functions:

Examine Returns
Prepare Organization Chart
Identify Return

In general, reading across the rows of this matrix we can

see the functions for which a given office or organizational unit is responsible, and reading down the columns we can identify the business function with the offices having responsibility for its execution.

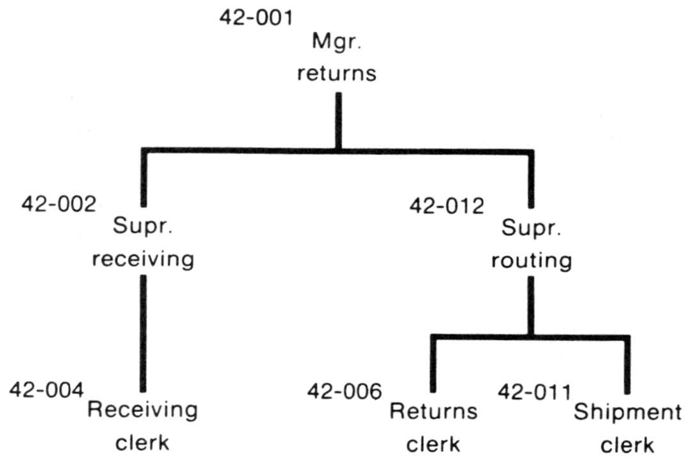

Figure 3.5/RETURNS ORGANIZATION CHART

The importance of the function-organization sharing matrix is that it identifies those who do the job with the job to be done. More importantly, those who do the job can provide information on its doing; the definition of the information that is employed in the job, the frequency of its execution, the speed with which it has to be accomplished, the volumes of information that are involved, etc. Furthermore, they can give us insights into the quality of the current information that they deal with in terms of its accuracy, timeliness, arrangement, etc. That is, these are the users from whom the data base requirement statement must be developed. Thus the first result of the overall process of the data base survey is to the users of information based on the functionality of the organization within which they perform their jobs.

	Function											
Organisation	Operate parts return	Receive returns	Examine returns	Prepare org. credit	Identify return	Determine routing	Return to supplier	Return for repair	Check for credit	Return for credit	Dispose of item	Return to stock
Mgr. returns	X											
Supr. receiving		X										
Receiving clerk			X	X	X							
Supr. routing						X					X	X
Shipment clerk							X	X				X
Returns clerk							X	X	X	X		

Figure 3.6/FUNCTION-ORGANIZATION SHARING

Service Sources

Everybody today is familiar with the data processing report and the formatted screens for direct input and output of information. These and the preprinted forms to be filled in and sent to the data input department make up the DP products that are the essential elements of the user's relationship to data processing. As we have pointed out in the sections above, it is such DP products that are identified with specific subfunctions of the functional decomposition. Furthermore, the non-DP information carrying media, such as forms, telephone communications, manual logs and tickler files, also contain information that supports the execution of these subfunctions.

But the execution of these functions and subfunctions is carried out by individuals in the organization, and it is these people who use both the DP and non-DP information carrying media for these purposes. In fact, as we have discussed in Chapters 1 and 2, the data processing system will deliver services to these users. These services will be in the form of DP products. In order to do that, we will have to gather detailed information regarding function, organization, and information and this, as well, comes from the user. The identification of the current DP products and the non-DP information carrying media is an essential step in this process. These represent not only the activities that a given individual carries out, but the information with which those activities are accomplished. We call these information carrying media -- both DP and non-DP -- service sources, and as a part of the data base survey we will collect, identify and organize these service sources.

A data processing service source might, for example, be a report. A specific user receives this report and uses it for accomplishing certain functions that are defined as part of his job. The information content of the report is in its rows, columns, headings and values. Some part of the report may be used to support a particular business function, and some user's job responsibility.

If a sample of such a report is available when we talk to the user about his detailed requirements, we will obviously have a far better opportunity to understand what he does, and his satisfaction and/or dissatisfaction with the current DP products he receives, what can be done to improve and optimize them, etc. That is, the DP service sources obviously are an essential tool in the structuring of the requirement statement. That portion of the overall data base system activity that uses the service sources in interviews with end users to produce the detailed information of the requirement statement has been briefly described earlier and is referred to as the service analysis. Therefore, the data processing service sources are collected in order to support this service analysis activity.

The non-DP service sources represent information recording and transfer between organizational units via media other than the computer and its products. In exactly the same way that a DP product supports the functional responsibilities of the end user and provides insight into the detailed requirement statement, so also does the non-DP service source. An example of a service source of this type can be seen in Figure 3.9. Clearly the kind of information called for on this form is associated with, and even descriptive of the sort of work that is necessary to accomplish the functional responsibilities of a particular job or jobs in an organization. Therefore an additional part of the data base survey is to collect such data processing service sources so that a complete array of all service sources of all types supporting the functionality of the organization and the individuals in it who execute that functionality can be organized and analyzed.

Inventory of DP Products

The first step in the overall procedure is to gather up all of the data processing service sources. With the completed functional decomposition and the structuring of the function-organization sharing matrix, we are able to identify whose DP service sources we are interested in.

With this in hand, we can now prepare an inventory of DP products that are currently employed by these users, along the lines shown in Figure 3.7. This consists of the product name, which serves to identify it, and for an estimate of the volume in terms of the number of lines produced, the frequency of the product's production and the names of the files that enter into its production. The next column lists maintenance sources. By this we mean the individuals in the organization who generate and provide input to the files that support the products listed in the inventory. Ultimate concern will be with the nature of the maintenance effort, quality of the data that is entered into the system, the frequency of that entry, its timing relative to the product's production, and so on. This will all be brought out in the service analysis, but the purpose here is to identify these maintenance sources so that we are able to determine not only the recipient of the information represented by the DP product, but the source of the data on which that information is based.

Product name	Report volume	Production frequency	Files			Maint. sources	Comments
			Input	output	Master		

Figure 3.7/DP PRODUCTS INVENTORY

Finally, the DP product inventory should include comments from those who must run the system in order to produce particular products. This is, of course, the operations group, and any comments that are specifically reflective of difficulties with the system in its execution, or general characteristics of the system that should be noted, are valuable in terms of the objectives for the data base survey.

Non-DP Service Sources

The second step is to develop the collection of DP service sources that provide information that transfer media for the organization's users. Again, we are only concerned with the service sources that have to do with those organizational units that are identified by the function-organization sharing matrix. In the simplest statement of the process we need only go to these end users and collect samples of the non-DP service sources they employ. These are forms, telephone communications, manual logs, tickler files and the like.

The form shown in Figure 3.8 is useful for documenting these non-DP service sources. Each form is associated with a particular unit or office, and in the first two columns identifies the service source by title and a unique identifying number. The next six columns refer to activities relative to the service source within the particular office. The first one asks whether or not the service source is generated in this office. If it is, then the space should be checked, but otherwise left blank. An office which generates a service source is responsible for the original information quality, and ultimately the data base system project will have to locate and identify all organizational users with such responsibilities for source data put into the data base in order to guarantee quality control for that data at its point of origin.

The next column designates the office from which the service source is received if it is not generated by this office. This will be an office in the organization that has previously used the form for some purpose, which in turn

Office__________

Title	No.	Gen	Rec'd From	Pro-cess	Sent to	Ret	Des	Business Function

Figure 3.8/NON-DP SERVICE SOURCES

means that it employs its information in common with the organizational unit we are now examining. The process column is to be broadly descriptive of the actions taken on the service source, and as such will represent some portion of the functional responsibility of this office since it defines one of the components of the functional decomposition. At this point in the form a number should be entered identifying the process and on a second form, to be discussed below, the process should be described.

The next column indicates to whom the service source is sent once the process is complete. This, again, is some office in the organizational structure. If, however, the service source is not forwarded but is retained in this office, then that should be noted in column 7, or if it is destroyed, in column 8. The final column identifies the business function with which this service source is associated. This is necessary since the given user may have a number of responsibilities related to several different business functions.

Figure 3.9 is an example of a DP service source. This is a return transmittal form that is completed by Receiving Clerks for delivery to the Supervisory Returns Routing after the return has been examined (see Figure 3.5). The form identifies the organization returning the item, giving its organization identification, the item description and its item stock number. The dates of issue, return and transmittal are included, and a coding for the reason for return is determined. These all represent processes carried out by the Return Clerk.

Figure 3.10 is an example of the use of the non-DP service source form. The office is the Receiving Clerk and the form is the Return Transmittal number R126. It is generated in this office and therefore is not received from some other office. The process applied to it is described in note 1 and the completed form is sent to the Supervisor of Routing. It is also noted that a copy of the form is retained in this office. This suggests that the information on this form is retained for later reference, and in the data base system environment may be the source of services for executing such a functional activity. Finally, it is noted that the business function supported is "Issue Acceptance Form" which is in the further detailed decomposition of Figure 3.4. The process applied to the transmittal form is described in summary manner by means of the process description form illustrated in Figure 3.11. Again, the office is identified and the title of the form noted. The process description indicates the activities carried out to complete the transmittal form prior to delivery to the Returns Routing Office.

Returns Transmittal

Returning organization ____ Organization ID ____

Item stock no. ____ Item description ____

Issue date ____ Return date ____

Issue order no. ____ Return order no. ____

Transmittal date ____ Reason for return ____

Rec'd by ____

Examiner ____ Return code ____

Form No. R126

Office receiving clerks

Title	No.	Gen	Rec'd from	Pro-cess	Sent to	Ret	Des	Business Function
returns transmittal	R126	X	—	1	supr. routing	X	—	issue acceptance form

Figure 3.10/NON-DP SERVICE SOURCE EXAMPLE

PROCESS
DESCRIPTION

Office receiving clerks

Title	Process Description
returns transmittal	Assign return order no. Establish transmittal date and validate return code.

Figure 3.11

It is useful to point out here that at some point in the data base system project an application program will be written to provide DP products that support this process. For example, the validation of a return code may call for the searching of the Returns Transmittal "reason" description to derive key words, and the employment of those key words in a key word index to get the proper return code value. This is clearly processing that is most easily carried out by the computer system, and given the nature of the information on which such a system would operate would very likely be well suited to the data base technique. Thus, the process description, as represented in a form such as that shown in Figure 3.11, is the beginning of the application program function specification that ultimately will have to be developed in order to deliver the new DP products to end users.

Information Entities

Once we have collected all the service sources, both DP

and non-DP, we can identify the information types that they carry. For example, the Returns Transmittal form of Figure 3.9 has RETURNING ORGANIZATION and ORGANIZATION ID as two of its information types. In general the headings of reports, the names of fields on a screen or preprinted form, as well as field names on non-DP service sources, represent these information types of interest.

The next step is designed to determine who uses a given information type across the organizational units being examined, and how these information types might be grouped together. This can be carried out by a simple mechanical process employing index cards. Figure 3.12 shows three such index cards, each of which has on it a specific information type, the ID of the form from which it is taken, and the organization that is associated with the form. In this example, the Receiving Clerk uses service sources (in this case, form R126) for which index cards representing RETURNING ORGANIZATION and ORGANIZATION ID have been prepared. In addition, Return Clerk index cards taken from form R096 have been prepared, among which is a card for ORGANIZATION ID. That is, each service source for a given organization will yield up a collection of index cards, one for each of the information types it holds. All of these cards taken together for a given office, and then taken together over all offices, will yield a deck of index cards representing all of the information types used by all of these organizations in DP and non-DP service sources. There is, of course, a good deal of redundancy among these cards insofar as the information types are concerned. This is illustrated in the ORGANIZATION ID information type cards in Figure 3.12. However, to determine the unique information types, we need only sort all the index cards by information type, and then aggregate the result of each unique information type.

This is shown in the left hand side of Figure 3.13. Here the sorting has resulted in three index card items that involve ORGANIZATION ID, and three other card items involving RETURNING ORGANIZATION. Each of these card sets

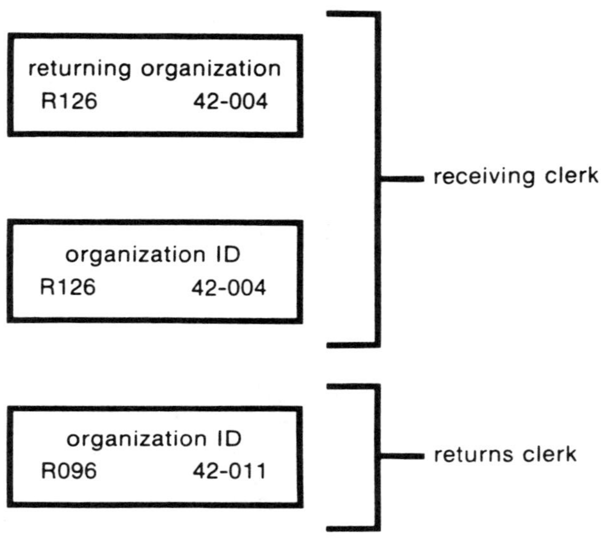

Figure 3.12/INFORMATION TYPE GROUPING

have been consolidated to give the collection of forms supported by the particular information type, with the set of offices they support shown by organization number. Note that the set of offices supported by the two information types are identical, and the implication to be drawn is that these two information types always appear together in the functions operated by these respective offices. We shall call such a grouping an information entity, and the next step is to prepare one card combining all of these information types that support a common set of offices, along with the forms on which these types appear. This is shown in the right hand portion of Figure 3.13. This information entity has been named ORG. UNIT and each reference to this information entity will directly imply the two information types ORGANIZATION ID and RETURNING ORGANIZATION. Given a file of such cards, containing both the information entity cards and the information element cards, we could then easily answer such questions as: "What organizations use ORGANIZATION ID?" and

"On what forms does the information entity ORG. UNIT appear?"

Such a structure is perhaps already familiar as the data dictionary. Indeed, the usual data dictionary provides just such a recording capability for data processing units known as data entities. In this example we have extended it to incorporate such facilities for the information entities of the service sources.

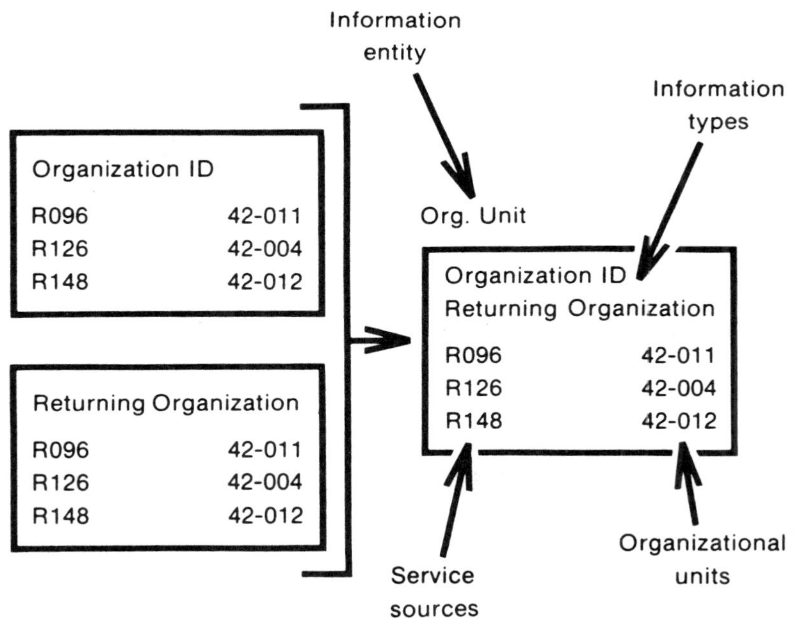

Figure 3.13/INFORMATION ENTITIES

Information/Organization Sharing

Starting with functionality, we have determined the organizational units responsible for its execution. This in turn has provided us with service sources which have yielded information types and information entities. That is, we have structured a relationship between organizations and the information they use. This can be seen in flow terms in the representation illustrated in Figure 3.14. Here, two organization units are shown with their respective processes relative to certain forms. For Organization Unit one, Form A is received from somewhere, the process is applied, and the result is Form B and an input to the computer system. Organization Unit two receives Form B, applies a process that results in Form C and an input to the computer system as well. Note that the input to the computer from Unit two derives an input to Organization Unit one and its process. Since both the DP and non-DP service sources have been associated with each of these organizations, and from them we have determined the information types and entities that their processes involve, we have, in effect, structured an information relationship between these two organizational units. In this structure the computer system acts as an information transfer medium, taking output from one process and providing it as input to another.

This relationship between organizations in terms of information can be effectively presented via the information-/organization sharing matrix. This is illustrated in Figure 3.15 showing organizational unit numbers as the row headings and information entities as the column headings. Each of these information entities consists of a certain specified set of information types, as in the case of the entity ORG. UNIT. For a given organization then, we are able to identify the collection of information entities which the organization needs to execute its functional responsibilities. For example, organization 42-012 (Supervisor Receiving, Figure 3.5) uses the following information entities:

RETURN DATA
STOCK DATA
ORG. UNIT

On the other hand, we may look at an information entity such as ISSUE DATA and determine from the information-/organization sharing matrix that four organizational units all employ the information types it contains.

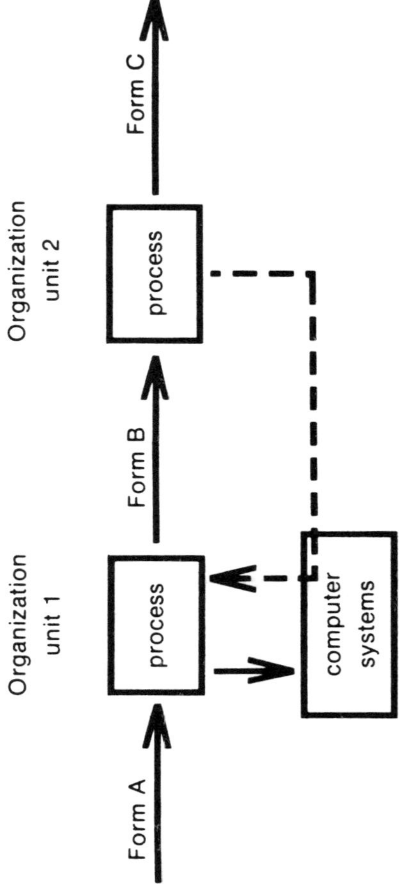

Figure 3.14/INFORMATION FLOW

Information entity

Organization	issue data	return data	stock data	org unit	restock	credit acct
42-001	X					X
42-002	X				X	
42-004	X			X	X	
42-012		X	X	X		
42-006		X				X
42-011	X		X	X		X

Figure 3.15/INFORMATION/ORGANIZATION SHARING

Information Function Sharing

If we have associated information entity types with organizations, and organizations with functions, then we should be able to associate information types with functions as well. This, in fact, is a straightforward process which is illustrated in Figure 3.16. Here the collection of functions for the decomposition shown in Figure 3.3 is listed on the left and the information entities determined by the service sources are shown as the columns. In this figure the information entities are taken from the example of Figure 3.15.

Each association of a function with an information entity has been marked in the matrix. The procedure is immediately apparent where one organizational unit corresponds to one and only one business function. Looking at Figure 3.6, this is the case for the office "Supervisor Receiving"

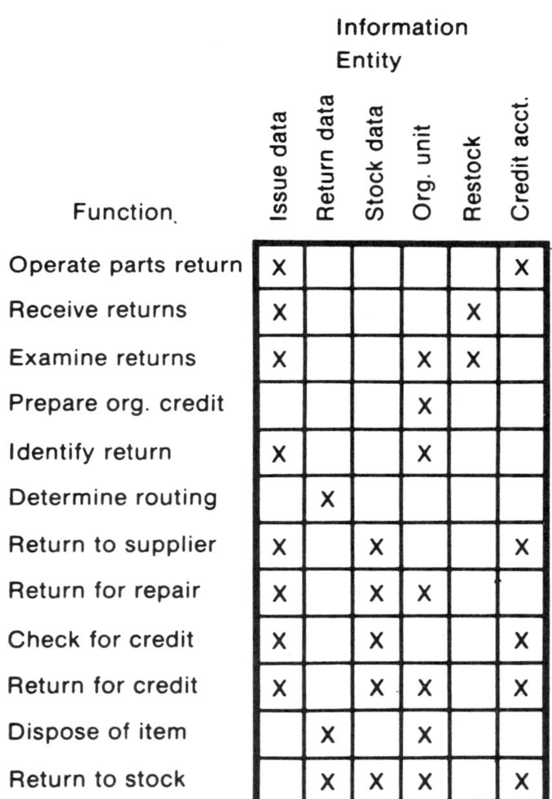

Information Entity

Function	Issue data	Return data	Stock data	Org. unit	Restock	Credit acct.
Operate parts return	X					X
Receive returns	X				X	
Examine returns	X			X	X	
Prepare org. credit				X		
Identify return	X			X		
Determine routing		X				
Return to supplier	X		X			X
Return for repair	X		X	X		
Check for credit	X		X			X
Return for credit	X		X	X		X
Dispose of item		X		X		
Return to stock		X	X	X		X

Figure 3.16/INFORMATION/FUNCTION SHARING — 1

and the business function "Receive Returns." The organizational identification for this office is 42/002 and in Figure 3.15 this corresponds to the two information entities ISSUE DATA and RESTOCK. Therefore, in forming the information/function sharing matrix of Figure 3.16, the "Receive Returns" row will have entries for the information entities ISSUE DATA and RESTOCK as indicated.

The process is slightly more complicated if one organizational unit corresponds to two or more business functions. Take "Shipment Clerk" as an example in Figure 3.6. This corresponds to the two functions "Return to Supplier" and "Return for Repair." The organization code is 42/006, and in Figure 3.15 we find that the two information entities RETURN DATA, CREDIT ACCT are employed in the execution of these two functions. However, the information that we have collected does not tell us, directly, which of the several information types is associated with each of the two business functions. To determine this, we need to go back to our data dictionary on index cards. Figure 3.13 indicates that there is an index card in our deck for each of the information entities. Therefore we could look up the card for, say, CREDIT ACCT, discover that it consists of a certain collection of information types and for each of these look up their respective information type cards in the dictionary which will in turn tell us the service source identification. We can now look at the service source, and in particular its documentation, to discover its identification with a business function. As a consequence, we are then able to fill in the rest of the information/function sharing matrix of Figure 3.16.

Each row of the information/function sharing matrix indicates the collection of information entities -- and through the data dictionary, the corresponding information types -- that are necessary to support the processes that are associated with that business function. Remember that these processes involve both current data processing and non-DP activities, since the information types have been drawn from both kinds of service sources. At the same time, the matrix indicates the functions that are supported by a particular information entity. For example, the entity RESTOCK and its associated information types support the two business functions "Receive Returns" and "Examine Returns." The information type ISSUE DATA supports eight out of twelve business functions, and represents the most widely used set of information types across this business function spectrum.

Data Resource Structuring

Between the minimal use of the RESTOCK information entity, and the maximal use of the ISSUE DATA information entity, there are varying degrees of usage among the other information types supporting these business functions. The question before us is how to organize this relationship between function and information entity so that we can identify a rational procedure for the implementation of functions which will both build on and expand the data base already created to support the business functions by prior stages.

This is accomplished by a two step procedure that we will refer to as data resource structuring. The first step is to rearrange the columns of the sharing matrix in Figure 3.16 so that the entity columns with the most entries are all on the left of the matrix and those with the least to the right. This has been accomplished in the sharing matrix of Figure 3.17. The next step is to do the same thing with respect to functions. That is, rearrange the rows so that the rows with the most entries are at the bottom of the matrix and those with the fewest are at the top. The result for our example is shown in Figure 3.18.

There are twelve functional elements in this example. Taken by itself, Figure 3.18 suggests that if a first stage of the project concentrated on the implementation of programs and program systems to deliver services supporting the first three of these functions, then a certain portion of the data base would have to be implemented in order to represent the information requirements of these functions. Following that, the figure suggests that implementation of the next four functions in a second stage would use certain portions of the data base already in

Function	Issue data	Org. unit	Credit acct.	Stock data	Return data	Restock
Operate parts return	X		X			
Receive returns	X					X
Examine returns	X	X				X
Prepare org. credit		X				
Identify return	X	X				
Determine routing					X	
Return to supplier	X		X	X		
Return for repair	X	X		X		
Check for credit	X		X	X		
Return for credit	X	X	X	X		
Dispose of item		X			X	
Return to stock		X	X	X	X	

Information Entity

Figure 3.17/INFORMATION/FUNCTION SHARING — 2

Function	Issue data	Org. unit	Credit acct.	Stock data	Returns data	Restock
Prepare org. credit		X				
Determine routing					X	
Identify return	X	X				
Operate parts return	X		X			
Receive returns	X					X
Dispose of item		X			X	
Return to supplier	X		X	X		
Return for repair	X	X		X		
Return for credit	X		X	X		
Examine returns	X	X				X
Check for credit	X	X	X	X		
Return to stock		X	X	X	X	

(Column group heading: Information Entity)

Figure 3.18/INFORMATION/FUNCTION SHARING — 3

place from stage one, and would also augment that data base by additional structures corresponding to the further information entity set required by the second stage functions. This is illustrated in Figure 3.19 which shows that the implementation of these seven functions and the data base associated with their information entity requirements will provide the data base required by the remaining five functions.

Functions	Information Entities
Prepared org. credit	Issue data
Determine routing	Org. unit
Identify return	Return data
Operate parts return	Credit acct.
Receive returns	Stock data
Dispose of item	Restock
Return to supplier	

Figure 3.19/FUNCTION IMPLEMENTATION SEQUENCE

More generally, we can say that by developing an information/function sharing matrix and carrying out the ordering steps described above, we should arrive at a matrix of information/function sharing which has the pattern shown in Figure 3.20. It is this pattern, indicated by the dashed border of the figure, which is of importance in determining the sequence in which a project can be staged so as to build and capitalize on the growing data resource. The general principal is that the first functions at the top of the list incorporate information entities which are required by the subsequent functions to be implemented. The successive stages therefore constantly build on the data resource already in place and augment that resource to support the next stage of the development.

Other Items to be Considered

The data resource matrix of Figure 3.18, or the more general structure shown in Figure 3.20, does not complete the effort for data base system project staging. In the first place, the implementation sequence implied by the matrix says nothing about the procedural order of function execution, or what is more important in the larger picture, complete benefit groups. We come to this issue directly in Chapter 6.

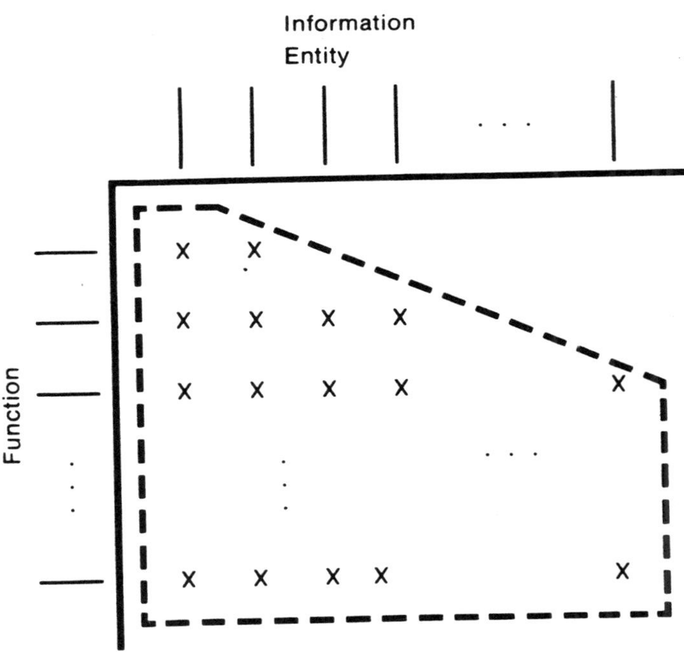

Figure 3.20/INFORMATION/FUNCTION SHARING PATTERN

CHAPTER 4
DATA BASE INTEGRITY AND PRIVACY

The quality of a data base system is ultimately defined in terms of the quality of the data it holds and the controls it provides for discrimination in its use. These two topics: the integrity of the data in a data base and the provision of data privacy are taken up in this chapter.

DATA BASE INTEGRITY

There are three major types of data in a data base and several subsidiary data types. These are discussed first and then each of the major data types is considered individually with particular attention paid to the nature of the integrity problem.

Data Base Types

We can identify three major types of data appearing in a data base. These are content, index data, and structure data. In addition, however, we can characterize other data that is, in effect, drawn from these three data types. These additional data types play further purposeful roles in a data base system environment and are referred to as derived data and overhead data.

Jointly, it is these five types of data which create the data totality on which a data base system is structured. This is characterized graphically in Figure 4.1.

Content Data

Content is the stuff of the data base, that which we usually think of as the raw data to be stored, retrieved and generally manipulated. It is the customer's name and

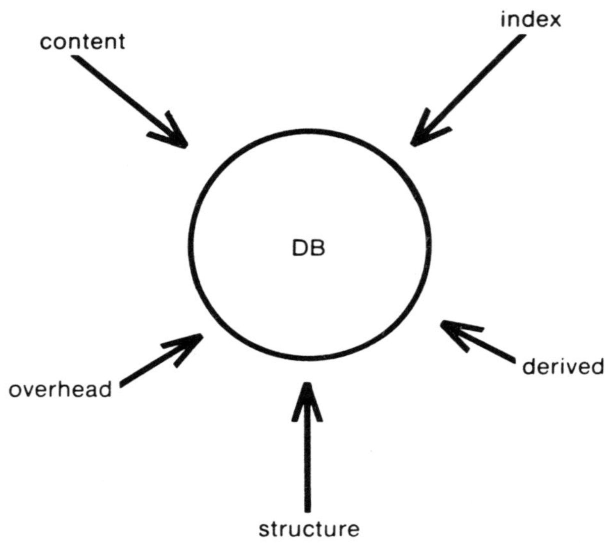

Figure 4.1/DATA BASE DATA TYPES

address, his order and the items that make it up, and so on. In general, we can say that the content is user supplied, and appears in the data base as the result of data base system services designed to input such data. At the same time, however, we might point out that such data is passive in nature. It creates no action on its own, but rather is the raw material out of which computational decisions are made. As a consequence, we may say that from the user's point of view, the quality of the content in the data base is the most overt evidence of the overall data base quality.

In Figure 4.2, we show three kinds of records that might appear in an order entry data base system. At the top of the figure, the first of these is a customer record and

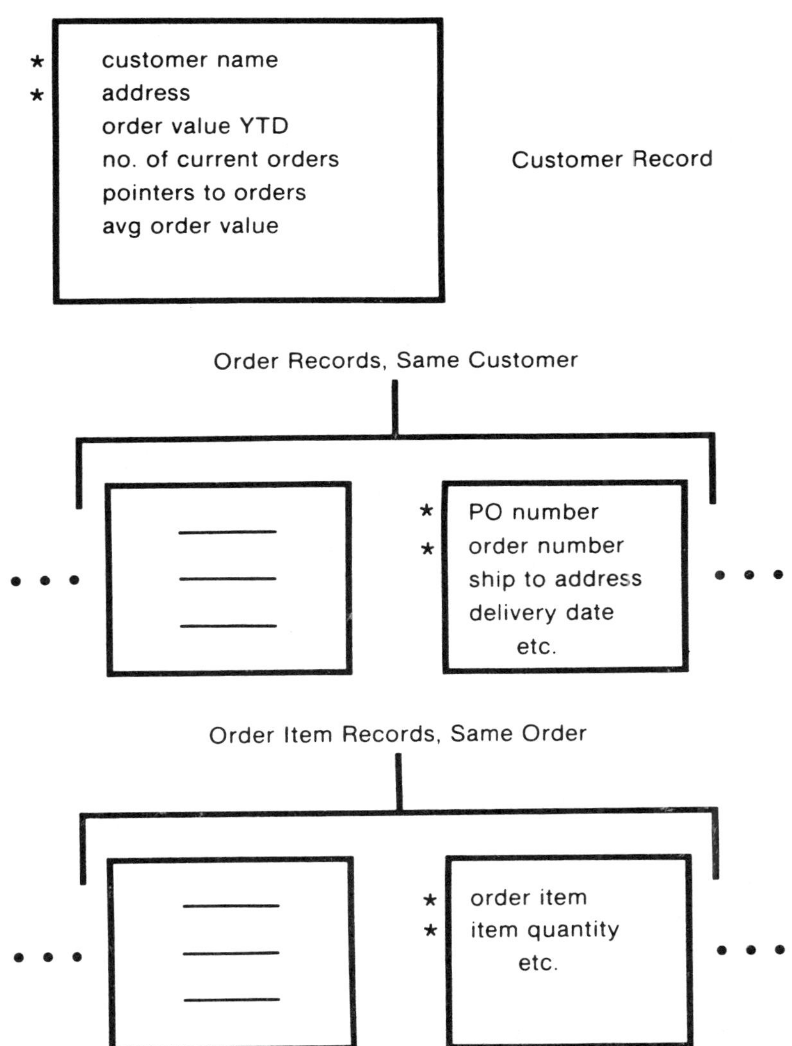

Figure 4.2/CONTENT DATA

contains the customer's name, address, and other data about orders held in the system for that customer. In these records such data as customer name and address represent content in the data base. At the next level down, we see a series of records which hold order data for the same customer. Within these records the purchase order number is another illustration of content. General examples of content data have been marked with an asterisk in this figure.

Index Data

In a file oriented system, we usually make reference to records by implying some knowledge of their current position in the data base. Thus, in a sequential file, we imply that the record we want next is, in fact, the next in the physical sequence of the file. In a data base system, the situation is rather reversed in that qualities of the data, charaterized by keys and key values setting forth conditions for selection, are employed to identify data to be selected from a data base. That is, we use data in the data base to discriminate between records in its various files. Data which is designated for this purpose is generally referred to as index data. It is usually supplied by the user and its discrimination role is designated by the user as well. These index data elements may be thought of as descriptors of the records in which they occur, where the specific values create the conditions for discrimination.

In general, any data element in a record may be thought of as index data and the concept would therefore be meaningless unless we were to make some distinctions as to index data types, known as primary and secondary index data. Primary index data represents a key for entry to the data base, and therefore when we present a mechanism which translates that key/key value pair into a physical position in a specific file of the data base.

The use of a primary key as a mechanism for entry is quite different from the use of an arbitrary data element as a means for discrimination. This is the role of the secondary index data; namely to serve as an additional qualification for records in the data base.

In Figure 4.3, we might have designed our data base system so that the purchase order number could act as primary index data and therefore serve as a key for entry to the order file. On the other hand, delivery date in the order record, in combination with order item in the item record, may jointly discriminate specific orders of interest. For example, we may be interested in orders with a delivery date prior to July 19, containing order items for speedometers. It should be evident therefore that the difference between primary and secondary index data is that the former is used to enter the data base, and therefore is a key available to the application program making the reference. The latter generally will not have a mechanism for data base entry, and is only employed as a further qualification for the data base reference.

We can make a further distinction in the types of index data by characterizing the descriptor as either unique or general. The unique descriptor is one for which the index data is not duplicated anywhere in the file. In Figure 4.3, order number and purchase order number will be unique descriptors. A general descriptor is one whose index data may be shared by more than one record. Delivery date is an example of a general descriptor. Clearly a unique descriptor serves to completely identify a specific record. In the example, each order in our order file will have its own unique order number. We will see later in our discussion of structure data that such a unique descriptor can be employed to create relationships between content data.

Derived Data

Derived data might be referred to as a secondary data type in a data base. It may appear as either index data or content or both, but is distinguished from these two by the fact that it is derived from the data already in the data base. We may say that content data plus a computer algorithm will produce derived data in the data base. For example, consider the case of determining the value of all

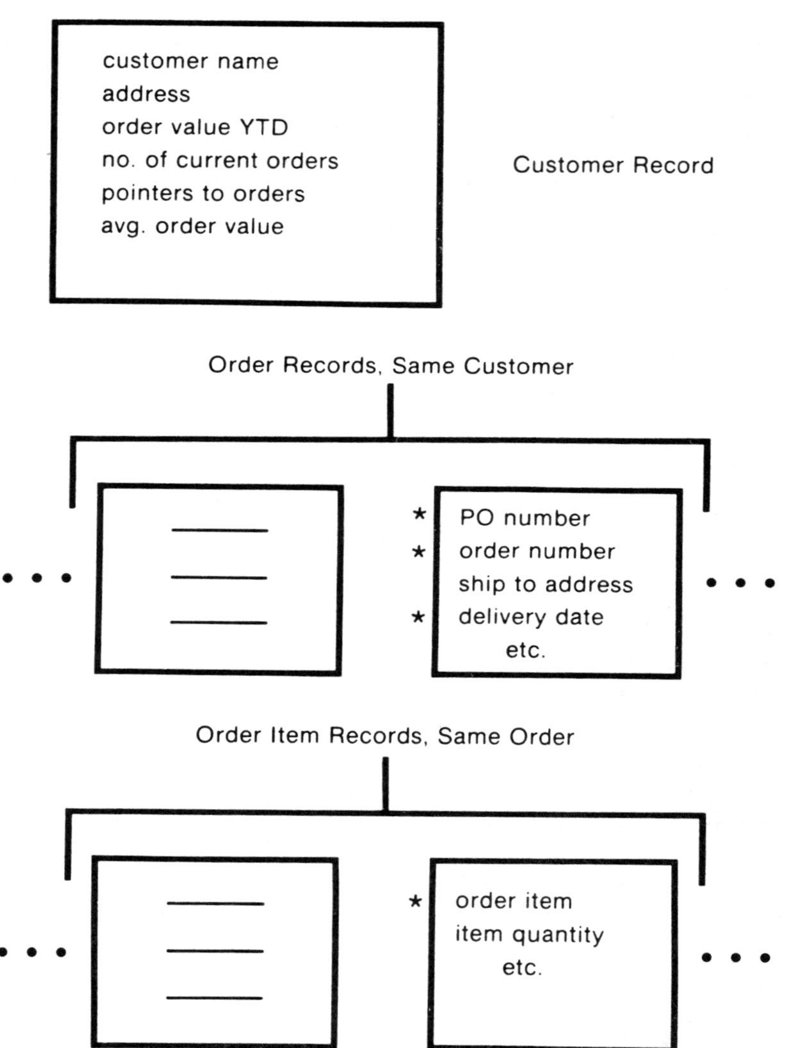

Figure 4.3/INDEX DATA

orders for a given customer and accumulating that total order value into a year-to-date value. Figure 4.4 illustrates the placement of this derived data value, which has been developed out of other content data in the data base. For example, consider the case of determining the value of all orders for a given customer and accumulating that total order value into a year-to-date value. Figure 4.4 illustrates the placement of this derived data value, which has been developed out of other content data in the data base. In this example, the derived value has been put into the customer record. The figure also shows other derived data, such as number of current orders and average order value. This last is computed by dividing the total order value by the number of current orders. This puts it in as a second level of derivation in the data base.

Derived data placed back into the data base is obviously content data. It may also be employed as index data. In this case, it will usually be a secondary descriptor and general in type, as opposed to unique. To illustrate this use of derived data as index data, we need only consider a reference to the data base seeking to find all customers for whom the number of current orders is greater than ten.

Structure Data

It is clear that if performance were not an issue we could always satisfy reference to a data base by means of passing all of the files that involve the data of interest. This brute force technique certainly would not be satisfying to the individual users of the system in terms of the turnaround performance they would receive, and surely would leave much to be desired in terms of throughput performance of the overall computing system. In fact, an important aspect of a data base system is the degree of relatability that it offers in its content data. Since content data appears in records, and records appear in files, the issue of relatability has to do with relationships between records within common files and across file boundaries. The purpose of structure data in the data base is to create these relationships. Such data is provided by the data base system for this purpose, and is usually managed by the

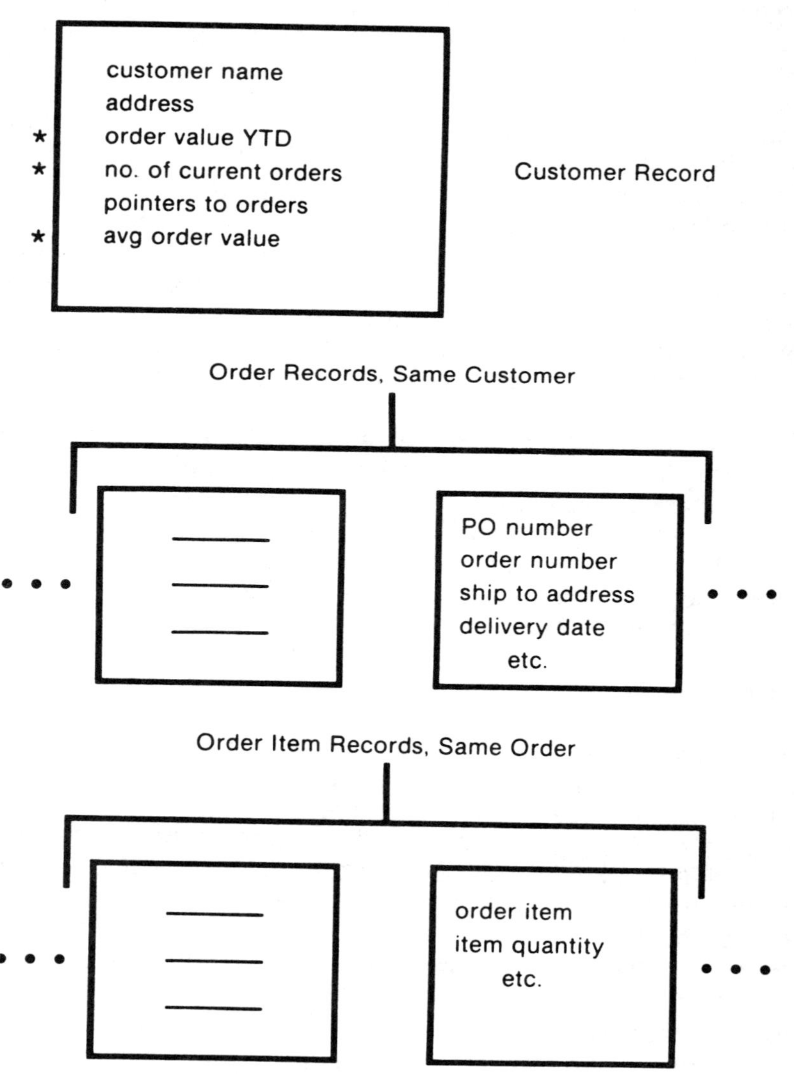

Figure 4.4/DERIVED DATA

system during its operation.

Figure 4.5 illustrates the employment of structure data for creating a relationship between a given customer record and the set of all order records for that customer. In the customer record itself, a pointer is carried which gives the location of one of the specific order records. This pointer generally is a device address indicating a position in the file that has been allocated to the order records. Within this file, a specific order record is picked out by this pointer, and thereby the association between the customer record and its associated order records is maintained.

It should be noted that structure data is actually employed to create the logical and physical file organizations that are designed to promote processing efficiencies in a data base system. In a later section, further characteristics of structure data will be examined.

Overhead Data

As the name suggests, overhead data might be considered as the price to be paid in order to gain a computational advantage. There are two types of overhead data in a data base system. The first is that created by the data base management system package, and the second by programs of the application environment. Overhead data added by the DBMS serves structural purposes that are necessary to the effective operation of the DBMS. Overhead data which is added by application programs, however, may be present in order to suit the needs of certain processes.

As an example, we might consider the tally of orders for a given customer, as illustrated in Figure 4.6, as overhead data, if its purpose in being there is to aid in a computational process. In this case, we may have established in our programs the rule that if the number of current orders is less than twenty and all of them must be sorted into a specified order, then that will be done within the application program. If, however, the number of orders is twenty or greater, the application program would not have enough storage space for an effective sorting and therefore an

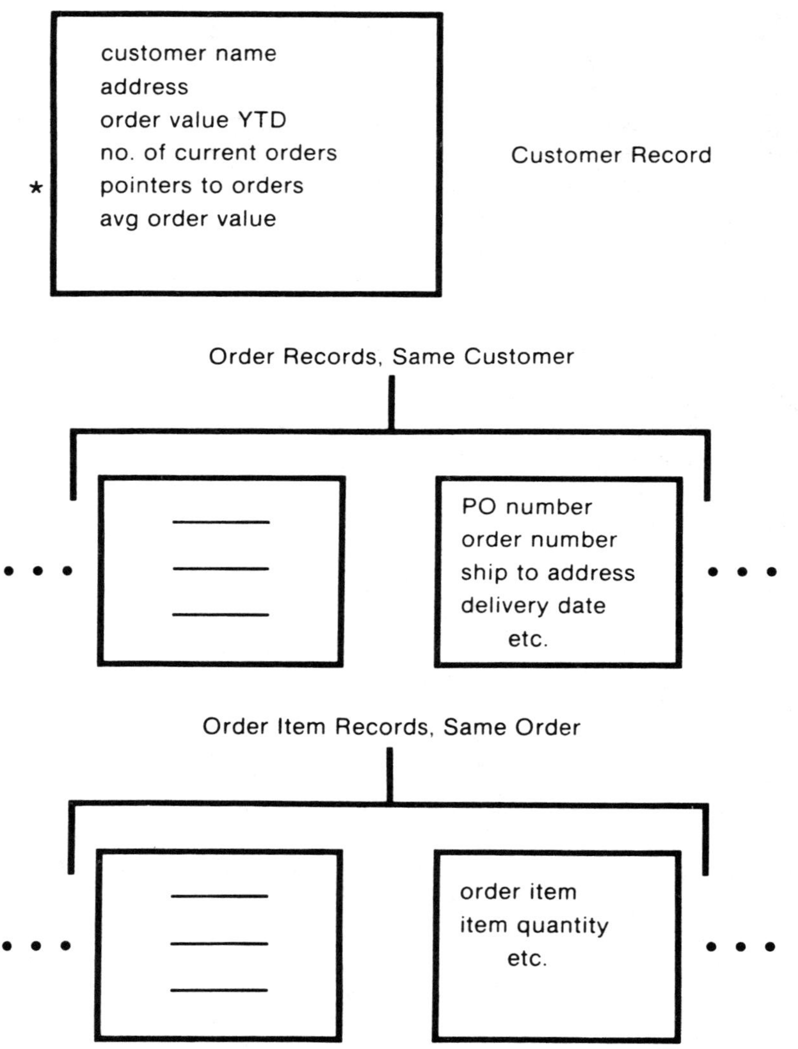

Figure 4.5/STRUCTURE DATA

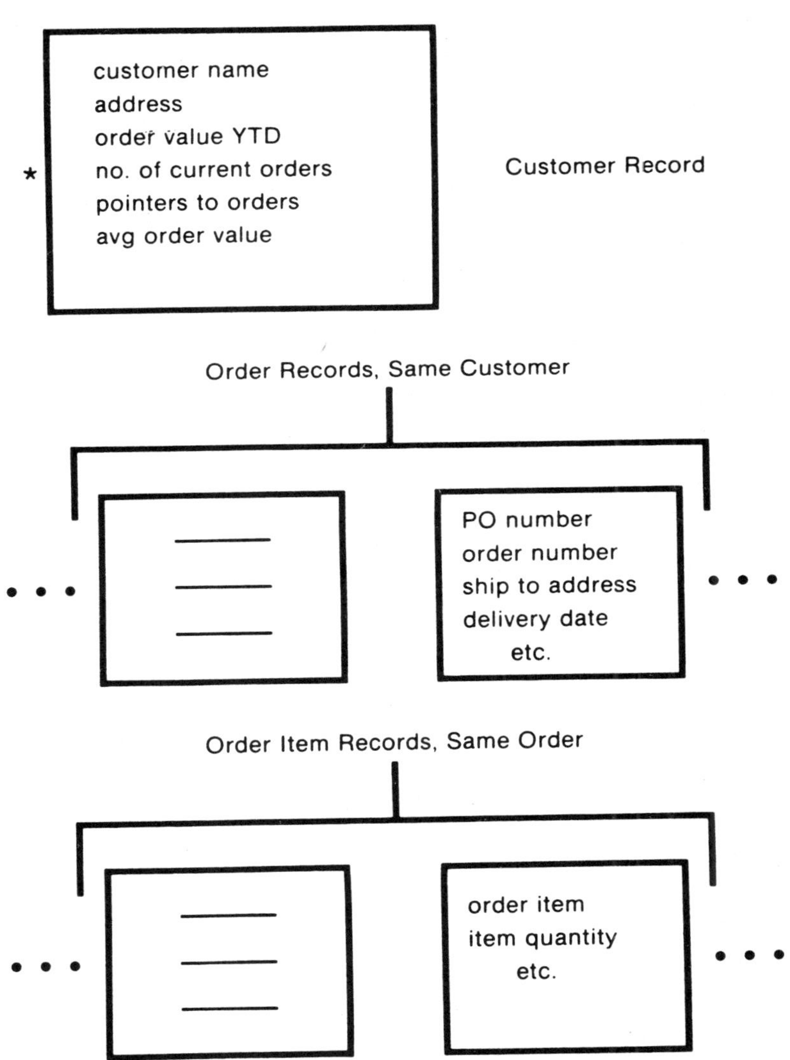

Figure 4.6/OVERHEAD DATA

external sort operation will be invoked. In this example, the count information has be employed to assist the application program in the execution of its data processing objectives. The objectives, of course, are aimed at performance, and we generally will find the overhead data in a data base is present for just that reason.

Finally, it should be pointed out that overhead data of the type under discussion is very frequently derived from either the data of the data base itself, or the current state of the data base. In this latter regard, consider overhead data which gives us the total number of additions and deletions that have occurred over a specified period of time. In particular file organizations, such information would be indicative of the degree of physical dispersion of the records of the file, and might allow an application program to decide between one method of processing and another, based on the dispersion estimators. In this case, we have clearly designed this overhead data to measure the current state of a portion of our data base.

CONTENT DATA INTEGRITY

The integrity of the content data of a data base is of concern upon the addition of data, and the modification of data already present. The maintenance of content data integrity is essential not only because of the so called "ripple effect" which will be discussed later.

Content Addition

The maintenance of data base integrity begins with the addition of data to the data base. If the data that is put into the data base is incorrect, then not only is the data retrieved incorrect, but the effects of the installed errors may ripple through the data base and multiply, as we will see. It follows therefore, that on the addition of content to a data base, it is necessary that we establish the validity of the data in at least three areas. The first of these is its format. This involves the types of codes allowed, whether the field is alphabetic, numeric or alphanumeric, left justified, right justified, with a properly inserted decimal point, and so on. In many data base management packages, no such checks are made on the data as it is added to the data base, and therefore this level of content data integrity is left to the application program.

The second area of integrity concern has to do with the range of the data values. The purpose here is to control the quality of the data within boundaries so that such things as negative paychecks and 30 inch yardsticks can not occur.

Finally, we must be concerned about special values that may or may not be allowed. Suppose that data to be entered is to designate sex. We might specifically require only the characters M or F, or the number 0, 1, with no other values allowed.

As mentioned above, such integrity checks are very often not made by the data base management system package, and this applies as well to range and special value controls. This is particularly the case where conditional rules for data integrity apply. To illustrate this, consider Figure 4.7. Here an order number is shown to consist of three letters followed by five numerals. This represents its format structure. The figure also shows that the range of the last three numbers must be between 350 and 990 if the first letter is in the range A through R.

Otherwise, the number range is 0 to 349. The example also illustrates a set of special values which are not allowed for the second and third letters of the order number. As we can see, content data integrity may develop some rather complicated conditional relationships among the elements of the data. This is difficult to control via a generalized tool such as a DBMS, and therefore it is frequently left up to the application program.

Content data integrity must also be of concern at the time when the data base is modified. Data modification occurs as the result of a retrieval operation, a correction to the data retrieved, and its return to the data base. In general, records are taken from the data base by the DBMS, and only the data specified is then delivered to the application program. Thus, the modification effect is only on a portion of the record rather than on the whole record. However, the modification itself may depend on other data in the record.

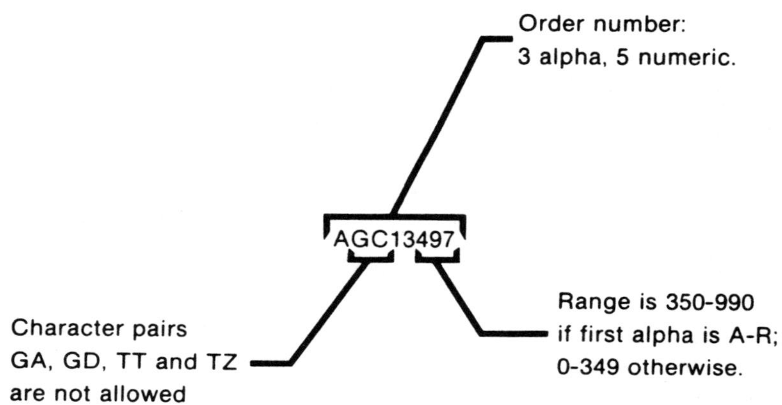

Figure 4.7/DATA INTEGRITY CONDITIONS

For example, consider the case where we would like to raise the assembly shop priority for all orders for which the order date is more than 15 days old, and the delivery date is less than 25 days away. This means that the modification of the priority value is dependent on other information, some of which is in the record. In this case, the order date and delivery date are in the record, while the current date must be supplied from a non-data base source. The point here is that the algorithm making the modification must correctly determine whether or not the modification is to be made, and this in turn is dependent on the content data of the data base. As we will see in the next section, if errors have occurred in other portions of the data base, such operations may end up being erroneous as well.

The Ripple Effect

It has been suggested in the discussion of content data integrity that an error at one point of the data base could propagate through the rest of the data base and seriously magnify that error. Consider, for example, the case where for marketing purposes we would like to rank our customers by their average order value. This is computer by accumulating the order value on a year-to-date basis for each customer and then dividing this accumulation by the current order count. The result is the average order value and the objective is to then rank our customers based on this value. Figure 4.8 suggests the impact of the ripple effect. Suppose that for some reason an order value was installed in error. Now, if we divide by the current order count, the average order value is in error. The ultimate result may be an embarrassment for marketing and a sharp memo from the president to the head of data processing. In this case, the error effect of the order value has rippled not only through a portion of our data base, but through a rather significant portion of our organization as well.

From this we can conclude that the nature of the data base system, which treats data as a homogeneous and centralized resource, is such that errors will tend to propagate along the lines of relationships that have been set up to create the content data associations. Thus, the data base is more vulnerable to failure than our isolated file oriented systems. This makes our concern with content data integrity all the more important in the data base context.

INDEX DATA INTEGRITY

The integrity of index data presents special problems in data base. This is immediately apparent if it is remembered that the purpose of index data is to provide for a discrimination capability within the content data of the data base. Loss of index data integrity will mean loss of

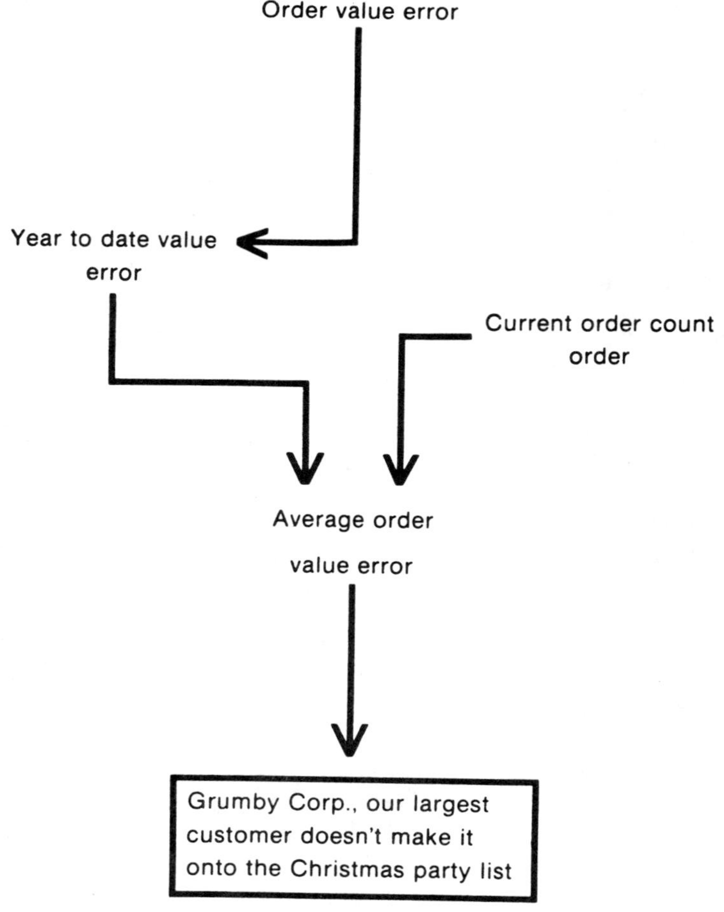

Figure 4.8/RIPPLE EFFECT

content data in terms of our inability to find it by means of its primary and secondary descriptors.

Unique Descriptors

If a particular field in a record of the data base has been designated as a unique descriptor for that record, then the index data which it contains may not be duplicated in any other records of a similar type. In an earlier example we considered order number to be a unique descriptor for each of the order records, and therefore each order number value was to be uniquely different and uniquely associated with a particluar order and its record. Clearly, the uniqueness of such a descriptor must be retained on both addition and modification of the record. If this uniqueness is lost by some error in the associated index data when a modification is made, then the record in which this index data error has occurred may be irretrievably lost.

This is particularly the case if the unique descriptor is employed as a key for entry to this file of the data base, and is the only way of entering it. In this case, the record is literally defined by its index data, and if an index data error occurs, then the record is as unavailable as if it were actually not present in the file.

This is illustrated in Figure 4.9, where several order records are shown schematically with the letters in each representing the associated order number index data. Suppose that record number one should have been assigned the order number value W, but by some error, at either input time or in application processing system, that value has been erroneously included in the record as V. Then any reference to order number W will not correspond to any record in the data base, so that in effect order record number 1 is inaccessible.

It may be that the error in the index data is such that the original index data value is erroneously changed to one that already exists in the data base. This violates the uniqueness assumption for the descriptor and might result in a situation as shown in records number two and three of Figure 4.9. Here the order number for record number three was originally to have been the value U and was erroneously changed to the value Y. This corresponds to the order number value assigned to record number two. As a consequence, there will be ambiguity in the employment of what is supposed to be a unique order number descriptor since the index data value Y corresponds to more than a single record. Thus, the one-to-one property that matches

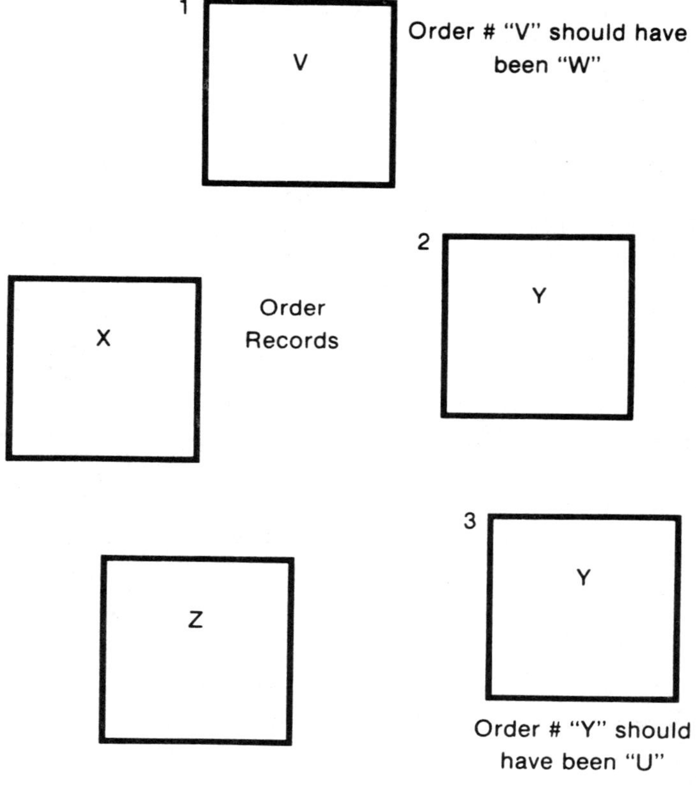

Figure 4.9/UNIQUE DESCRIPTOR ERRORS

the unique index data values to individual records of a file of the data base is lost. If this type of error is not discovered, then a further difficulty will result when an attempt to delete either record number two or three is made, since no other discrimination is available and the wrong record might just as easily be deleted as the right one.

General Description

The index data associated with a general descriptor for a record does not uniquely define that record, but rather describes it as a member of a class of records having this descriptor value in common. This characteristic of the index data for a general descriptor is illustrated in Figure 4.10 which shows a collection of order records in the order file. Records number one and two will have a common descriptor value for customer identification. This is also true with records three and four. The problem with failure in index data integrity for general descriptors is that an error in addition or modification of the data base may shift the group membership implied by the index data. For example, if an error was made with record number five on its addition to the file, or at some point when it was modified, so that the proper customer identification A was inadvertently changed to the value B, then the order becomes associated with the wrong group of orders in this file.

In general, relationships implied between records of a file with common descriptor values are realized via file organization mechanisms that, in turn, are achieved by means of structure data. However, if the association is in error as in the example of Figure 4.10, then the structure data relationships will implement that error so that the only way the mistake will become apparent is by examination of the data itself, usually by its users. It might also be pointed out that this erroneous association will later create errors when deletions are made from the data base. In the case of the order records in the example, there is one less order record for customer A to be deleted, and one more record for customer B to be deleted. If counts of orders were maintained in the customer's record, as suggested in previous examples, then these counts might be wrong as well. In terms of the ripple effect, a direct consequence would be an error in any derived data in which count by order record per customer more involved.

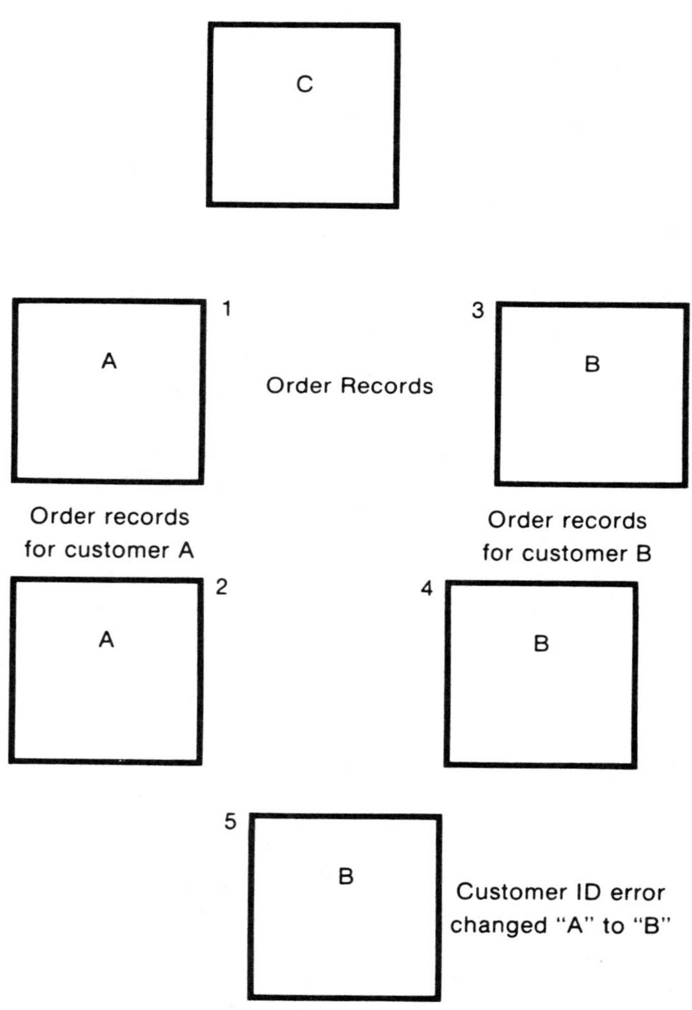

Figure 4.10/DESCRIPTOR ASSOCIATION ERRORS

Associated Derived Data

In the example of Figure 4.6, we referred to the accumulated year-to-date value of all orders for a customer, and indicated in that example that the derived data would be stored in the customer record. In many data base system designs it is useful to store derived data values in other files of the data base so that their structure, utilization and performance characteristics can be arranged independently of the files holding the data from which they are derived. This is illustrated in Figure 4.11 where certain derived data has been placed into a file of its own. This example illustrates only the year-to-date accumulation, which in this case has been removed from the customer file and placed into a derived data file, along with the customer ID with which it associates. In the first place, we should note that the customer ID serves as index data for a unique descriptor in this file. If there is an error in this index data, either in the original index data, either in the original customer file or at the time the data is placed into the derived data file or updated in that file, then its association with its customer record will be lost. That is, if on entry to the customer file we are looking for the year-to-date accumulation data associated with customer number 1, we would enter the customer file, pick out the customer record, and from it abstract the customer ID, in this case ID1. We would then apply that to our indexing technique, which would presumably lead us into the derived data file and to the associated derived data record for this customer. Clearly, however, if the index data is in error, then this second step of the process will not work correctly.

STRUCTURE DATA INTEGRITY

The failure of structure data in a data base is perhaps the most insidious type of error that can occur. The effects can be disastrous, difficult to identify and very expensive to rectify. In order to understand the impact of structure data failure in the data base system, however, it is necessary to understand the role of structure data and the two data types that are employed to create structure data. We can then discuss the implications of structure data failure.

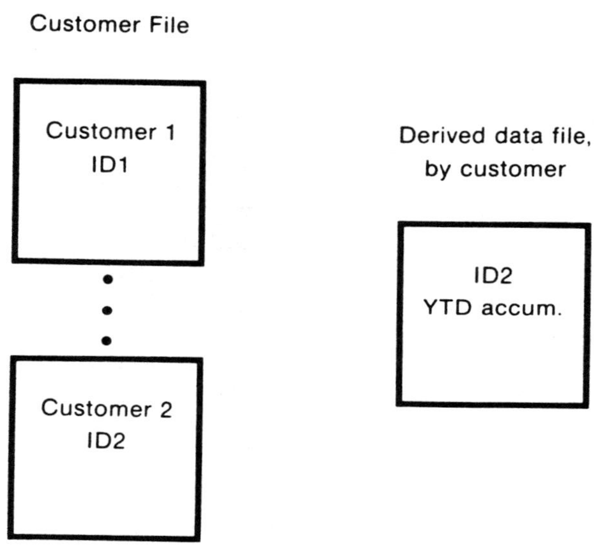

Figure 4.11/DERIVED DATA ASSOCIATION ERRORS

Role of Structure Data

It was mentioned earlier that if performance were not considered as an issue in the data base system, we could satisfy all references to a data base by the simple expedient of passing all files involved in the reference. In this process, we would look at every record in the file, test each record for the reference conditions, and from those records that satisfied these conditions would pick out the data values that are to be delivered to the user. Such an approach does not require primary descriptors, and all data in the data base could be considered as secondary descriptors. More importantly, since we are passing all records of each file involved in the reference, there is no need for file organization, and as a consequence no need for structure data.

That is another way of saying that the purpose of structure data is to provide short cuts through the file in order to improve the efficiency of the overall data base system's operations and its performance for individual references. These short cuts are referred to as file organization, and as mentioned earlier are realized by means of structure data in the data base. The role of structure data may be restated by saying that its purpose is to aggregate records of a file into subsets that have certain characteristics or qualities in common. These characteristics and qualities are defined by the designated descriptors in the records. Figure 4.12 illustrates this with the records of the order file. The circle represents all of the records of the order file, while the indicated records, linked together by the directional pointers, imply an association between that subset of order records which go with a particular customer X. If we were able to find the first record in this association, then that record indicates the next, which indicates the next and so on, thereby creating the relationship. This, by the way, is the file organizational form known as a simple list. Its effect is to identify a specific, usually small group of records in the total order file as having a certain characteristic of data processing interest to our users; e.g., association by common customer. If we are interested in the order records associated with this particular customer, then rather than dealing with all the records of the order file, we are able to operate on this much smaller subset.

Structure Data Types

Structure data is the means by which relationships are created between content data, with different arrangements and applicationss of structure data leading to specific file organizations. That is, structure data is the fundamental tool of file organization, and here we point out that there are two basic structure data types, each with its own characteristics.

The first of these is called physical structure data and is simply a pointer carried in one record indicating the position of the next record in the association. The term "pointer" is used in discussing structure data because its graphical representation is in terms of an arrow drawn from the record in which the structure data resides to the record that its value indicates. This is illustrated in Figure 4.13 where a collection of records in the order file is shown in schematic form. These records contain the purchase order number, the order number and, among the remaining data carried in the order record, a pointer to the next order record having the same customer association. That is, the purpose of the structure data in this example is to bring together all order records in the order file in a logical assocation by customer. Therefore the first record, residing in position 20019 of the storage device carries in it the position number 25678 of the next record in the association. At that location, as the figure shows, we have the next order record with its data and its pointer to the record which follows it in this logical association.

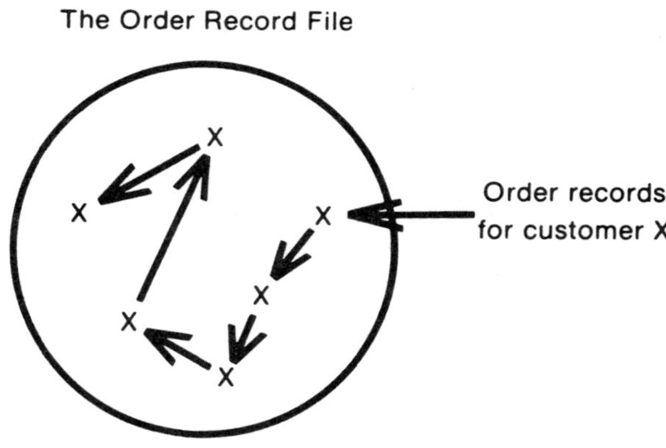

Figure 4.12/ROLE OF STRUCTURE DATA

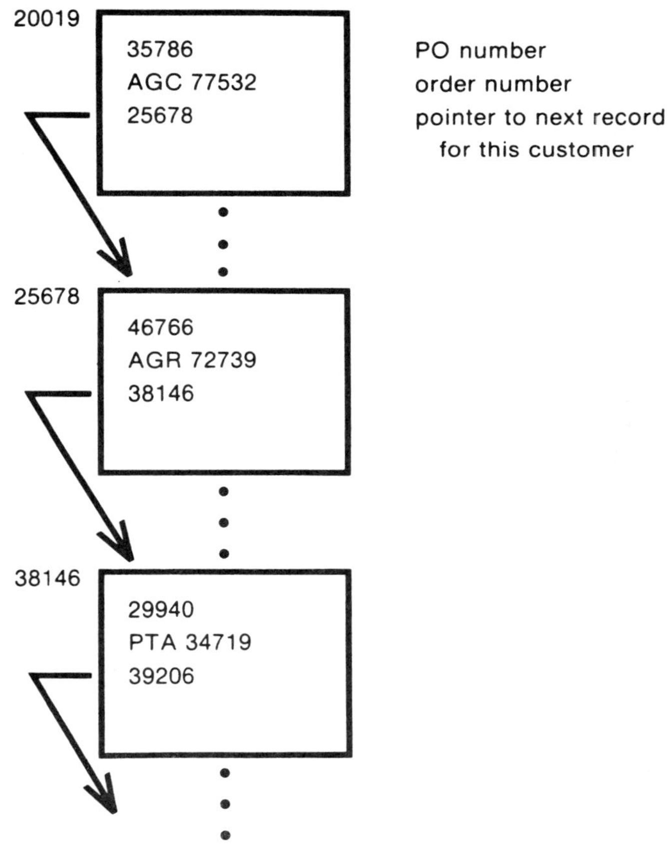

Figure 4.13/PHYSICAL STRUCTURE DATA

It is important to note that physical structure data is specific about the existence of a next record in the association, and explicit about its location. If the record in position 38146 were moved for some reason to a different physical location in the storage device, then the pointer value in the order record located at 25678 would have to be modified.

The second type of structure data is referred to as logical structure data. This involves a unique descriptor in the record, and its associated index data values and indexing method. As described earlier, a unique descriptor is a key for entry to a file of the data base, and an indexing method provides the mechanism for translating a given value for a particular key into a physical location in the file. If we have such a unique descriptor available, and an indexing method for it, then we may substitute index data for the physical pointers of the example of Figure 4.13. This is illustrated in Figure 4.14. The same order records in the order file are shown, but instead of a physical pointer in the record in position 20019 giving the address of the next order record in the association as 25678, the order record carries the order number of that next record. That is, the order number value AGR72739 is the order number for the order record in position 25678. We, therefore, take this order number value out of the first order record, pass it through our indexing method whose job is to translate it into position 25678, and then use this position value to reference the next order record of our relationship.

Clearly this approach to structure data ony works if the descriptor is unique, providing a key to the file, and if the system has an indexing method for that key. Given these two conditions, then the virtue of this approach to structure data is that each record in the relationship is positionally independent of the other members of the set. That is, the record in position 38146 may be moved to another physical location. The indexing method for the key obviously will have to be updated in order to maintain its validity. In so doing, the relationship of the order record in position 25678 to the next order in the association is automatically maintained as well. Thus, we may

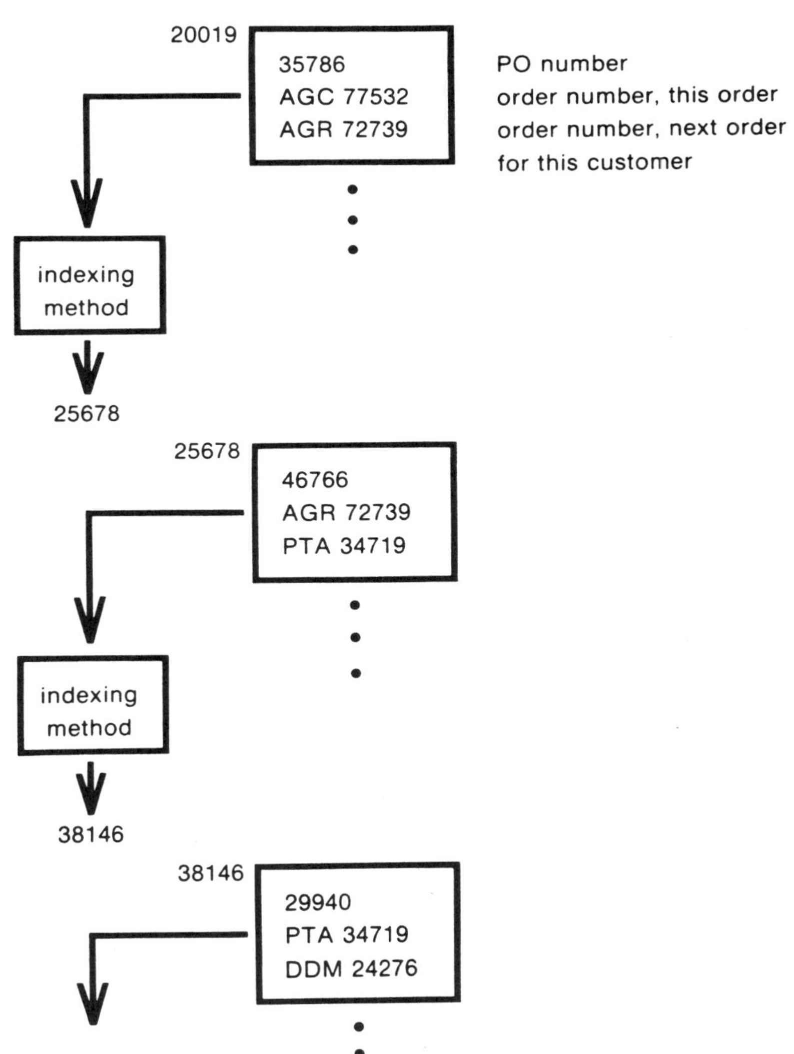

Figure 4.14/LOGICAL STRUCTURE DATA

say that logical structure data also implies the existence of a next record in the relationship, but gives its location in the file only indirectly through the associated indexing method.

Ordering Rules

From the foregoing examples and the discussions of structure data it should be evident that in many cases we are bringing together records according to some criteria of association and providing them with a serial order via structure data. By serial order, we mean a precedence relationship among these records so that there is a first, a last, and each record in between has an identifiable position. This implies that there is a rule for ordering the records, which rule must be observed when new records are added or when modification of data in a record causes a change in its serial position in the association. The concept of an ordering rule is illustrated by the example in Figure 4.15 where serial order for a collectin of order records by order date within customer is shown. In this example, the records for customer X are arranged from the most recent order on 2/14/77 through the oldest on 11/13/76. A similar ordering rule would be applied to records for customers Y and Z, and so on, so that in our file we might say that an ordering rule has been imposed over all orders by customer based on the order date.

Obviously if a file is to have a set of ordering rules based on specific data elements, then when new records are added, some function must take responsibility for maintaining the ordering rule. If a new order record is added for customer X in the example of Figure 4.15, then the pointers in the serial association for that customer wil have to be suitably modified. In the same way, if an order record is deleted from the association, or if a modification affecting, say, the order date is made, then a rearrangement of the structure data is required in order to maintain the integrity of the association in the first place and its specific ordering rule in the second. If this is not done, then although the structure data itself may be correct in the purely mechanical sense that the given structure data is legitimate and indicates the next record in the association, that record may not be in the proper ordering rule sequence.

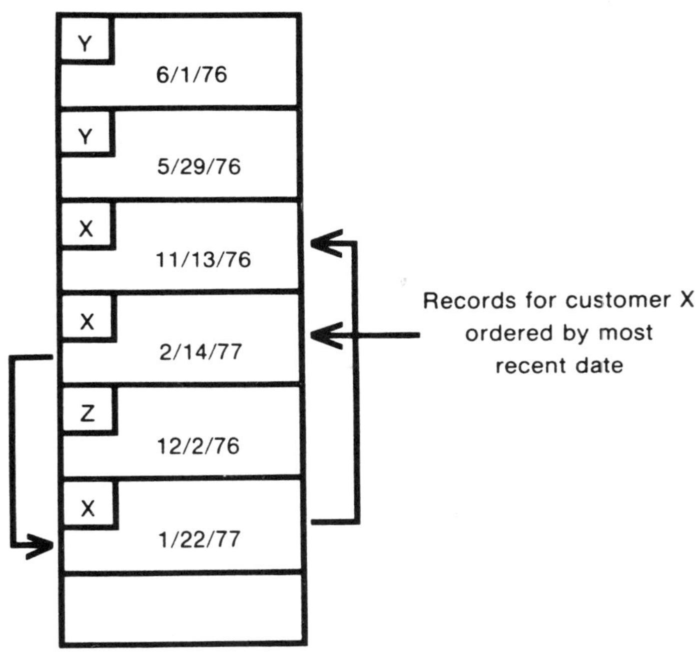

Figure 4.15/SERIAL ORDER

Structure Data Failure

When structure data fails, either the pointer, whether it be physical or logical, is simply invalid in terms of the file in which it resides, or is erroneous and does not indicate the proper record of the file. In the first case, physical structure data may given an address that is erroneous for the storage device and cause a hardware error, or just as bad, may provide a legitimate address on the storage device that has absolutely nothing to do with this file or any associations within it. That is, the pointer value may send the association off into the nether regions of the device and land it in the middle of a device storage area which is meaningless and unintelligible to the data base system. Unfortunately, unless specific track is being kept of the legitimacy of pointer values, a data base system will never know the difference and will deliver junk data to the application program making the reference. In all probability, the application program will know junk data when it sees it and will make an appropriate signal, thereby identifying a failure in the data base. It may, however, take some digging to come to that conclusion, since application programs usually make such signals by simply failing. This leaves it up to some programmer, shovel in hand.

A logical structure data failure occurs in two ways. There may be a failure in the indexing method itself, in which case the index data picked out of one record will incorrectly identify a next record in the association, or worse yet will lead to some device storage position outside of the file that it totally irrelevant to the organizational structure. The second kind of error may be as a consequence of erroneous index data appearing in one record of the association which then leads to an equally erroneous next record in the association through the indexing method.

Figure 4.16 illustrates one of the serious difficulties that can occur because of a structure data failure. In this example a number of order records are shown in an order file that should be associated by means of structure data either physical or logical. However, after the second record of the association an error has occurred. In the illustration, the error has created a false association with a record in a second file. In this case, the file is accounts receivable, so that in the sequence of orders being considered, there appears some unidentifiable accounts receivable record. Clearly, the data of the accounts receivable record will be unacceptable to the program processing order records and a program execution error will occur. But what happens to the remaining records of the association? If the only indexing method available in the order

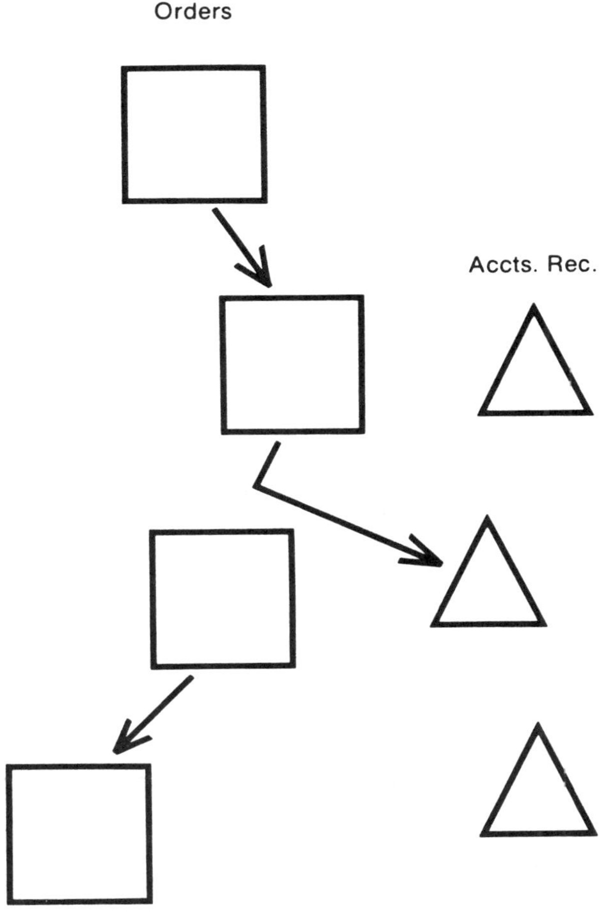

Figure 4.16/STRUCTURE DATA FAILURE

file leads to the first of this series of order records and no other structure data associations existed, then the order records beyond the break point would be lost and gone forever. That is, under the conditions suggested above, there is no other way to find them in the file short of passing the entire order file and looking explicitly for these records by a known order number, purchase order number, or any other known unique descriptor value. Otherwise, we will have an extremely difficult time in determining what data is missing from the association and where it is located in the order file.

DATA BASE PRIVACY

The purpose of instigating data base privacy controls is to provide a means for the authorization of use of the data base system and the data base it contains. In this section, the general problem of data base privacy is considered, including levels of privacy controls throughout the data base system, general methods for instituting these controls, and the tracking of privacy violations.

The problem of maintaining control of the authorized use of data in a data processing system has a long and significant history in computing. However, that problem, as difficult as it may be in our more familiar file oriented systems, is extended and expanded in the data base context. The scope of the privacy problem for data base is also associated with the four primitive operations on the data base, and the user's objectives and intentions.

Privacy and File Oriented Systems

The system and its programs are directly related to the associated files in a file oriented environment. Furthermore, the number of these files is usually rather small, and as a consequence physical control is more easily accomplished. Under such circumstances, the files of these systems would be mounted and demounted as the system is run. This provides a point of usage control in that such mounting had to be called for in the first place, and in the second approved by the operator of the system. To a certain degree then, there was a physical and visual authorization associated with the use of a particular file. In addition, the file oriented system either provided no keys at all or minimized the number of such keys. In the most popular random access method, only a single key is allowed, and as a consequence, there are few if any entry points to the file itself, other than that offered by physical passing of the file in sequential order. Finally, such file oriented system rarely were concerned with the integration of data in different files, and as a consequence, system growth and the associated privacy questions were never raised. In many respects, in fact, the privacy question for file oriented systems can be likened to a maze such as that illustrated in Figure 4.17. This maze would have only one entrance to the maze itself, and then only one entrance to the center containing the file under control. A sentry at this one entry point in the center would be more than sufficient to control access to the file.

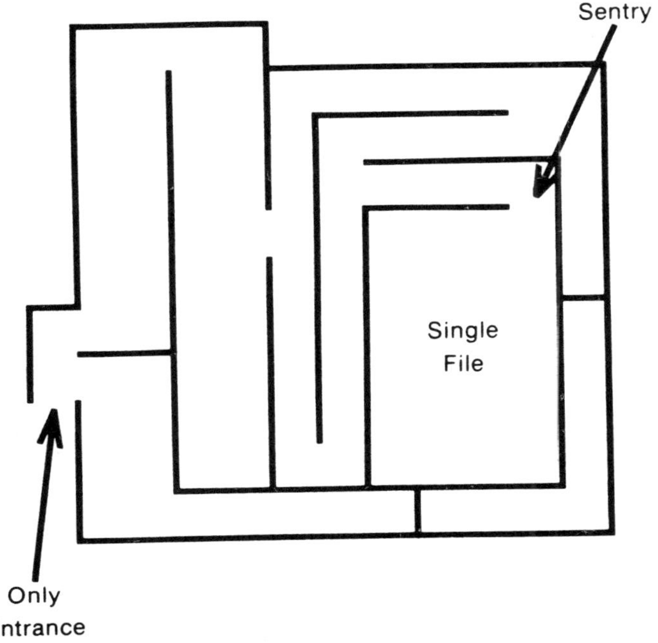

Figure 4.17/FILE ORIENTED SYSTEM PRIVACY

Data Base Privacy

In a data base system environment, the data base is generally always on the system and is usually always available. Furthermore, by definition, a data base system is a data resource that is designed to be available under arbitrary conditions of access, up to the privacy consraints, to all users of the data base system. This means in turn that there are many keys for entry to the data base system, and these keys allow for entry at many points. In addition, the relatability characteristics of a data base system insure that entry to the data base at any one of the key points will provide access to not only dta within the file of entry but in all likelihood access to many of the other files of the data base via the file organization routes that had been designed into that architecture. Finally, an objective purpose of the data base architecture and the overall design of the data base system is growth, and therefore integration. Thus, users of the current data base could very easily have access to and become users of the new data base portions that are integrated without privacy controls.

We might liken the data base privacy problems in this context to a maze in which the center contains the many files of the data base. This maze, however, has many entrances and the repository for the files at its center may also have points of access. This is illustrated in Figure 4.18.

It was suggested in the preceding that the relatability of a data base system implies that access to one or more files of the data base in turn implies access to the others. This is clearly the case in the context of any data base having some degree of generality built into its architecture. As a consequence, it is necessary to be very careful indeed about the way in which specific files of data base and the data that they contain are protected. But note that although we may build rather solid looking privacy walls around specific files of the data base, relatability may easily and inadvertently provide a pathway to that protected data via the unprotected files of the data base.

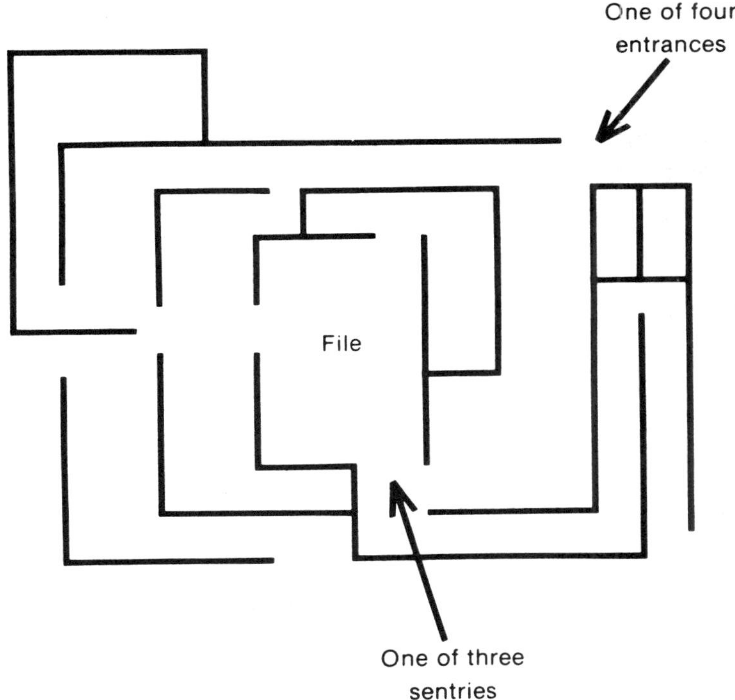

Figure 4.18/DATA BASE PRIVACY

Scope of the Privacy Problem

When we consider the issue of the privacy of data, the circumstance of use that comes to mind most readily is that of retrieval. This, however, is only one of the primitive operations available to users of a data base. That is, the privacy problem must be extended to the addition, deletion and modification functions as well. To put this in another way, it is not enough to develop and operate privacy controls for retrieval alone, but rather we must ensure that only authorized individuals are allowed to add data to the data base, delete data from it, or make changes to the data it already contains.

This much broader scope for the privacy problem is absolutely essential, as innumerable cases cropping up in both commercial and governmental data processing have attested. Three such motives for attempting unauthorized use and abuse of the data of a data base are suggested in Figure 4.19.

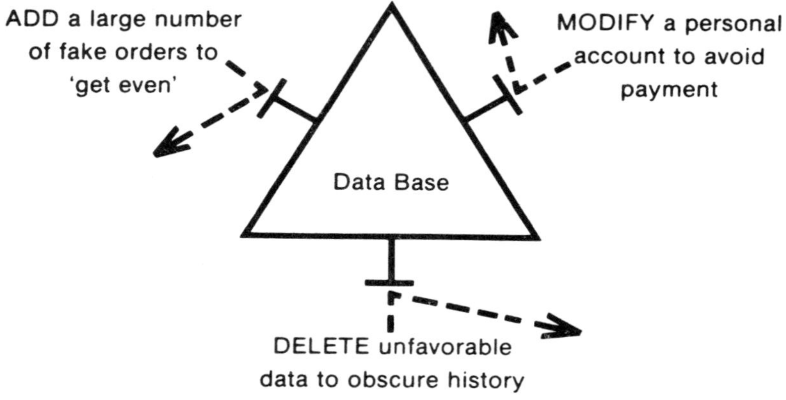

Figure 4.19/SCOPE OF PRIVACY PROTECTION

Cooperative and Uncooperative Users

From the point of view of imposing and exercising privacy controls, we have to understand that there are two kinds of users of the data base system. The first of these is the cooperative user who not only understand but appreciates the need for these privacy controls, and who inadvertently violates the privacy ground rules on occasion. Such a user in all likelihood welcomes notification of the privacy violations he has committed because these violations have slowed down his own development effort with aborted runs and privacy violation messages that need interpretation via manuals that may not be readily at hand. For this user, the purpose of privacy controls are to remind him that there are boundaries on the range of the programming systems that he develops, and these privacy controls may in fact be interpreted by such a cooperative user as designed to prevent an information loss in his systems. In this sense then we might think of the application of privacy controls to the cooperative user as a mechanism to inform him of the errors that his system makes in the privacy environment that has been established for the data base.

The uncooperative user, on the other hand, is a totally different story. This user is seeking unauthorized access to the data base to retrieve, modify, delete, or add to it. We must assume for this type of user that the motives are essentially illegal, that telling him about the mistakes he makes does not inform him of procedures for correcting these errors, but rather provides him with further information on how to defeat the privacy controls that have been established. For this user therefore it is clearly necessary that the privacy controls be rather positive in the sense of preventing unauthorized access when such attempts are intentional, and furthermore such attempts be documented so that the uncooperative user can be identified.

LEVELS OF PRIVACY CONTROL

What has been suggested in the foregoing is that we wish to protect the data of the data base from unauthorized access relative to the individual primitive operations of the data base. This, however, is a rather gross expression of the privacy problem and the qualities of privacy control that might indeed be instigated. In fact, we can identify a rather specific hierarchy of privacy levels at which it may be desirable to exercise privacy controls. The levels of a data processing system which incorporate data base are illustrated in Figure 4.20. These system levels begin at the user and his system entry device. These devices are keyboards, consoles, RJE equipment, card readers and even the job submission window at the computer center. Whatever the entry mechanism, the user is represented in the computing system by either a job or a transaction, and this must ultimately be transmitted to an application program. If the operations of the application program involve the use of a data base, then at some point calls are made on the DBMS, which in turn will reference the data base. This reference will be via keys to files in order to operate on the data base content.

Imposed over this hierarchy of computer system use in the data base context is a hierarchy for privacy controls. These necessarily begin with the user, and in this section we discuss the additional possibilities for maintaining data base privacy.

Referencing Equipment

When we think of data base privacy, the two entities that usually come to mind are the user in the first place, and the explicit data of the data base in the second. These represent the extremes of such control, and between them we will find a number of areas of equal importance. The first of these is the equipment made available to the user for referencing the computing system in general, and the data base in particular.

We may say that with respect to the data base system environment, referencing equipment represents both data sources and data sinks. That is, it is the point not only of entry to the system by the user, but as well the point at which results are delivered to him. In a particular data base system we may want to raise legitimate questions about the association of a particular user with specific referencing equipment for both entry and delivery of data bse results. That is, privacy controls may extend to controlling sources of entry and sources of information delivered. We may say that in this context the objective of the privacy system is to ensure that the user is right for the equipment he is using.

Figure 4.21 is an example of data source and sink control in terms of the referencing equipment. This example

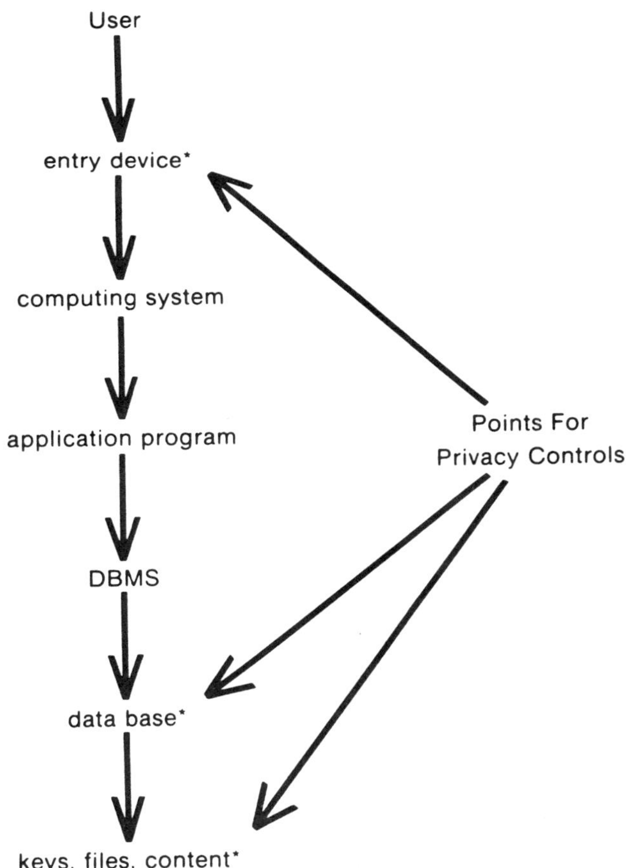

Figure 4.20/PRIVACY HIERARCHY

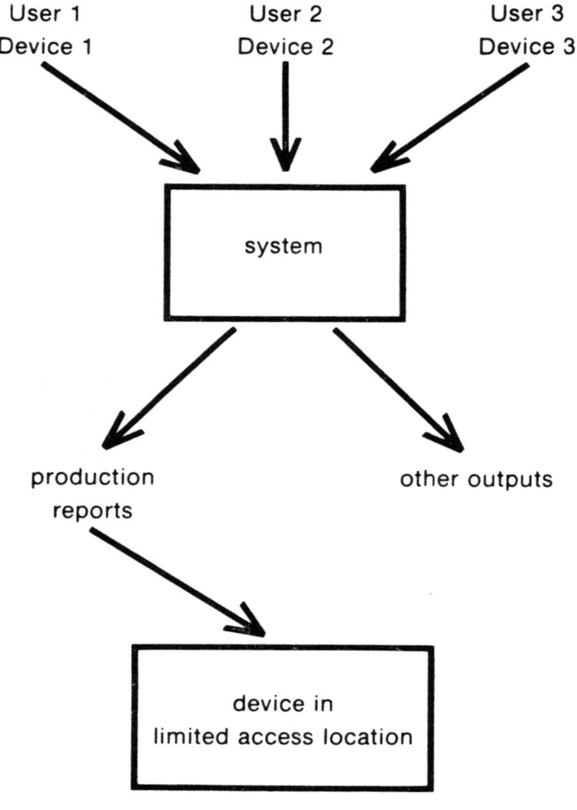

Figure 4.21/DATA SOURCE & SINK CONTROL

shows several users and the devices with which they are associated. These devices all lead to the system, and for particular users produce particular outputs. In certain cases, some of these outputs represent production reports, and it is necessary in order to preserve the privacy of production information that the production report be delivered to the proper device. In this example, the concern with privacy has been extended to the physical location for delivery of the production report in that the delivery equipment has been placed in a location to which limited physical access is allowed. In this sense then, the privacy system must ensure that a user at an input device is properly associated with the device designated for delivery of the associated results.

The Data Base

Once we have gotten past the issue of controlling the referencing equipment relative to the users of data base, we may consider privacy controls at more detailed levels of the data base system. The first of these that we will encounter is clearly the data base itself. If we view the data base system as a collection of interrelated files such that entry at one point leads to data in a specific file, which in turn may lead to data in either that file or other files of the data base, then controlling access to the data base itself does not discriminate against the files which it contains. In this sense, a privacy control on the entire data base is of perhaps limited use, as illustrated in Figure 4.22. This model suggests that given the proper credentials, we can get into the data base system, after which anything it contains is fair game for reference. This means that the entire content of the data base is available, all of its index data via the keys supplied, and any of its file organization and consequent data relationships. This is admittedly a gross level of privacy control.

Keys

Keys represent information classes for entry to the base. We may think of a key as the user's expression for locating data of interest so that if privacy controls are applied to the keys of the data base, access has been restricted to data normally reachable via these keys. This extends as well to secondary keys which are developed as a result of an initial entrance to the data base. Figure 4.23 illustrates an example of this level of privacy control and the concern over secondary keys. The example assumes that purchase order number is a key to the order file and indicates an entry via the indexing method to the order file with a given purchase order number. The illustration shows that the order records all contain among their general information an assigned customer ID value. If there exists an indexing method for customer ID that will lead to records in the customer file, then customer ID is a secondary key. Clearly then, the key level of privacy control must extend to secondary keys if access is to be limited.

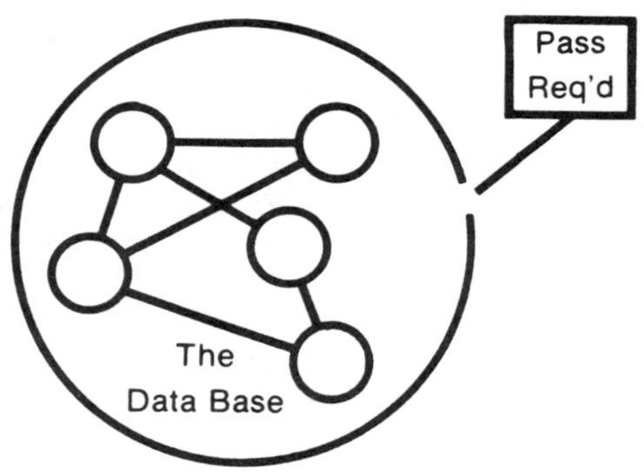

Figure 4.22/DATA BASE PRIVACY

Where the key represents an information class for reference and entry to a data base, the key value represents a specific condition for satisfying the referencing requirement. Thus, salary may be an allowable key for the individual user, but we may wish to control the range or level of salaries that can be used for key reference to a file. In this example, we might restrict certain users of the personnel file from seeing names of individuals whose salaries are greater than, say, $15,000 per year. This is key value protection and represents a further dimension of privacy control at the key level.

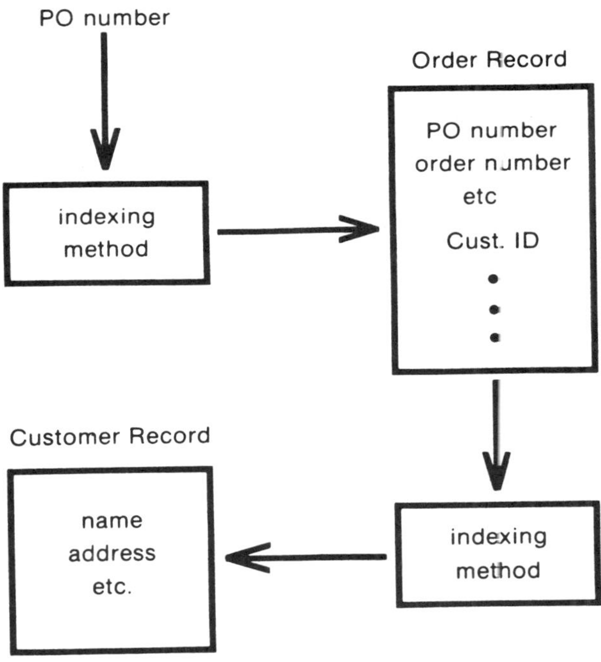

Figure 4.23/KEY PROTECTION

Files

It is one thing to control access to a data base and thereby all of the files that it contains, and quite another to control access to individual files of a data base. That is, a collection of users may jointly have access to a data base, but within that collection of users specific users may be allowed or disallowed access to specific files. This raises problems of controlling the structure data making up the file organizational architecture of the data base and creating the interfile relationships. This was illustrated in the last example, Figure 4.23. There, logical structure data formed the connection between an order record and an associated customer record by means fo customer ID logical structure data. This logical structure data was put through the indexing method for customer ID on the customer file and resulted in the connection. If we wanted to allow a user access to the order file but would like to restrict access to the customer file, then we must devise some mechanism to prevent the use of this logical structure data. As described in the previous section, controlling the secondary keys would satisfy this requirement. If, however, the connection were via physical structure data, other techniques must be developed. An example of this problem is illustrated in Figure 4.24. Again, we show customer and order records. A set of customer records for individual customers A, B, C, etc., are each individually associated with a subset of order records in the order file. This is illustrated for customer D. The way in which the relationship has been developed in this illustration is by means of a simple ring structure in which the customer record enters into a list relationship, as indicated by the pointers, with the order records for that customer. Thus if we are dealing in customer order records and move around this ring, we would eventually come to the customer record. Should we desire to control access to the customer file and the records that it contains, we must provide controls for this structure data in the order file as well.

Content

The ultimate objective of privacy controls is to limit access to the content of the data base. These are the data elements of the records in the various files of the data base, and if privacy controls are instigated at this level, then many users may have access to the records of a file, but the control is to be applied at the data element level after the record access has been made. It must be remembered, however, that keys are used to enter files and a file organization is employed to locate these records. These

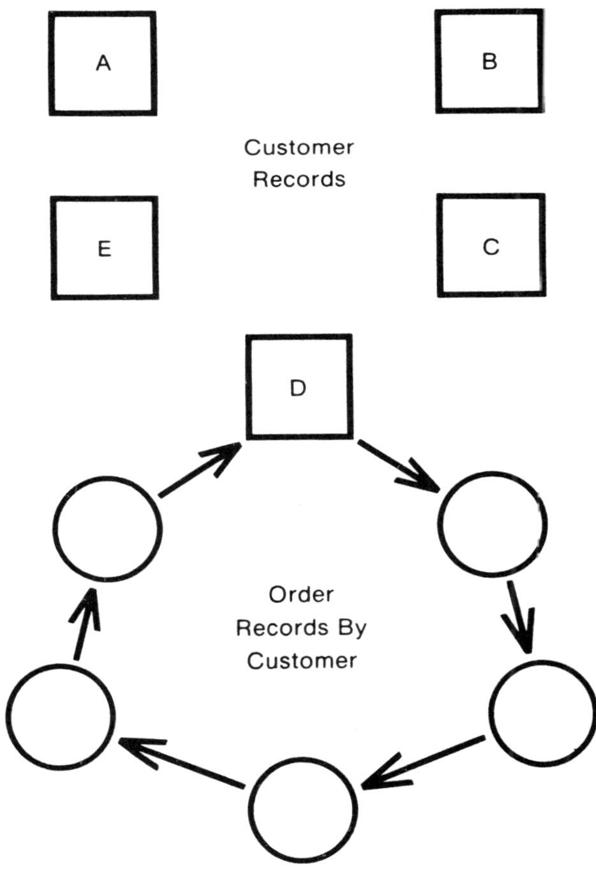

Figure 4.24/FILE PROTECTION

location activities are carried out using descriptors and their associated index data. For example, suppose that the Jones Corporation has called in to ask for a list of their purchase order numbers for all orders dated prior to 4/26. In this circumstance, it is necessary for us to enter the customer file with the name of the customer, pick up the file organization connection to the associated set of order records, follow the list of these order records, and pick out purchase order numbers for orders that satisfy the date condition. On the other hand, if we choose to protect the purchase order data and restrict its use to authorized individuals in the customer's organization, then it is necessary to provide privacy controls at the content level if others in the organization are allowed to have access to the data in the same order record.

Controlling privacy at the data element level, and particularly at the level of data element values, can have many important effects on structure and operation of the data base system. Consider a case where we compute an aged account receivable index above which the account is so far in arrears that we place it in collection. This does not mean, however, that we must remove the data for the account from our data base. In the more usual approach to such data processing problems, we would probably remove the account from one portion of the data base and place it into a special "deadbeat" file. Privacy controls, however, may allow us to avoid the introducation of a new file to our data base system, its attendant organization and management problems and associated indexing methods. In considering this question, the point is made that the deadbeat record is virtually identical in every way to the normal customer record, differing only in the value of a particular data element. When this aged account receivable index value exceeds the allowable limit, then we wish to allow access to this record only by certain authorized individuals in our organization. This clearly falls within the scope of the privacy problem at the data element value level.

METHODS OF PRIVACY CONTROL

In the precious section, the various levels of privacy controls were identified and briefly described. In this section, methods for creating and maintaining privacy controls at these various levels are introduced. The section closes with a discussion of certain problems related to the management or privacy data.

User and Device Identification

For any privacy system to work it must be able to identify a particular user, and this is accomplished by means of an assigned user password. The user password is employed on entry to the system in order to establish identification for referencing the data base. Generally, when a display device is employed by the user for entry to the data base system, and "enter password" command is invoked by the user, and then the password itself is entered. However, the system usually blanks the screen or does not echo the typed characters on a printing device, so that there is no visual record of the password entered by the user for other eyes to see.

Figure 4.25 illustrates a user/device matrix that would then apply privacy controls by user and device for entry to the system. Each device is identified in this matrix, and the matrix then notes whether or not a particular user is allowed to employ that device.

Device	1	2	3	4
User A	Y	Y		
B		Y		
C	Y		Y	Y

Figure 4.25/USER/DEVICE MATRIX

Figure 4.26 extends the notion of the user/device matrix so that time controls may be incorporated into the privacy system. The table shows the time periods which are under control, applies a code to each of them, and associates that code by user and device in the user/device matrix.

Period Table

Time	Code
8 - 10	1
9 - 12	2
12 - 2	3
12:30 - 4	4
4 - 6	5
All	6
None	7

Device	1	2	3	4
User A	1	2, 3	7	7
B	7	6	7	7
C	4	7	4	6

Figure 4.26/USER-DEVICE MATRIX WITH TIME CONTROLS

The point of such a matrix is that on acceptance of a user password, it can be searched on the identification of the device that was employed for data entry. Presumably the device identification is automatically and electronically made available to the system, thus validating the legitimacy of this user password for the selected device.

Data Base

A data base is a named collection of files having an integrated relationship to one another via structure data that overall creates a file organization architecture for the data base. However, a data base system may contain several physically disparate data bases. This means that the several data bases, while representing interconnections among the files which they individually contain, will not have physical interconnections between them. Thus, if we wish to provide privacy controls at the data base level so that we may selectively allow access to a data base, then a straightforward approach to accomplishing this objective is to employ the user/device matrix. The overall principle is illustrated in Figure 4.27. Here a user number and a device number enter the user/device matrix, which carries not only the authorization for a user's employment of a particular device for reference, but as well the allowable data bases that may be reached via that device by the particular user.

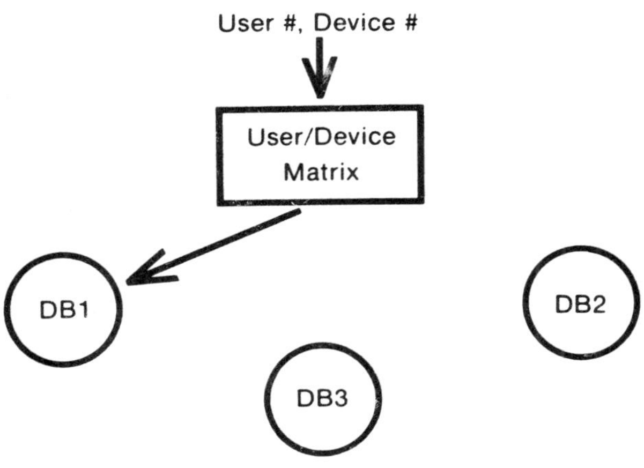

Figure 4.27/DATA BASE CONTROLS

Figure 4.28 shows one way in which such information might be organized. In this matrix, the user is associated with each of the data bases available in the data base system. The matrix connects user and data base to the set of reference devices. The body of the matrix then encodes whether or not the user may have access to a particular data base via a specific device and for a particular primitive operation. Thus, user A may reference data base number two for both addition and deletion operations from device one only. He may not reference data base two from any other device.

Keys

Any technique that is going to provide privacy controls to access by key and key value clearly is going to have to associate the user with an allowed set of keys and an allowed set of values. Figure 4.29 illustrates an approach to achieving this. This associates the user via his password with the set of keys allowed to that user. In this example, user A has access to order number. This may be one of a number of keys allowed to user A. For the particular key in this example, any order number value not in the range AGCxxxx - ALRxxxx may be employed as the key value by this user. The additional qualification is that within this range of disallowed key values, one particular key value AHIxxxx is accpetable. This ilustrates that the set of specific values may be used to qualify the allowed and disallowed values in the given ranges. This association of user and privacy data by key and key value may be extended to primitive functions as well, if that is of concern to the system. Such control is illustrated in Figure 4.30. In this case, the allowable primitive functions that might be applied using a particular key are listed by user. In this example, user A is allowed to employ order number only for retrieval of data, and is restricted from using the order number key for any other primitive operations on the order file.

At this point, it should be clear that there is a degree of independence between user and device privacy controls, and those at the key and key value level of the data base.

	device	1	2	3	4
user	A, DB1	1	5	6	6
	A, DB2	1, 2	6	6	6
	A, DB3	6	6	6	6
	B, DB1	6	4	6	6
	etc.				

Primitive Functions

function	code
add	1
del	2
mod	3
retr.	4
all	5
none	6

Figure 4.28/DATA BASE CONTROLS BY PRIMITIVE FUNCTION

		Range		Values	
User	Key	Allowed	Not Allowed	Allowed	Not Allowed
A	Order #		AGCxxxx—ALRxxxx	AHIxxxx	
etc.					

Figure 4.29/KEY VALUE CONTROL

User / Key	Order #	PO #	Cust. ID	Order Date
A	4	4	4	5
B	6	6	2, 3, 4	2, 3, 4
C	6	6	6	2, 3, 4

Primitive Functions

function	code
add	1
del	2
mod	3
retr.	4
all	5
none	6

Figure 4.30/KEY CONTROL BY PRIMITIVE FUNCTION

That is, we must independently qualify a user for employment of a specific referencing device which, on satisfaction, then leads to our concern about controlling that user's access to the data base itself via specific keys and their values. It should be noted in this regard therefore that since the same key may appear in two or more physically disparate data bases of the overall data base system, it follows that key privacy control may call for data base privacy control as well, as described above. With data base privacy control then, we may allow an individual user access by a given key to one data base, but not allow access to a second data base via that key if our privacy constraints so demand.

Files

As discussed earlier, it may well be that within a particular data base it is necessary to control access to specific files. This is generally accomplished by recording the file names within the data base and associating those file names with the allowable user. This, however, is equivalent to controlling pointers, since movement between files of a data base, once a key entry has been made, is generally via structure data. These pointers may be physical or logical, and in the latter case imply key control as discussed earlier.

In all events, it is clearly necessary to first control access to the data base by user and device, and possibly time, and the allowed data base. At this point, control over the file then requires a user/function/file mechanism along the lines illustrated in Figure 4.31. This example shows the user first clearing the password controls and then the device and data base controls, after which entry is allowed to some specific file of the data base where again the controls are placed on the primitive functions to be carried out. Once entry has been made to a file and its file organization, and the reference moves around the data base, we must be able to check whether or not the physical and/or logical pointers of the file organization will next take the reference activity across the file boundary and into a new file. If logical structure data is employed, then key value

User check
Device check
Data base check

User	Primitive Function	File
A	1, 2	4
A	5	7
B	4	4

Primitive Functions

function	code
add	1
del	2
mod	3
retr.	4
all	5
none	6

Figure 4.31FILE ACCESS CONTROL

controls come into play. If physical structure data is employed, then it is necessary to have file boundary information relative to the file on its assigned device, and its data space within that device, so that the pointer value can be compared to the boundary values. If the boundary values are exceeded, then reference is being made to another file of the data base, and before that reference can be completed, privacy controls must be actuated.

There is a small complication in effecting such privacy controls, since the pointer does not name the file to which it is going once it leaves the boundaries of the file from which it has come. However, the pointer value itself can be used to enter a device map which associates ranges of device positions with file names. The pointer value will lie in one of these ranges and therefore the file name will be identifiable. This will then allow us to apply the privacy control tests using structures such as those illustrated in Figure 4.31.

Content

The control of both the general data elements of a data base and the values in these data elements is the final level of privacy control. Clearly all front end controls concerning the user and the referencing device, the data base and allowable files, must first be applied. Controls by user function and data element are then possible. Under these circumstances, we must associate with each user the set of allowable data elements and the functions that he may invoke on the data in those data elements. As in the case of keys, we may also apply such controls on the values of the data element, so that allowed and disallowed value ranges are noted, as well as specific values that are allowed or disallowed.

Managing Privacy Data

It should be clear at this point that because of the number of data elements and the function and user combinations that are possible, the data processing problems are difficult, to say the least. In fact, overall we may say that the privacy problem requires a significant amount of data, particularly if it is implemented at all applicable system levels. To bring this point home, consider that a given user is associated with allowable reference devices, times of entry, data bases of access, files within those data bases, keys and their values, and data elements and their values. Overall we may impose a further dimension of control by primitive function. This can total up to a significant amount of data, and it represents certain difficulties in its management. One general approach is to formulate the required privacy data so that it can be put into the data base itself, and we can then use the DBMS as the referencing mechanism. This is a powerful approach to the management of privacy data, and should be given consideration.

TRACKING PRIVACY PERFORMANCE

The purpose of privacy controls is to prevent unauthorized access to the data of a data base, but it is equally necessary to record when such accesses occur, as well as where, and what violation of the privacy control conditions were noted. The objective here is to inform the cooperative user so that he may learn to avoid these errors in the future, and to track down and uncover the uncooperative user. The violations log and privacy statistics are the basic tools for tracking privacy performance.

The Violations Log

If the data base system overall has privacy controls at several levels, then it is necessary to identify violations at the specific level at which these violations occur. This requires that identification of the violator be available at all levels. This identification will be the user password. In identifying the privacy level in the violations log we must also identify the kind of privacy violation, i.e., the conditions at that level which have been violated and the time of the violation. If the violation occurs at a level that is beyond the application program boundaries of the system, then it is also useful to identify the program from which the DBMS call was made which resulted in the privacy violation. This will allow the cooperative user to review the actions of his programs and program system so as to make corrections as needed. It will also allow the data base administrator to review the privacy log to possibly locate an uncooperative user who has been attempting to broach the system's privacy controls.

Privacy Statistics

Finally, it should be pointed out that a privacy log represents an interesting collection of information about the privacy performance of the system and the nature of violations that occur. Sometimes the privacy controls themselves may be in error, and privacy statistics could very well indicate this. In general, however, the objective is to produce information about violations, violators, and the areas of the data base violated over the running history of the data base system.

CHAPTER 5
DATA BASE SYSTEMS SECURITY AND RECOVERY

In earlier chapters we have discussed the problem of data integrity and its maintenance in a data base system environment. This has to do with the quality of the data base in terms that are specific to the data itself and with concerns that directly impact the individual user. Data base system security and recovery, however, focuses on the types of data base and data base system failures that can occur, methods of recovering the data base from these failures, and the problems of restarting the data base system after a recovery has been effected. This chapter deals first with data base security, and then the idea of check points is examined and recovery questions are investigated. This provides a context for analysis of the restart problem.

THE DATA BASE SECURITY PROBLEM

There are several major dimensions to what is described as the security problem for data base systems. The first of these is general and involves failure of the hardware configuration and/or the data base management system package. This is sometimes referred to as a hard failure and is rather different from a soft failure and its consequences. The security problem also involves user lockout and user deadlock, and must deal with the question of individual program failure.

Hard Failure

Whenever a component of the hardware configuration or the data base system fails such that further operation of the data base system is not possible, we say that a hard failure has occurred. The most dramatic example of hard failure is a disk arm dropping onto the rotating disk plate. The problem is immediately audible, and clearly use of the data base system involving this disk and possibly the entire disk drive must be prevented. The problem is similar if power is lost at the main frame and it fails. A non-hardware problem with the same effect is a failure of the DBMS. This, of course, is due to a bug in the DBMS and, under the circumstances which we associate with a hard failure, would probably cause an ABEND condition. While not quite as noisy, it is equally as dramatic as a physical device failure.

Generally we can say that hard failures result in circumstances which make the failure immediately apparent. Though these failures are often traumatic in terms of the loss of data, there is at least the saving grace that we know that the failure has occurred. For other failure types this unfortunately is not the case, as we will see.

When hard failure occurs, several problems immediately present themselves. These problems have to do with the current status of processing in the overall data base system environment and in the data base itself. These status conditions are illustrated in Figure 5.1. This example suggests that there is a current queue of incoming transactions from users of the system. These are distributed to associated application programs so that at the point of failure we may assume that a particular application program is involved in some current user transaction. This program is in the middle of some process for the transaction which probably involves a certain state relative to the DBMS and references to the data base. The DBMS itself is aware of this status and reflects the fact that activities within the data base have been accomplished to a certain point, and that further activities will perhaps continue from this point. The problems that hard failure raises, therefore, are connected with maintaining a proper position in the queue of incoming user transactions, the status of current processing for individual programs relative to particular transactions associated with them, and the several status conditions held by the DBMS with respect to each of the application programs referencing the data

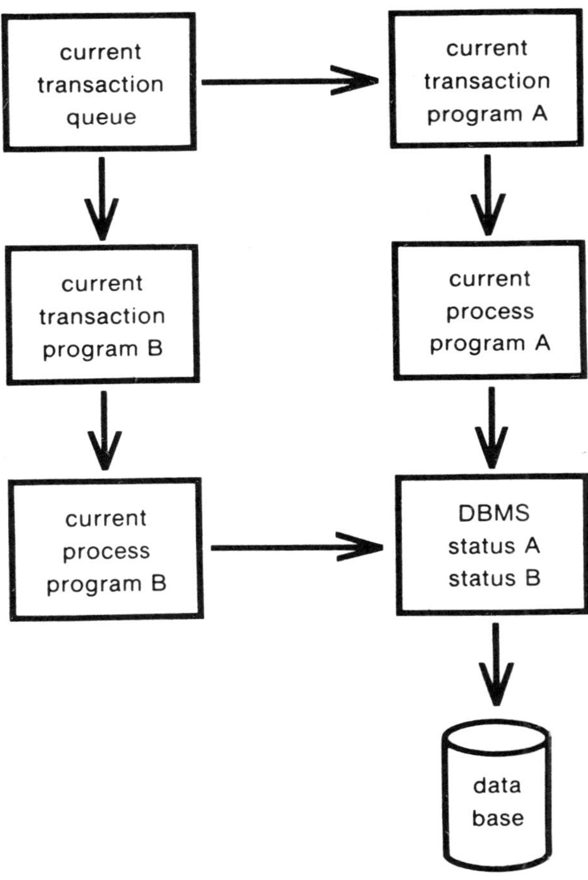

Figure 5.1/HARD FAILURE PROBLEMS

base. It is these various system states which must jointly be recovered when a hard failure occurs.

Soft Failure

Soft failures have virtually no dramatics associated with them, but create problems in the data base system that are sometimes extremely difficult to resolve. Soft failure occurs, for example, as the result of a transient error that has not stopped the system. In general, the failure does not signal that it has occurred and requires that its effects be undone once the consequences of the failure are discovered. Hardware transients are the most easily understood of the soft failures. These may happen when a disk controller generates an erroneous timing signal so that a record is placed in a wrong position on the disk. However, a data base management system package may have a bug in it which computes a wrong address, or one of the indexing methods in the package may, under certain rare conditions, place a record in the wrong position in some file of the data base. Application programs also make errors, and such program bugs may put erroneous index data into a record, wrong content, or even have everything right except some particular detail of the call statement to the DBMS. In systems which allow concurrent access to the data base for simultaneous use, the control of this access may fail because of a bug in the DBMS. Thus, any number of error sources can cause soft failure, and in general such failure is not immediately apparent. That is, the data base system continues operating and the error goes unnoticed. At some later point, however, the quality of the data base system will deteriorate and the soft failure will be discovered.

An example of the notion of soft failure and its delayed effects is illustrated in Figure 5.2. Here a collection of payroll records, involving among other things a pay code, is being treated by two independent processes. The first one is processing all of the records for crane operators, seeking to change those pay codes from their current value to the value 7. Out of the collection of personnel records, one is illustrated in this example where the job is crane operator

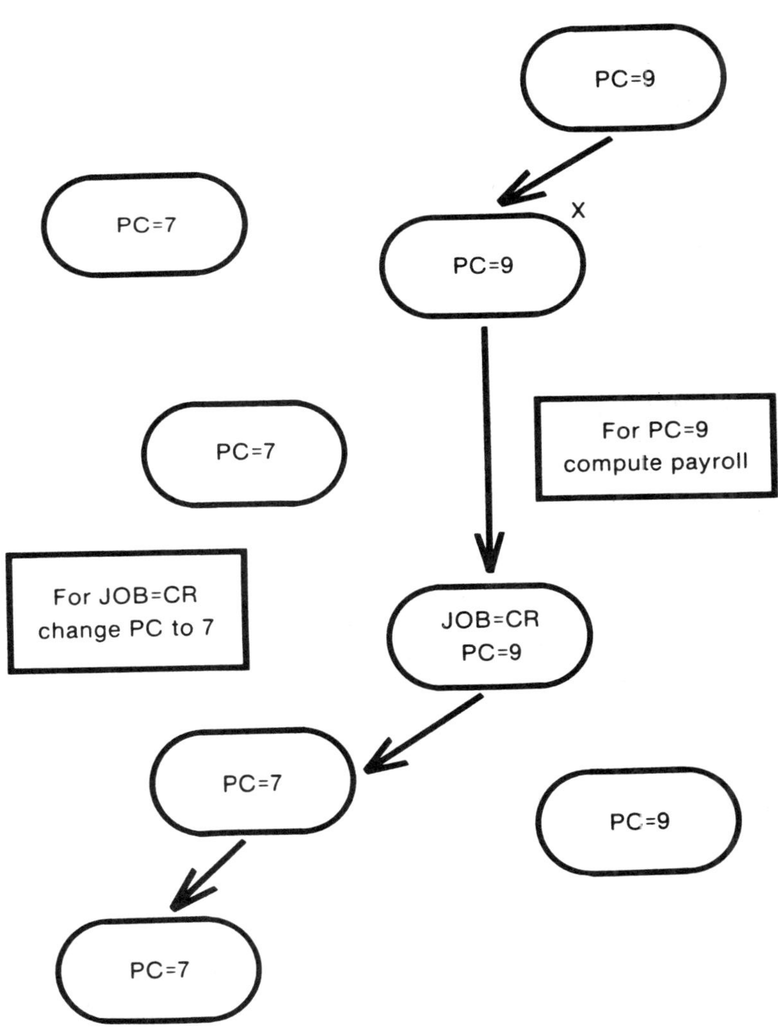

Figure 5.2/SYNCHRONIZATION FAILURE

and the pay code is equal to 9. This is changed to 7 so that the record for this individual will now be in the group of PC=7 records shown.

At the same time, an independent process is computing the payroll for all individuals with PC=9. Now consider the case where the first process retrieves the record for the crane operator with a pay code of nine. As this process looks at the record and makes its modification, the second process retrieves the prior record in the PC=9 group (marked X) and carries out its payroll computations. Meanwhile, the first process has completed its modification and changed the value of the pay code from nine to seven and logically has inserted this record into the set of PC=7 records. This means that the pointer in the last record in the payroll process (marked X) indicates a next record which is now in the middle of the PC=7 group, and unless it checks explicitly for the pay code value, it would continue its process in the wrong pay code set.

The problem is resolvable by controlling usage of the data at various organizational levels of the data base system, as will be discussed later in this chapter. The point here is that if such an error should occur, it may well go undetected until a large number of employees discover they have no paycheck.

Lockout problems

The only way to prevent difficulties of the sort described in the preceding section is to control the independent users in synchronism with their joint use of the data base and the overall data base system. This is called locking out, and it creates several data processing constraints. These lockout problems occur at various levels of the system: the data base level, files within the data base, records within the files, and fields within the records.

If we effect a lockout control at the data base level, then clearly we should not run into the difficulties described in the previous example. Here, only one user at a time would be allowed to operate within the set of files of a given data base and clearly no synchronization problems would arise. Similarly, locking out users at the file level will have the desired synchronization effect, since only one user at a time can operate on the data within the file. The difficulty with lockout at the data base and the file level is that a single user carrying out elaborate operations on files of a data base may tie it up for a significant period of time and as a consequence might lock other users out of not only the information in these files and data bases, but out of any performance of their own processing as well.

In order to get around this difficulty, it is necessary to consider the possibility of locking individual users out at lower organizational levels of the data base. The first of these is the physical record level. Of course, the user is not generally delivered all of the fields in a record, but the physical record must be delivered onto the main frame if the fields required are to be abstracted and the data forwarded to the application program. Therefore, it is interesting to consider arranging the security controls so that only one program at a time can use or operate on a specific record of the data base.

At first glance it might appear that resolution of the lockout problem at the record level could be realized by means of controlling the keys. That is, if key lockout were applied, then only one user at a time could use a particular key. This however, would fail in a multikey file, since a multiplicity of keys implies that there are a number of different ways of getting to a given record in the file via the several keys the data base system makes available.

The final level for considering the application of security controls in the context of lockout is on the fields of the data base. That is, several users may be allowed simultaneous access to a given record, but only one user at a time is allowed access to a specific field in that record. However, this creates significant data processing problems for the DBMS, and as a consequence, few packages bother with controlling the lockout at the field level. The more usual lockout controls are applied at the record and/or file level of the data base system, with some system providing lockout at the data base. These latter systems are sometimes referred to as single thread systems.

Deadlock

Quite often the logic of an application program which is modifying the data base will involve more than one file in what is referred to as a dependent update. That is, data in one file will be picked up and used to find data in a second file, which data will then be employed in a modification of the first file. If lockout occurs at the file level, then these two files must be seized by the application program for the duration of its update activity. In a similar way, we may lock out pairs of records if lockout is offered at that level of a data base. The problem is that a deadlock situation can occur when two independent programs simultaneously attempt to seize a common pair of files or records. When this happens, each of them manages to lock out one of the elements of the pair, thus preventing the other from using the element it does not control. As a consequence, neither of them can go any further, being locked out by one another, and in this situation we say the application programs are in a deadlock situation.

Deadlock at the file level is illustrated by the example in Figure 5.3. Here, process A is involved in an activity in file 2 first and then file 1. These are two independent and asynchronous problems and their processes therefore have virtually nothing to do with one another. However, the timing is such that file 1 has been seized by process A, but before it can get to file 2, that file has been seized by process B. Process A needs file 2 to complete its activity, and process B requires file 1. Each of these two processes then discover that the second file they need in order to complte their respective activities is seized. At this point they are individually stalled, and the two processes are jointly in a deadlock.

Deadlock can occur at the record level in a number of ways. Figure 5.4 illustrates a dependent update being carried out by two different processes. These again are asynchronous and independent of one another. Process A is going to carry out an update function that will involve the records labeled A1, A2, A3, and A4, while process B will employ the records B1, B2, B3, and B4. However, the timing of the operations is such that process A has gotten through record A3 and is ready to go for record A4, when it discovers that process B has already passed through its record B2, which is the required record A4 for process A. Therefore that record is seized and process A is stalled. This situation is mirrored when process B seeks to move from its record B3 to the record B4, and finds it has already been seized by process A.

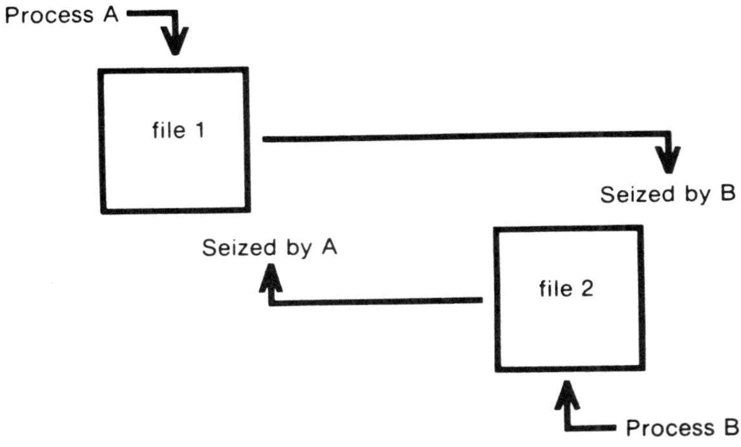

Figure 5.3/FILE DEADLOCK

The deadlock problem at the file level would, at first glance, seem to have relatively simple solutions. One of these might be to not allow any application program to seize two files at the same time. But this may create soft failure, as described earlier, because the program must make synchronized, dependent updates in several files concurrently. However, if it is desired to allow an application to make modification reference to two or more files of a data base simultaneously, then one approach is to have that application program announce its intention by naming those files in advance. This will allow a properly structured DBMS to check on potential file use by the various application programs so that the processes do not create a deadlock at the file level on files that they access simultaneously.

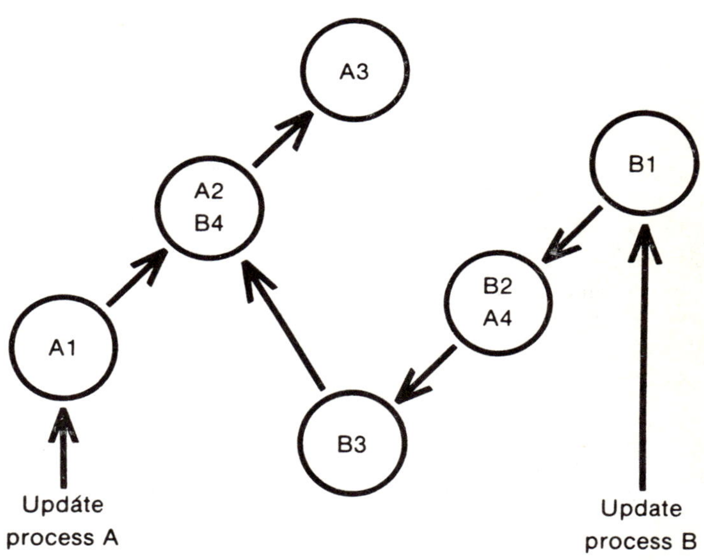

Figure 5.4/DEADLOCKED RECORDS

The problem is far more difficult at the record level, since record updates may be a rather heuristic process. That is, the process itself may determine where it is going next based on what it has discovered in the data of the last record dealt with. As a consequence, it would be very difficult, if not impossible, to announce in advance the specific records that will be employed in the update process. Therefore the best approach to avoiding the deadlock problem is to allow a process to seize only one record of a data base at a time. Another approach is to require that the application program announce in advance the set of keys that will be employed in making its references, so that no two processes will be allowed to simultaneously access particular key. Since keys are the means for locating specific records, this goes a long way toward the resolution of the lockout problem, but presents a serious data processing difficulty to the DBMS that provides this facility.

Program Failure

A severe problem occurs in the data base when an application program making a series of updates fails in the middle of its updating process and is terminated by the operating system of the computer. As a consequence, some of the changes have been made to the data base while others that must be made in order to make these changes valid are not completed. This means that we are left with a half formed set of modifications to the data base, and the net result is an error. As a simple example, consider the case where the modification of an order amount includes modifying the total order value. If the application program modifying order amount fails before it is able to make the necessary changes in order value, then there is a clear error in the content of the data base. There are two ways to approach this difficulty in the data base system environment. The first is to insure that any modifications made by the application program prior to its failure are removed from or backed out of the data base. The second approach is to isolate the program's modification effects until the modifications are complete and the program has run successfully. Then these modifications are applied to the data base in actuality. This is referred to as shadow recording. The example of Figure 5.5 shows a record that is to be modified in a file of the data base. Instead of making the modification to the record itself, this record is marked as being in an update process and a copy of that record is moved to a separate file of the data base, referred to as the shadow file. The update activity is then carried out in the shadow file. All records involved in the update activity for this application program are so treated, and when the application program successfully completes its operations and terminates, the actual updates are made to the object file by using the images in the shadow file. Obviously, this is an effective procedure to prevent the difficulties created by an aborted program, but at the same time clearly involves duplicating the updating process, since we must reference the object file to draw records into the shadow file, carry out the update process there, and then repeat it again in the object file once the application program has successfully terminated.

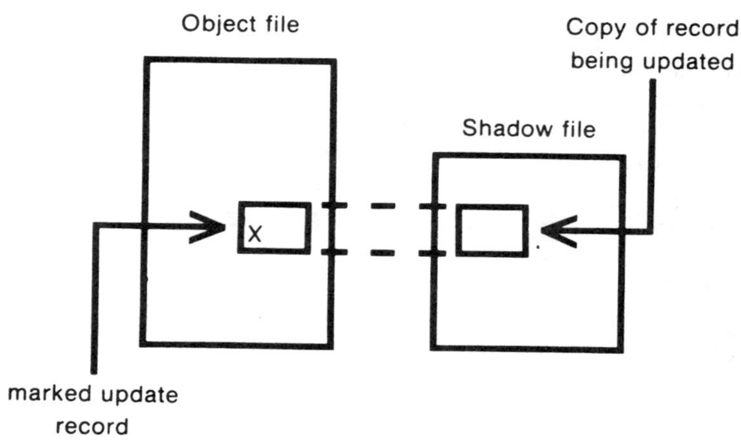

Figure 5.5/SHADOW RECORDING

Shadow recording and updating is a preventive measure that is sometimes built into a data base management system so that it will not be necessary to roll back the data base. This latter is a recovery technique and is treated at a later point in this chapter.

SECURITY LOGGING

Any recovery from a data base failure of any type is going to depend on the availability of certain information. This is referred to as log file data, and in what follows, we consider the objectives of logging, the type of data required, the content of the full audit trail, and the methods of structuring and storing this data.

Logging Objectives

As we will see in a later section, there are several different motives for the recovery process and a variety of calls for recovery techniques which themselves are different. In all of these, however, there is the common thread of having available a record of the changes that are made or are required to be made to the data base. This means making a record of all incoming transactions that imply change to the data base. In this regard, we must distinguish between transactions that are generated by users and delivered to application programs, and the resulting transactions created by application program which cause modifications in the data base to take place via actions of the DBMS.

This is illustrated in Figure 5.6. User transactions come into the system and are associated by a routing mechanism with a particular application program. This application program in turn creates a set of program transactions in a logical sequence and under the control of the application program. These are forwarded to the DBMS which then operates on the data base to effect these modifications, all of which jointly satisfy the modification service invoked originally by the user. The objective for logging, therefore, is to generate a record of not only the incoming user transactions, but of all program transactions that are created as a consequence.

Log File Data

The transaction events that affect a data base must be recorded in the chronological sequence in which they

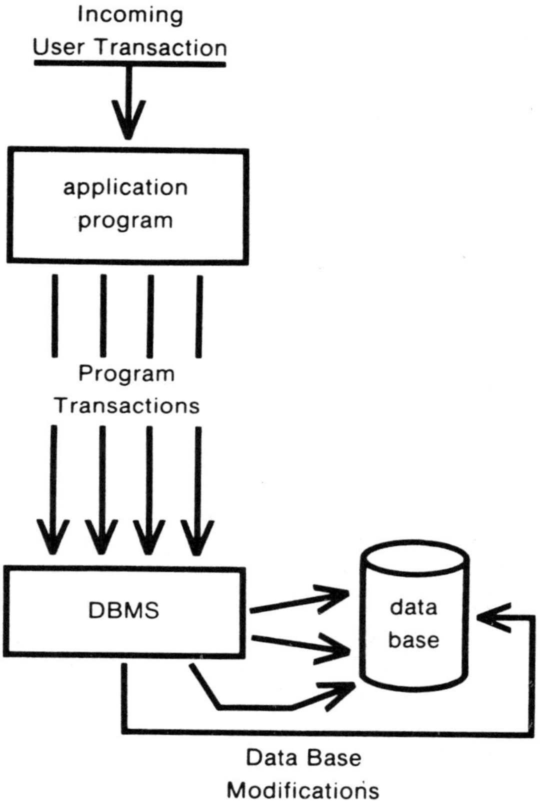

Figure 5.6/USER AND PROGRAM TRANSACTIONS

occur. In addition, the transaction text, or original user transaction must be recorded, particularly if recovery from an image copy of the data base is to be effected, as will be described later. Certain data base management system packages provide the user with a rather self-contained referencing mechanism so that the DBMS call in the application program not only designates the data to be modified, but the modification as well. Under these circumstances, it is sufficient to collect the name of the program creating the data base transactions and the set of

DBMS calls in the sequence in which they are created. The process is illustrated in Figure 5.7. Here the program produces a modification transaction which is then sent as a call on the DBMS to the package for application to the data base. In addition, the DBMS will log the details of the call, the time of the call, and so on.

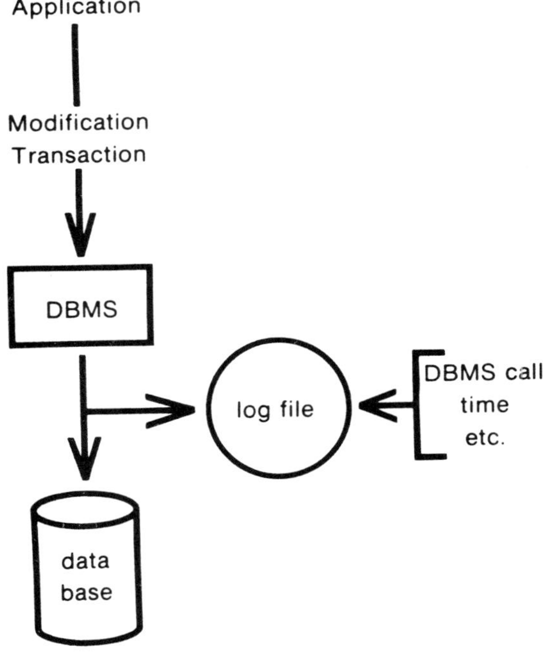

Figure 5.7/LOG FILE DATA

When the call language cannot be so complete that it includes the modification as well as the reference to the data base, then that modification will result from the execution of logic in the application program itself. This is a circumstance where an algorithm update is required. In Figure 5.8, for example, the application program is looking for orders in a class referred to as "express delivery orders" to determine if any of the delivery dates are greater than 50 days from the order date. The handling fee charge is reduced by 2% in such cases.

When transactions of this type appear in the data base system environment, it is clearly not enough to store just the DBMS calls. We must also keep a record of the program process that operates on the results of these calls and produces the data base modifications. The log file data will have to contain not only the calls on the DBMS, but also the algorithms and any other log file data required. Since there is little point in storing pieces of code from an application program, and indeed little point in storing the whole application program in the log file, it should be sufficient to store the name of the application program so that its individual processes can be invoked.

As we will see below, it makes more sense to more directly log events occurring at the data base. Most logging systems for security purposes are structured in this fashion because of the greater generality of the data log and the flexibility that it offers in recovery from data base failures.

The Full Audit Trail

As mentioned above, the logging data collected is most frequently made up of explicit data events and the times of their occurrences. There are five basic ingredients to this kind of logging, two of which have been referred to earlier; namely, the user transaction and the times of occurrence of these events. In addition, however, we will consider each call on the DBMS to be a transaction. These transactions refer to a file of the data base, a key or set of keys and their associated values for the reference, and a

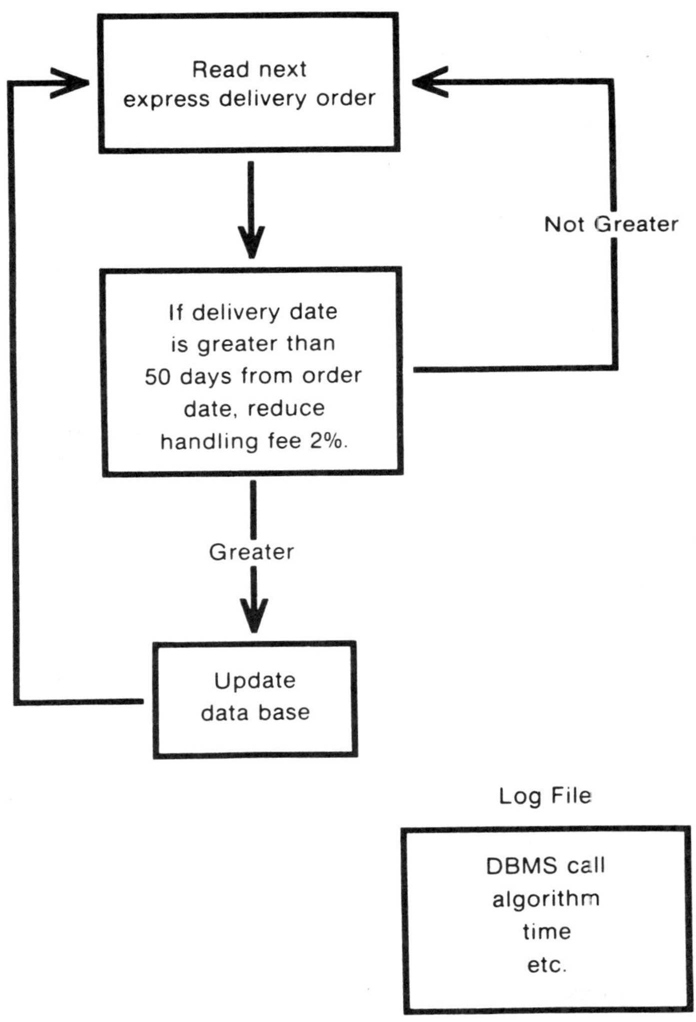

Figure 5.8/ALGORITHMIC UPDATES

primitive function specific action. This last part of the DBMS call specifies whether an addition, deletion, or modification operation is being invoked in the DBMS.

In addition to the DBMS call information, the "before" image of the record, what it looked like before the modification took place, is also recorded along with its data base position. And finally, the "after" image of the record, taken after the modification occurred, is recorded as well with its data base position. All of these elements together make up what is known as a full audit trail.

The full audit trail is generally organized chronologically by event time in the log file. Figure 5.9 illustrates how the various events from different application program processes may be mixed together as a consequence of asynchronous actions at the data base. In this example, the first action in the chronological sequence observed is an incoming transaction from user A. The next event was created by the program associated with this transaction and records its time, DBMS call, and before and after images for the records in the data base that have been affected by the operation.

The next event recorded on the log file in chronological sequence is for a created transaction from program B which is associated with an entirely different user transaction. Its DBMS call time and record images are also recorded. Thus, the full audit trail data is a chronological ordering of these events from all program sources, including a record of the termination of a program's execution, as illustrated in the example.

Log File Media

If it is necessary to collect data about events that change the data base, and we have a number of users over a period of time which create such events, clearly we will have a large amount of data to be stored. Storage requires a computing media for the data, and the natural inclination is to employ the disk. However, if the purpose of the security measures is to collect information so as to

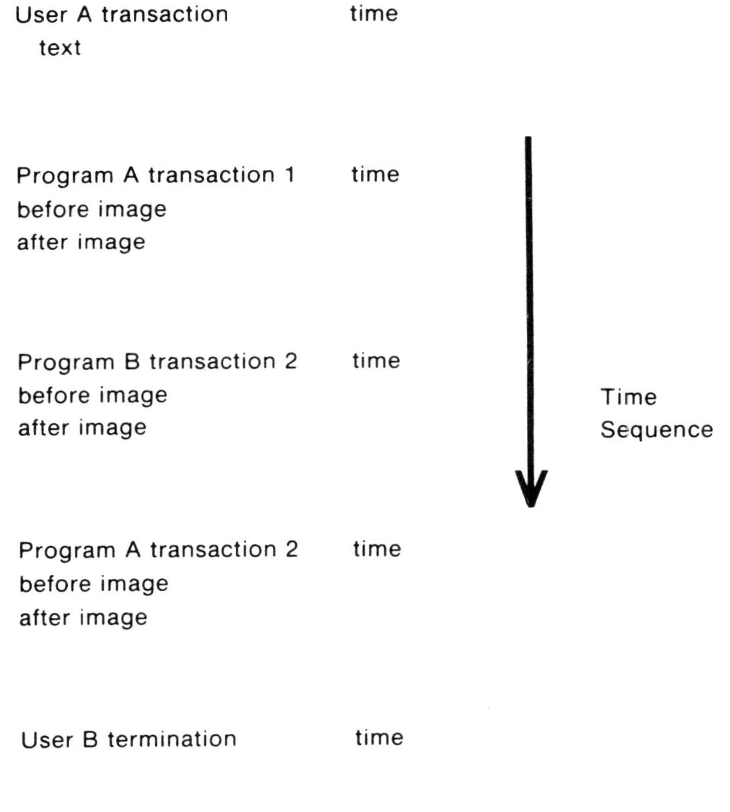

Figure 5.9/FULL AUDIT TRAIL DATA

recover from a failure, we are vulnerable to both hard and soft failures in the logging disk. This would make the log file almost totally useless and completely defeat the purpose of the logging activity. The usual alternative is to log the data on a magnetic tape. Tapes are exceptionally reliable, and furthermore the use of a tape for logging purposes would not interfere with other data processing activities, as the use of a disk pack very well might.

Next we must raise the question of a blocking factor for the data being logged. If we arbitrarily collected the data into larger buffer blocks, we again make our system vulnerable to memory failures or transient errors and bugs in systems and application programs. This suggests that the safest approach is to use magnetic tape and to send each individual logging element out to the tape with a blocking factor of one. Unfortunately, the effect on the length of tape employed will be enormous, if not entirely prohibitive. This is because the interrecord gap between each small record will in all likelihood be larger than the record itself. Hence the tape will be mostly given over to unused space in the form of these gaps, and the result will be a lot of tape swapping, not to mention the inconvenience of using this data in the recovery effort.

A middle ground tradeoff between the safety of a minimum blocking factor on the one hand and the potential loss of logging data on the other is illustrated in Figure 5.10. This is an approach that associates each application program operating on the data base with a DBMS buffer storage area. As the application program operates on the data base via its created transactions, the DBMS collects the required log data in the buffer assigned to that program. When that buffer is full, it is emptied into the log file, cleared, and made available for further log data from the program. One result of this approach is that the data appearing on the log tape is not in strict chronological order. However, the data does appear in relatively large blocks which makes efficient use of the tape. The only risk is in a failure in the main frame, with some data being lost. However, this approach associates the loss with only one user transaction for each program, and if the original

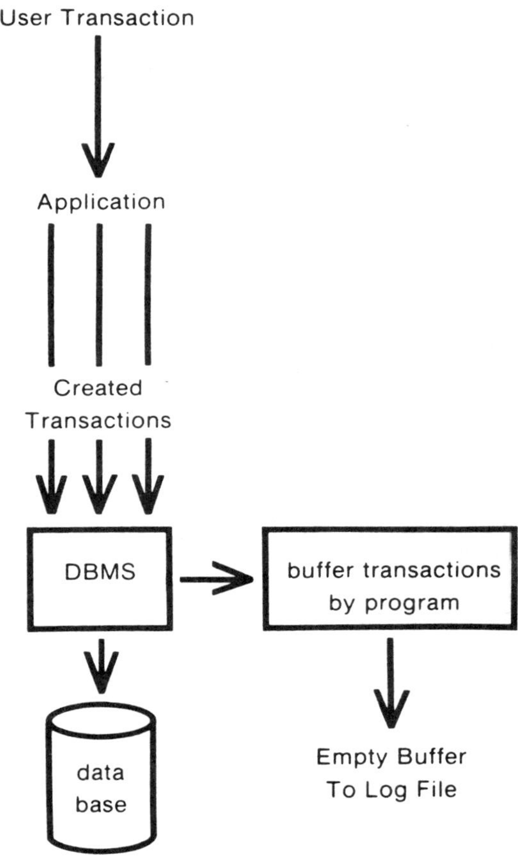

Figure 5.10/LOG FILE MANAGEMENT

user transaction was logged, then by rerunning that program we should be able to recover the set of log data it created in operating on the data base. In this approach then, the tradeoff is between some lost data and potential difficulties in recovering it if a mainframe failure should occur, vis-a-vis storage and general resource savings. Finally, it should be pointed out that a difficulty with this technique, and a data processing price to be paid, is that the log tape will require sorting into strict chronological order before it can be applied to any of the recovery processes that will be described later.

Log File Structure

In closing the discussion of security logging, it must be remembered that the purpose of the log data is to provide a means for recovering from a data base failure. The data that is logged is for data base modification references to many files via transactions delivered from many users and executed by many application programs. It is clearly of use to be able to separate the log file data by data base, file record, and user and program, with time the controlling factor. If this can be accomplished, then the log file data can be used selectively by data base, by file, by user, etc. On the other hand, if our logging media is magnetic tape, it is difficult to build such structures logically, and as a consequence difficult to be selective about the log data to be employed in effecting a recovery from a specific failure situation. For this reason there is a great temptation to put the log file data onto a disk pack, and even into the data base so that it is under the contorl of the DBMS. This would provide a very high degree of logical control over the data, but as mentioned earlier, at a vastly increased risk. It is interesting to contemplate the idea of using disk as the storage media and the DBMS as the mechanism for structure of and reference to the log file data. Then a tape image of the log file, while a less than convenient form, would provide ultimate if clumsy safety on the rare occasion of a disk log file failure event.

CHECK POINTS

Before any serious discussion of recovery can be undertaken, it must be recognized that synchronism among the several elements of the overall data base system must occur. These elements are the application program, the DBMS, and the data base. Check points provide the required synchronization.

An image copy of a data base, or portion of a data base, represents a check point for the data. This must be understood in the context that any operation on the data base which modifies it creates an on-going version of the data base that is a function of time. The purpose of the image copy is to represent a point in time at which the content of the data base can be considered as fixed. This may be thought of as a point relative to which the DBMS and application programs may be synchronized as part of the recovery process. This is illustrated in Figure 5.11.

Log data provides for recovery from errors starting at a checking point position; i.e., an image copy for the data base. Application programs recover by execution, and the check point is a place from which to begin such recovery. On the other hand, we may have to consider recovery of the overall data base system and, as a consequence, must provide for a system check point via the DBMS. These two check point types are discussed below.

Program Check Points

The program check point is invoked by the program itself and is activated at some stage of the processing where a unit of logical activity has been completed. The purpose of the check point is to establish a position from which the application program can be restarted once the data base condition has been synchronized to its state at that point in time. Check points are usually established at an easily identifiable point in the processing logic of the program. Thus on completion of a batch of updates, program check pointing prior to the initiation of a next batch of updates would presumably allow the program to be restarted from

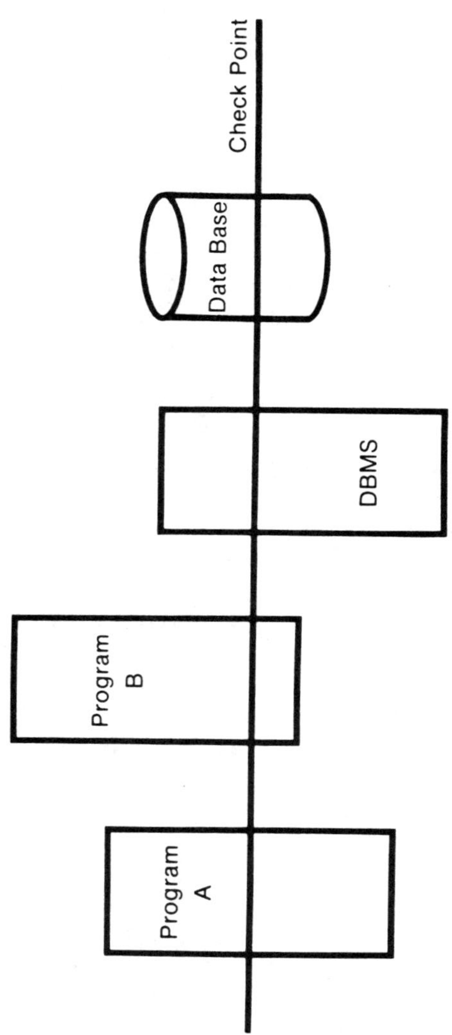

Figure 5.11/CHECK POINT SYNCHRONIZATION

this point once the data base itself had been re-established to the corresponding point in time. Under other circumstances, a check point may be associated with the completion of all data base acitivites created by a user transaction that has come into the application program. Such user transactions, as described earlier, will create activities on the data base, and check pointing between different users allows for restart at a more convenient "quiet" point in the program's execution rather than in the midst of its data base processes.

Check points are also of use in application programs where the major function is retrieval. That is, such programs may only be pulling data from the data base in order to, say, create a report. Suppose that such a report has been produced and it is discovered by operations that a data base error has occurred at a time that predates the production of the report. The user therefore would be interested in rerunning that portion of his system which produced the report once the data base has been recovered to the proper point in time.

By properly constructing the application program, check pointing can be simplified. If the check points are associated with breaks in general data based data processing activity, then buffer contents, current data base position, and so on, need not be stored and check pointing then becomes much easier. Under these circumstances, the only thing that is necessary is the saving of the check point location in the application program itself, and the time of the check point so that synchronization with the data base condition can be established. With this approach, the check point process is not time consuming and does not require extensive storage space.

System Check Points

The system check point is a rather more complicated affair than the program check point. The system check point is one taken by the DBMS for the overall data base system. In effect, at a given point in time a snapshot of all the data base system constituents is recorded so that the system can be returned to this point in time for rerunning with a properly synchronized data base. This check point must record the current status of the overall data base system environment, and this will include for each application program the content of its buffers, several state variable values for that program and, of course, the program name. This is for each of the programs, while for all programs jointly it is necessary to establish the open/close status of each of the files of the data base, and for the individual programs their current position in the data bases. Finally, the DBMS will operate one or more buffers which pool input/output space for all the current application programs jointly. The status of this buffer pool must be recorded as well.

The state variables for an application program include not only its current execution position, but the status of registers, any currently active DBMS call statement, and so on. That is, the state of the program relative to the data base system is exactly that set of data necessary for the resumption of the execution of that program in a multiprogramming environment. To put this in a different perspective, if we recognize that check pointing for the data base system is accomplished by the DBMS, then with respect to the DBMS, application programs are in one of two run time states. In the first of these, the application program has created a call on the DBMS and transferred control to it. Such application programs therefore may be considered dormant until the DBMS completes the called for activities and returns control to the application program. There may be several such programs in the system in this first state. The second state is the set of all application programs which are engaged in non-DBMS activities at the moment. When the CPU is assigned to execution of the DBMS, each of these programs is being multiprogrammed by the operating system and, therefore, the system check point must be able to recognize in which of these two states each of the application programs is to be found. It is clear, however, that with regard to restarting the system from this type of check point, if the state of each such application program is re-established, then there should be relatively little difficulty in their individual restarting. The problems occur in collecting the system check point information in the first place, and in applying that information to the restart in the second. The required information types for system check point activity are illustrated in Figure 5.12, which shows the joint recording of data necessary for both application programs and the DBMS within the context of the system check point function.

Finally, it should be pointed out that the purpose of the system check point is to provide a single point of system control, as opposed to individual user controls. Check points are usually taken after the DBMS has quiesced all data base activity. This means that it completes all current data base activities and accepts no new commands for execution. This means that the check point data itself is clean and a clear cut point of synchronization for data base recovery is provided. If recovery is carried out from an image copy of the data base, then it is usually the case that the image copy cycle will contain a number of DBMS check points within it.

RECOVERY METHODS

There are five general techniques for recovering from a data base system failure. These involve the direct correction of the data in the data base, setting up a check point/restart status via an image copy of the data base, and then three recovery methods that are designed for resolution of specific data base failure problems. These are roll forward, roll back and back out.

Direct Correction

Let us suppose that several days after placing an order, the customer receives a copy of that order in complete detail. This detail includes item quantity for each item in the order, and the customer discovers an error in the quantity value. By notifying the order entry department, the error can be corrected by direct modification of the proper field of the data base. Similarly, if the customer

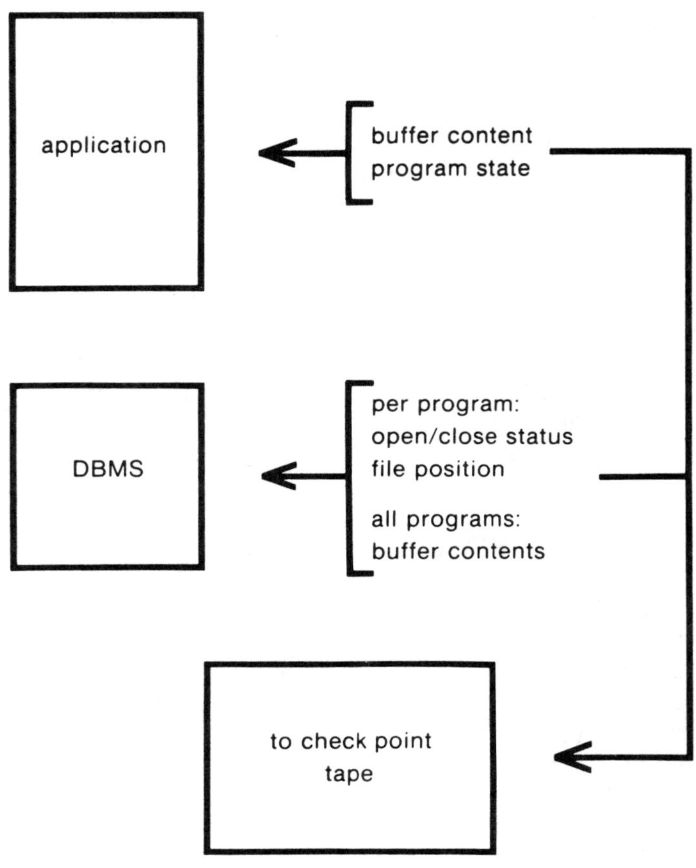

Figure 5.12/SYSTEM CHECKPOINT INFORMATION

address were found to be wrong, a direct correction could be made.

This approach to recovering from a discovered error in the data base depends on being able to identify the error with a specific position or record of the data base. It also requires that we be aware of any associations this changed data has in the data base. If for example, item quantity is accumulated for each individual item, then the accumulation is affected and must be modified as well. In an actual order entry inventory control system, order quantity is used to relieve the inventory, and therefore modifications must be made for certain parts of the inventory data base in order for the recovery to be complete.

What has been said in fact, is that if the data element which is corrected directly involves derived data, then the derived data must be corrected as well. On the other hand, if only content is at issue, it should be clear that the recovery problem is the direct equivalent of a data base modification function. However, there may be a larger impact if index data is to be corrected. This is because index data may not be only a means for entry and discrimination throughout the data base, but also for association in file organization methods. If it enters into logical structure data, then the effects of an error in index data may be much more widespread throughout the data base. In fact, it if is determined that certain index data is in error, and as a consequence certain content is in error, then in all probability the failure which impacted the index data has caused errors that have yet to be discovered in a number of other places of the data base. It is wise to not only correct the data base to effect a recovery to the extent to which the failure is identified, but to look in logical places within the data base for other possible failures that may be connected with the present one.

Image Copies

When a data base disaster occurs, such as an arm falling on the disk plate, large volumes of data are irretrievably lost. This may involve several tracks of the data base and even whole cylinders. In some instances, where the wreckage is so tangled that the disk cannot be removed without destruction, entire data bases may be lost.

Admittedly, it is rare when such a calamity occurs in the computing room. However, the fact that it does and that its effects can be so disastrous demands that some method of backing up the data base be provided. An image copy of the data base is the technique generally used. This is a copy for each physical data base of the overall data base system, file by file within each data base. Image copies are created at a certain point in time, and the image of the data bases is associated with that time. The other constituents of the data base system, namely the incoming transaction queues, the application programs, and the data base management system, are all check pointed so as provide a means of synchronizing the image copy with the various status points of these data base system elements.

Figure 5.13 is an illustration of the image copy cycle. In most image copy systems it is first necessary to quiesce all current data base operations. This means that all current calls on the DBMS are completed and results sent back to the application program, and as these data base system activities are brought to conclusion, no new activities are accepted by the DBMS. When all activities relative to the data base are at a standstill, the DBMS then records the current status of the queues, the programs and its own internal status for the programs, followed by a copy of the data base as it currently stands. When this is completed, the data base system is then started up again and run until the next preplanned time for a data base image copy.

The purpose of having an image copy is to be able to recover from a hard failure in the data base system. Suppose that the log data we have accumulated in the operation of our data base system consists of the incoming user transactions, the time of their arrival, and the name of the application program to which these transactions are applied. If at a certain point during the execution of the data base system we then have need to recover from a failure, the image copy, plus the log file synchronized to the first transaction following the image coy time, gives us the means for recovery. The image copy file is mounted in place of the current failed data base, and the log file is run forward from the synchronization point. The log file data introduces each user transaction in the proper time sequence and provides the system with the application program name which must be loaded and executed. The execution of this application program operating on the incoming user transaction reproduces the data base events that occurred prior to the hard failure. All of these together will reconstitute the data base and provide a recovery.

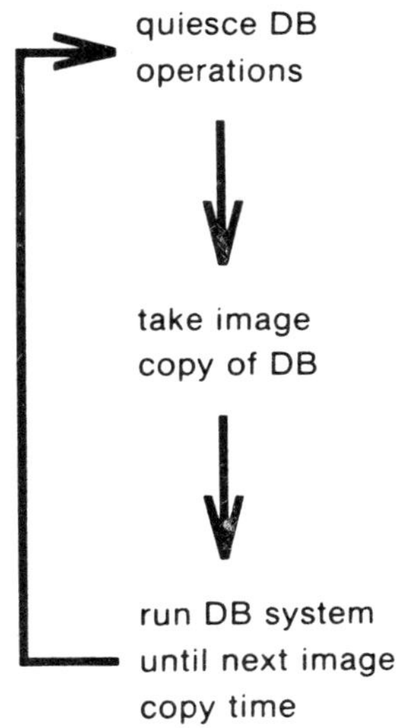

Figure 5.13/IMAGE COPY CYCLE

To accomplish this is obviously expensive. If an hour has gone by since the last image copy time, and 75% of the activities in that hour were associated with operations that modified the data base, then all of that data processing activity will have to be reproduced. Clearly, if idle time was encountered relative to the data base system in that hour, it does not have to be reproduced, but a large portion of the overall data based data processing load will indeed have to be executed again. Of course, while this is happening users are not allowed access to the data base. Thus, all current data based data processing must be stopped for what may turn into a significant time period. However, one advantage of the image copy approach to recovery is that because each of the incoming transactions are executed by their respective application programs to reproduce the data base from the image coyp, problems with any derived data in the data base are taken care of automatically.

Figure 5.14 illustrates the overall process of recovering with an image copy. Failure occurs at the current time T1, and the recovery via the log file of transactions with the application programs applied to the image copy of the data base as it was at time T0. This results in the restored data base at the current T1, plus whatever recovery time is required.

Roll Forward

The difficulty with recovery via an image copy and the incoming user transactions is that all computations must be reproduced. The roll forward technique is designed to significantly reduce the computational effort required to recover from a hard failure using an image copy of the data base. In this case, the log file contains all record images after modification to those records occurred. These "after" images are made available from the log file in chronological order. To recover from a hard failure using the image copy at a time T0, that copy is mounted on the computing system and the proper synchronization point on the log file is determined.

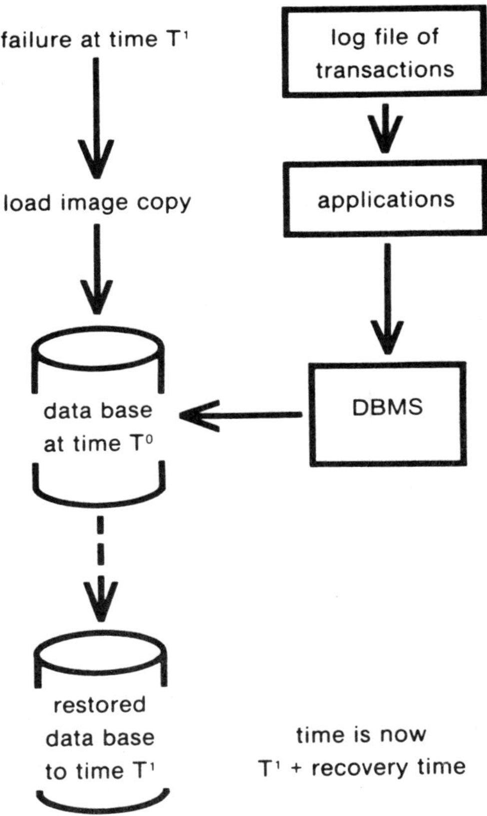

Figure 5.14/RECOVERY WITH AN IMAGE COPY

Roll forward recovery is illustrated in Figure 5.15. This log file of "after" images, starting from a time T0 forward to T1 is then processed against the image copy of the data base as it was at time T0. The process consists merely of applying each after-image on the log file in chronological order to the corresponding record in the image copy. When all of these after-images have been applied to the proper positions of the image copy, data base recovery has been effected and the data base can then be considered as restored to its condition at the time of failure.

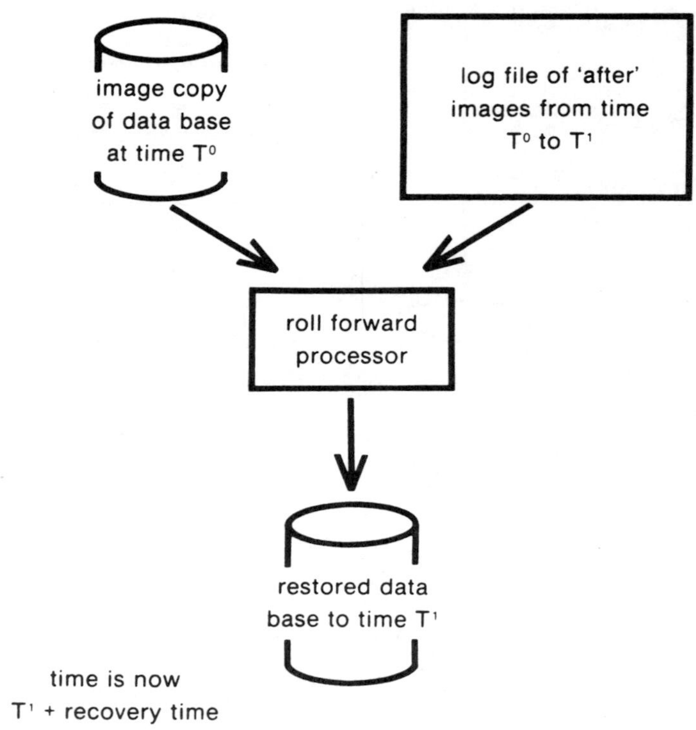

Figure 5.15/ROLL FORWARD RECOVERY

It should be evident that the roll forward method of recovery from an image copy following a hard data base system failure is much more rapidly accomplished than reproducing each of the transaction executions as described in the previous section. Since each after-image in the log file represents the data base as it was on completion of the modification activity with which it is associated, each such step moves the recovery forward one increment in time. Furthermore, each of these steps is a simple record replacement operation based on the position data that was originally logged with the after-image. No computation in an application program is involved and, therefore, roll forward recovery should proceed rapidly.

At first glance, the roll forward technique might appear to offer some difficulties with respect to derived data since the derivation functions are not executed. However, if derived data is involved in a modification process, then the execution of the associated function results in a further modification to the data base. This in turn creates an additional after-image at a later time. Recording this "after" image, the time, and the physical position of the modified record in the data base simply adds yet another step to the recovery process and accomplishes the necessary recovery for associated derived data.

Roll Back

We earlier discussed the problem of program failure during updating activities. There we described the difficulties that might be encountered if an application program failed to complete all updating activities and was terminated. As a consequence, a number of records in the data base will have been updated, but the overall update is not correct until all updates have been completed. If such a program termination occurs under these circumstances and the method of shadow recording and updating has not been employed, then we must find some means for removing the effects of the terminated program from the data base. The purpose of roll back recovery is just this.

To effect a roll back recovery from a program failure we must record "before" images in the log file. That is, a copy of the physical record to be modified during an update activity is taken, along with the time of the modification and its physical position in the data base. The log file now makes "before" images available in reverse chronological order. The roll back recovery process is illustrated in Figure 5.16. Here, the before images, starting from the present failure time T1, and backward to the start of the job whose program has failed at T0, are made available. These before images are applied in the reverse chronological order to the data base as it stands at failure time T1.

The roll back processor then replaces each current after image found in the data base with its corresponding before image.

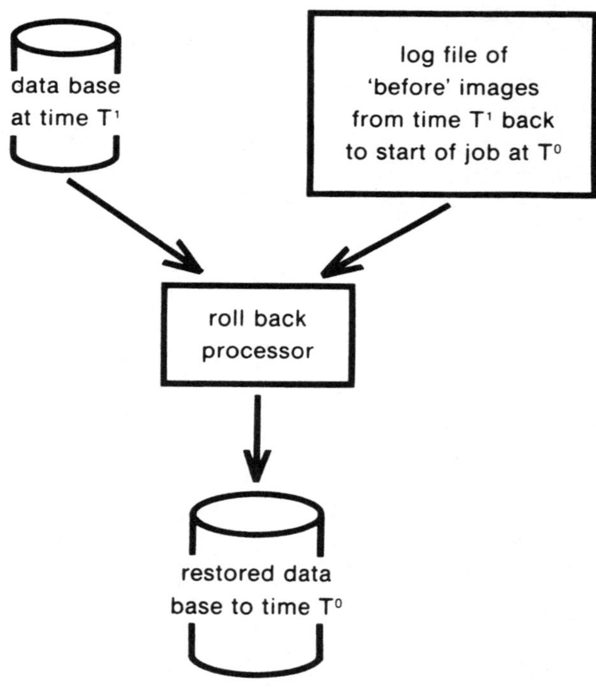

Figure 5.16/ROLL BACK RECOVERY

This is carried out in reverse chronological order so that each step in the roll back recovery process moves the status of the data base back one increment in time. Each such step backward undoes a specific update effect. Of course, update effects from all application program activities are included, and it is, therefore, necessary for the roll back processor to monitor this recovery process so that when their respective effects are removed from the data base, the roll back processing may stop. At this point, the data base is in the state that obtained at an earlier time, T0, just prior to entry into the system of the job whose update program activity failed.

In order to complete the roll back recovery, it is now necessary to bring the state of the data base up to the present time, T1. This is accomplished by rolling forward from T0. The roll forward, of course, requires that the after images be available. These after images were those replaced by the before images of the roll back process. Thus, as roll back recovery is effected, each replaced record must be retained so that it may play the role of after image in the ensuing roll forward operation. However, the after images of records associated with the offending job need not be retained since the roll forward operation is carried out as if the offending job were never run.

Back Out

In the discussions thus far we have considered recovey techniques in response to hard failure of the system. Soft failure is a different and more difficult matter. As described earlier, a soft failure is either due to some transient effect in an unknown constituent of the hardware/ software environment, or may be due to an error in an incoming transaction that has not been caught by the associated application program. In both of these cases, the technique of data base back out provides a method for recovery.

In order to accomplish a back out recovery, it is necessary that the log file record both the before and the after images resulting from operations on the data base. These record image pairs are associated with their physical position in the data base, and with the time of the occurrence of the event which caused the modification. Figure 5.17 illustrates the back out process.

The log file of before and after images is employed in reverse chronological order. The back out processor compares the next after image with what should be its identical counterpart in the data base at the designated physical position. If this is not the point at which the error in the data base is noted, then an incremental roll back step is executed using the associated before image from the log file. In this way, the data base is rolled back incrementally, but with a validity test for continuing the roll back operation. This process is repeated until some after image comparison fails. At this point we have determined the location of the data base error, not only in the data base but in terms of position in the log file as well. If now we continue the roll back process for all of the transactions which were created by the same job, back to and including the original incoming transaction on the log file, then the source of the difficulty will have been removed from the log file and its effect from the data base. Once this is accomplished the data base can then be rolled forward using the after images on the log file but, of course, skipping those associated with the offending user transaction.

At first glance it might appear that the test to compare after images with their counterparts in the data base is unnecessary since we know where in the data base the error occurred, and we have on the log file the address of the after image. However, it should be remembered that the error we are seeking to rectify in the data base in all likelihood occurred rather earlier in time, and therefore there may have been a number of legitimate updates to the data in the particular record following the update which created the error.

Finally, if the error is a transient and not a failure in some transaction, then the above described procedure will still work satisfactorily. That is, the effect of the transient was to cause an erroneous entry into the data base during an update operation. The back out process will locate the error in terms of after images that do not compare, and then remove the transaction and all of its effects. Clearly, however, since the error was a transient, the user

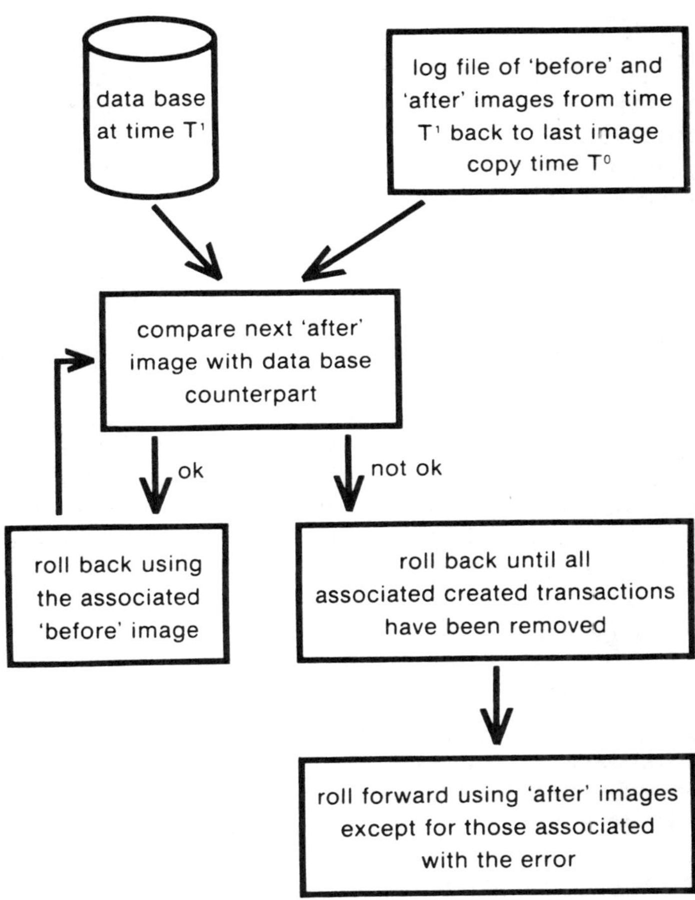

Figure 5.17/BACK OUT RECOVERY

transaction itself and the associated created transactions were not at fault. However, it seems impossible to make such a discrimination, so at worst, one user transaction is lost. Under these circumstances it would seem only fair to notify the user of the action taken.

Random Transients

In considering the last section, it may have occurred to the reader that a random transient may have been the cause of the observed problem in the data base. That is, the transient error occurring in a constituent of the hardware/ software environment during a data base reference activity results in some record in the data base being changed at random. The record that is in error has no connection with any of the changes that are being made and, therefore, no connection with any information stored on the log file. As a consequence, we can only back out from the current time until we return to the time of the last image copy of the data base. At this point we can conclude that the observed error was a random transient, and the best that can be done is to roll the data base forward to the current time and then effect the best direct correction to the error record and any associated corrections that the logic of the data base suggests.

Recovery Performance

A final remark concerning recovery techniques is in order. In the discussion of recovery, it may appear that the operations are extremely difficult in data processing terms and may be rather expensive and time consuming in the overall operation of the data base system. Of course, the error itself is a problem and its detection may take time. The effect of the error in the data base clearly must be removed if the integrity of the data base is to be preserved along with the faith of its users in data processing. On the other hand, if we look more closely at the kind of operations that are involved in the several recovery techniques discussed, we see that essentially direct replacement of data base records accounts for the major data processing activity. Granted, these records may be spread rather widely over the storage device resulting in a large amount of arm movement, but consider the circumstance where an image copy of the data base is made available file by file at, say, one hour intervals.

If our average incoming user transaction rate in an hour is, say, three thousand transactions, and each creates an average of five program transactions, then the log file will contain approximately 15,000 before and after image pairs. The roll back part of the back out operation will read these 30,000 log file images (presumably sequentially from the log file) and will read 15,000 after images from the data base and replace them with 15,000 before images from the log file. Thus 30,000 records will be read sequentially and 30,000 records will be read and written at random. If we assume that 40 milliseconds would be required for each of these data trasfers (even though the sequential reading from the log file would go much more rapidly) then the maximum time to accomplish the back out activity would be about 40 minutes. The corresponding roll forward operation would then replace the before images with the after images, with each one read again from the log file. This would represent a total of 30,000 records read and written. Again assuming 40 milliseconds per average operation, an additional 20 minutes would be required. Therefore, a total data base back out would require something on the order of one hour.

Now consider that on the average we would expect to back out half way in order to discover our error transaction. But suppose that we record in the log file data not only the before and after images along with the data base physical positions, but information that tells us whether or not this update had an associated dependent update in another file. We will also need to identify each of the image pairs on the log file with the data base file from which they came. With this information in the log file, we then can dramatically enhance the performance of data base back out because we can localize the back out operation to the file in which the problem has been observed. This means choosing before and after images from the log file selectively by the file name in which the problem exists. If the log file information indicates that a dependent update has occurred, then the log file data for the associated file is used to create additional back out operations. Thus, we need to apply the back out method only to the file in which the error has occurred, and to any dependent files that may appear during the back out activity. This should cut the back out recovery time by an order of magnitude, which seems a relatively small price to pay for maintenance of data base integrity.

DATA BASE SYSTEM RESTART

The purpose of the log file is to provide a basis for recovery of the data base. The purpose of check points for application programs, the DBMS, and the data base system in general is to provide a basis for restarting the data base system with respect to a recovered data base. In what follows we will discuss some of the types of data base system restart processes and the components of the restart problem. There are essentially two circumstances under which the restarting of the data base system must be considered. These are warm and cold restarts, and each are given consideration below.

Warm Restart

In its simplest statement, the purpose of a warm restart is to pick up and continue the execution of the data base system from the point at which it was interrupted. The warm restart, however, can rarely be executed at exactly the point of failure, but rather must be accomplished at some earlier time. This means that data base recovery must be accomplished to that point in time, and then the restarting of the application programs and the data base system in general must be synchronized with the data base. The synchronization problem is illustrated in Figure 5.18. The synchronization occurs with respect to the check point positions of the several application programs that are associated with the data base system at the point of data base recovery. In this figure, application program A is shown with three check points, and program B with two check points. The check points are numbered in chronological order and are listed below each of these programs. The data base is therefore recovered to the latest point in time that is consistent with check points associated with the application programs in the system at that point in time. That is, as the data base system progresses from state to state over time, there will be a variation in the membership of the set of application programs in the system producing these changes.

The difficult problem in restarting a data base system derives from the fact that we must determine at which point in time recovery of the data base is to be made, and this determination must be based on the available program check points. In Figure 5.18, the data base recovery is carried to a point such that no effects of program A past its check point number 2, and no effects of program B past its check point number 1, are present. This allows the restart operation to synchronize the data base with these two programs at their respective check points CP2 and CP1 so that the programs may be run from these check points forward. This is a difficult and delicate determination and requires that significant information concerning program check points, the times of these check points, and control of data base recovery be available to the restart operator.

A warm restart is then accomplished by resetting the application programs and the DBMS with the check point information. The warm restart process is illustrated in Figure 5.19, and as a result of this first step allows the operator to determine a common synchronization time. The recovery processor will then operate on the image copy of the data base, or the data base as rolled back to some suitable point, the log file, and the synchronization time. The log file will be applied to the image copy or the rolled back version of the data base, and the recovery will be made forward to the point in time when a warm restart has been determined as possible. This delivers a recovered data base at a point in time that is synchronous with the check points of the several application programs and the check point information for the DBMS.

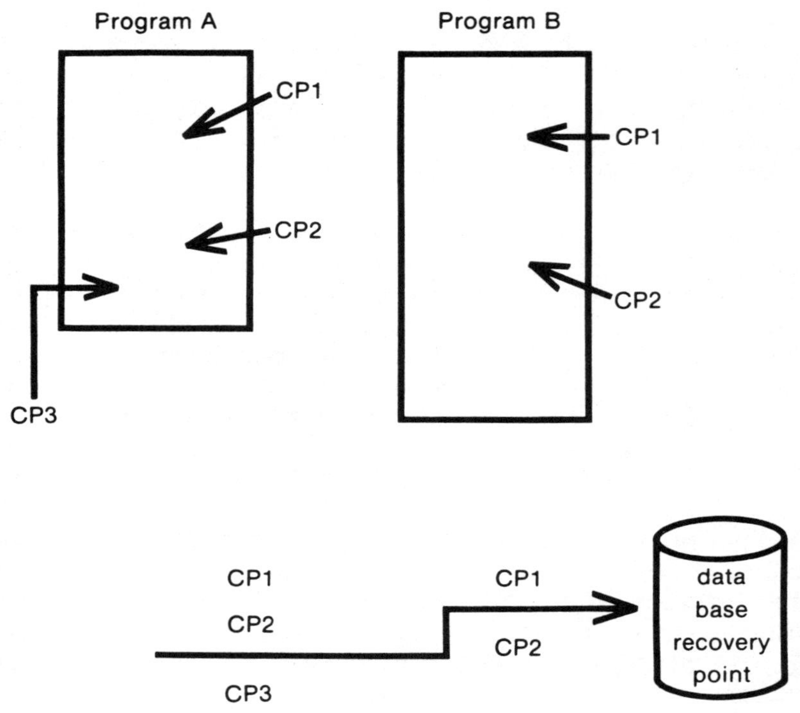

Figure 5.18/DATA BASE -- CHECK POINT SYNCHRONIZATION

Cold Restart

When a hard failure occurs in the data base system environment, it is not only immediately evident but, in general, significant amounts of data are lost. As a consequence, it is usually necessary to go back to a check point for the data base via an image copy and to reconstruct the data base forward to some suitable restart point in time.

Figure 5.20 illustrates the way in which a hard failure might occur in the run time environment of the data base system.

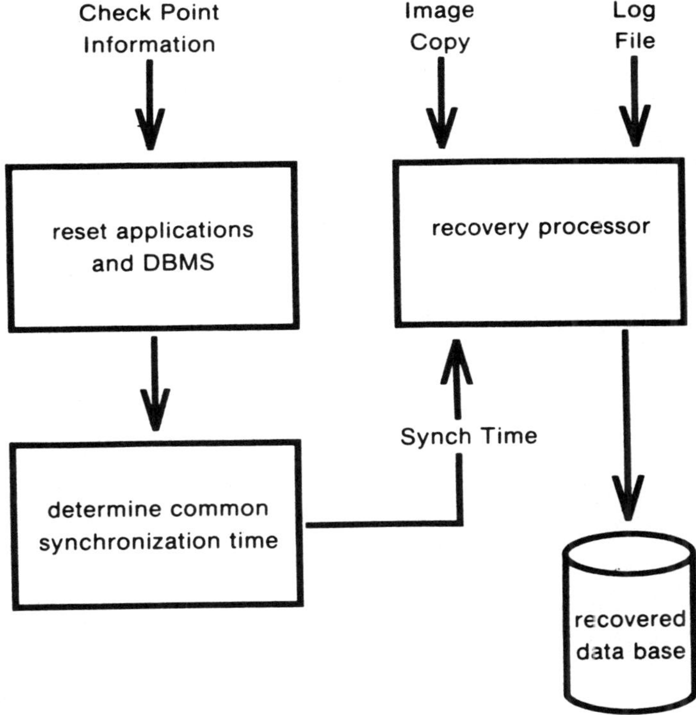

Figure 5.19/WARM RESTART

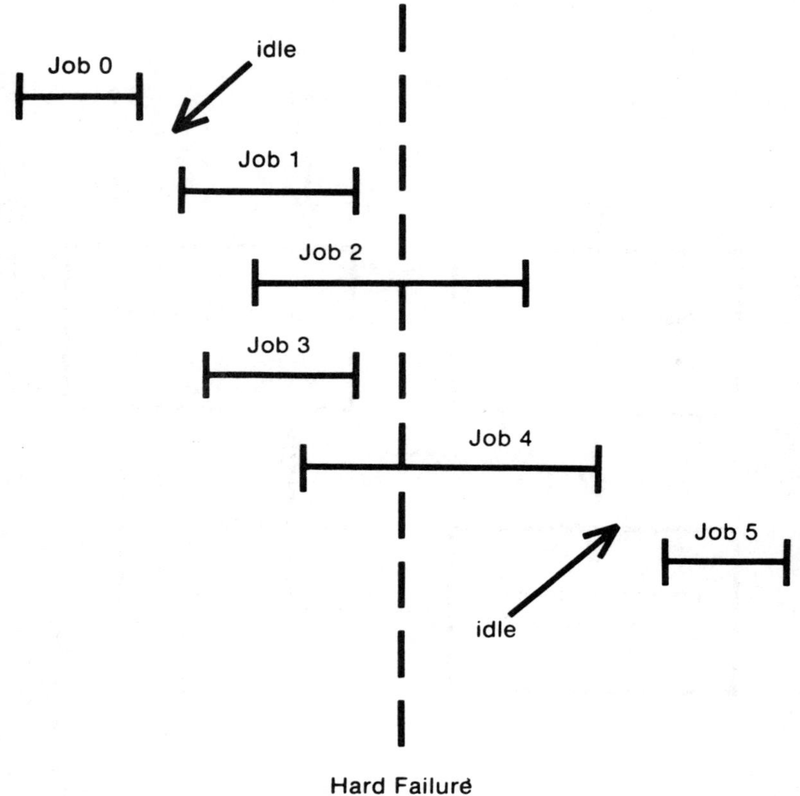

Figure 5.20/HARD FAILURE OCCURRENCE

In this example, at the time of occurrence, jobs 2 and 4 are present in the computer and the dotted line indicates the point at which the hard failure interrupts the operation of the system. That is, jobs 2 and 4 are present when the crash occurs, and the restarting of the data base system must take this into account. At first glance, however, it would seem that bringing the system forward from any image copy point that is earlier than the starting time of job 2 up to the point where job 2 begins would be sufficient to carry out the recovery. That is, the data base recovered to this point, plus execution of job 2 followed by job 4 should then satisfactorily continue the operation of the data base system. However, it must be remembered that the effects of job 1 and job 3 on the data base prior to their respective terminations, but during the executions of jobs 2 and 4, will have some impact on these jobs, their modes of operation, and the results they produce both for their users and in the data base as well.

This follows directly from the fact that by definition a data base is a common repository for data available to all users up to privacy constraints. This implies then, that the data base should either be reconstructed up to the beginning of job 1 or up to the end of job 3, with a warm restart for jobs 2 and 4.

The difficulty with this last approach is that the hard failure may have obliterated data in the data base back to a time that is earlier than the termination time of job 3 and, therefore, the completion of job 3 and its joint effects on the data base with jobs 2 and 4 must be reconstructed as well. Thus, the first suggestion, namely reconstructing up to the beginning of job 1 and rerunning from that point, can now be seen as probably the most sensible point at which to effectively restart this system. The reason for this is that job 1 is preceded by an idle period. We are therefore guaranteed that since there were no jobs in the computer, the DBMS was not active and no data base events were in progress. If such idle points in the system, or more specifically in the data base system portion of the overall computing environment, can be identified by the operator at the outset of the restart function following a hard failure, then the most recent idle point represents the ideal position from which to inaugurate the cold restart function. Since an idle point in data base system operations is a good place at which to initiate restart operations, if such idle points could be created or forced by the DBMS, then the frequency of opportunities for cold restart could be increased so that the computational time lost due to having to back up to an earlier point after a hard failure can be minimized. The problem of forcing an idle state on the data base system is that it can only be managed for the non-online portions, that is, in the background data base operations. In this case, the operator is instrumental in effecting these idle data base system periods.

A large scale overview of the cold restart process is illustrated in Figure 5.21. Here it is suggested that data base system idle time can be represented by the situation where no data base files are open. This might be taken as the criterion for forcing the data base system idle time so that a cold restart check point could be created. Later, at a point where data base recovery must be accomplished, the most recent data base idle time commensurate with a recoverable data base then becomes the cold restart point for the overall data base system. This, of course, involves the log file for the data base. When the restart is effected, we are in actuality inaugurating the job stream at the cold restart point.

Restart Components

It has been mentioned at several points that the data base system constituents are each associated with the security, check point, recovery, and restart problems. These constituents are the data base, application programs, and the DBMS. In addition, log files of the data base system and the overall logging function must be restarted.

The Data Base System

The data base system consists of application programs, the DBMS, and the data base; and, as we have discussed in this chapter, it is these components which must each be synch

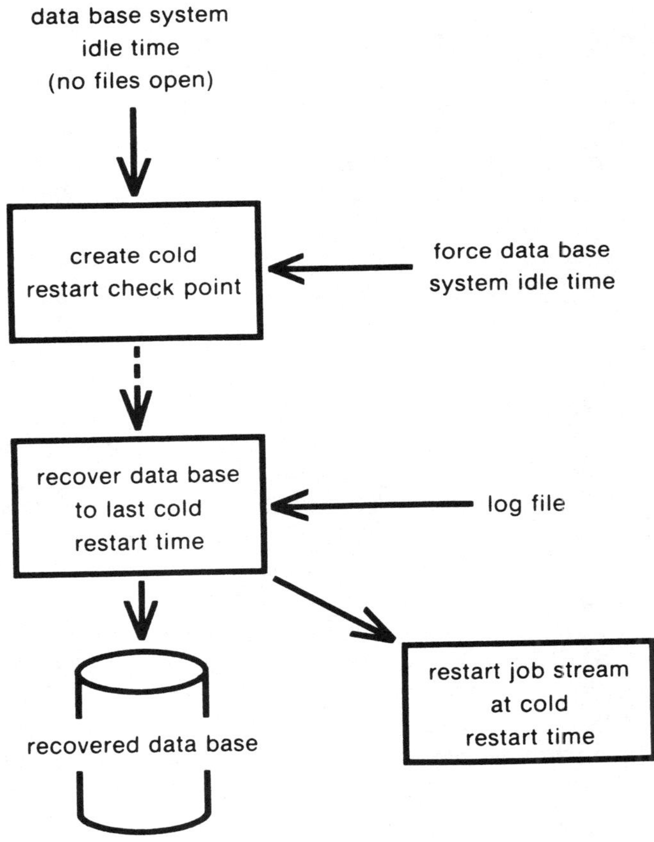

Figure 5.21/COLD RESTART

ronized with the point at which restart will be inaugurated. This is a point in time that is associated with program and/or system check points, the state of the data base, and the current state of the DBMS. Although the subject has not been brought up in this discussion of data base system security and recovery, the data base system may be operating in an online context. In all likelihood, this means there will be input and output transaction streams which on the one hand accept data base references from the users, and on the other return data base results to them. Since the members of these queues appear in chronological order, it follows that recovery and restart should be concerned with these queues as well. This is an obvious problem which, however, is part of a larger issue concerning data communications in a data base context, and is beyond the scope of this book.

Log File

Log files can be thought of as one of the generated outputs of the data base system. The log file is a recording of all events which modify the data base, and these events have a chronological order. Therefore, it is also necessary to synchronize the log file position with that of the rest of the data base system with respect to the time of the restart. There is a further point to consider in restarting the log file. This is illustrated in Figure 5.22 and is associated with that logging technique whereby each program has its own log buffer which is not written until all generated program transactions resulting from an incoming user transaction have been completed. For each program, then, there is an associated log file position to which its next log file output will be written and, furthermore, this log file buffer must be restored with the proper values for the restart time. If restart times are chosen according to well-defined check point conditions, then it would be wise to insure that these log file buffers are all flushed for each of the application programs, so that at restart time the buffers do not have to be restored. The flushing of the buffers corresponds to the completion of all data base events associated with an incoming user transaction. This was earlier defined as a logical place to create a program check point. In addition, it should be noted that when a data base system is idle, programs are not actively engaged in the use of the data base system, and as a consequence, there are no data base events. This means, in turn, that the log file buffers are empty, which contributes to simplifying the restart problem.

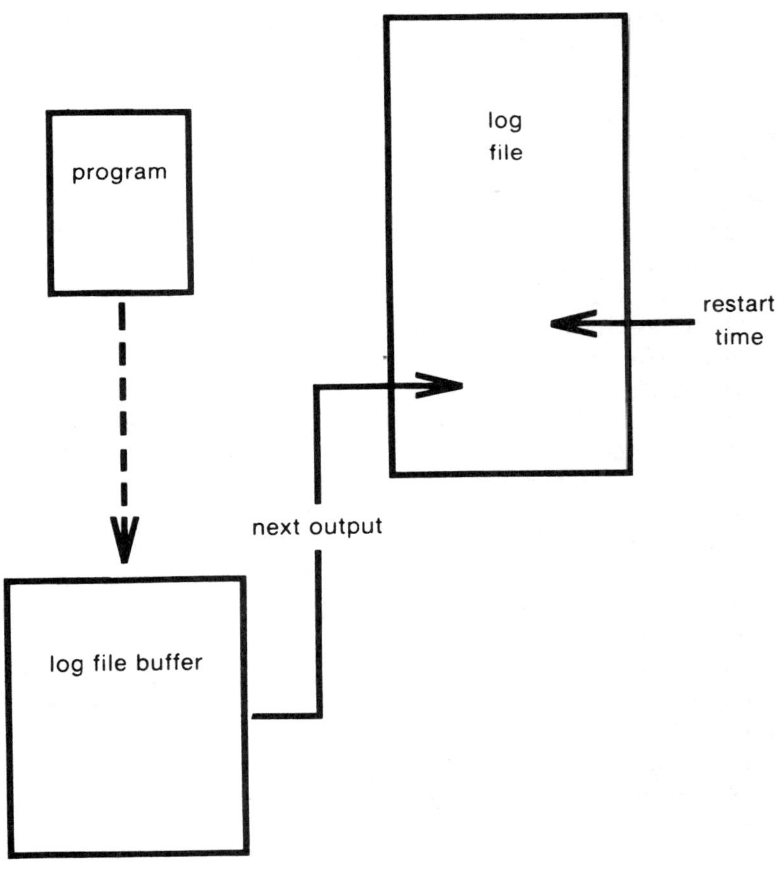

Figure 5.22/LOG FILE RESTART

Restart Validation

To widely varying degrees, the data base management system packages commercially available for use in the development and operation of a data base system provide security, check point, recovery, and restart services. In all of these packages it can safely be said that there is relatively little in the restart process that is automated. Of course, the mechanics of restarting, such as reloading buffers, restoring status, and so on, are accomplished as restart functions of the package, but the problem of synchronism generally is not.

Operator Role

The essential gear in the machinery of the restart function for any data base system is the restart operator. It is his function to guide the system through its various restart activities and to make the crucial decisions concerning synchronization. For this purpose it is useful that the system provide certain tools which aid the restart operator in successfully accomplishing this task. Perhaps the most important of these tools is making available an inventory of check point times by program, system check point times, times of available image copies, and times associated with the log file. Of course, it is unreasonable to expect that all of these times in these several categories will always be available. But a judiciously selected set of them involving the most recent of each of the several types of event times should be summarized somewhere in the system and be easily accessed. Once the restart operator has assessed the nature of the damage, he can then use such information to determine the recovery methods to be employed, the point to which recovery will be made, and the point at which the restart synchronization will be carried out.

In order to make such data available, it might be wise to consider the idea of collecting that data on a safe medium such as magnetic tape. Then, a reporting mechanism should be able to pass the tape, searching for such things as recent idle points, coincidence of image copy time with other check point times, and so on.

User Notification

In this chapter we have generally discussed the basic principles of data base security, logging, check point, recovery and restart. It should be evident to the reader that to a large extent a variety of methodologies must be employed, some intelligence must be built into the data base system, and all of it must be handled with degrees of wisdom. There is little in the security and recovery problem area that one can call clean cut and algorithmic and, in fact, we must expect less than perfect results in our efforts to recover from failures in the data base system.

This demands that we establish in our data base system environment a formal mechanism for reporting to its users the failure event and some summary of the potential loss of information that may have occurred. This is difficult to accomplish in any precise way but it cannot be overemphasized that user confidence in the data base system is built on confidence in those who build, maintain, and operate it. Errors and failures are expected and acceptable if attention is being paid to the circumstances which create them, and if the user is aware of the possible impacts on his use of the data base, the data base system, and the information environment within which he functions.

CHAPTER 6
PROJECT STAGING

In Chapter 3 we devoted extensive discussion to the subject of identifying the data resource. The vertical analysis of organizational structure identified reasonable organizational boundaries within which to examine business functionality in the detailed decomposition. This led to the discovery of the three-way relationship between function, organization and information, and ultimately to the data resource matrix of Figure 3.18. That is, this part of the project planning activity has identified the detailed business functions, and has provided us with a means for ordering business functions so that we can determine an optimum sequence of this implementation for the data base with respect to the development of the corporate data resource.

This, however, does not settle the issue of project staging. There is a logic to the execution of detailed business functions that will aggregate them into subsets to be referred to as business procedures. As we will see below, this provides identification of cost benefit groups, as discussed in Chapter 1, and in all probability, alternatives for the first project stage.

Business Procedures

The detailed subfunctions of a functional decomposition merely identifies the constituents of major functions of interest. The decomposition chart has only a top to bottom order which represents a precedence or definitional relationship. There is no implied order, such as left to right or line by line in a decomposition chart. In this sense then, the functional decomposition represents only the "what" of business function, not the "how" for that business function's execution. However, a major business function will have, among its collection of detailed subfunctions, aggregations into procedural units. These represent specific groups of functional activities that must be carried out in order to achieve a specific business objective. The reality of business function execution is that the function aggregations or business procedures are often carried on simultaneously and synchronously in the organization. Using the decomposition elements of Figures 3.3. and 3.4, the collection of subfunctions listed below has been selected, and, in the order presented, represents a business procedure.

RECEIVE RETURNS
IDENTIFY RETURNS
EXAMINE RETURNS
ESTIMATE REPAIRS
ISSUE DAMAGE SLIP

This is the "how" of some part of the organization and represents the sequence of business function executions that must occur for a damaged return item.

There will be many such business procedures to be extracted from the functional decomposition. Furthermore, individual functions of the decomposition may appear in several of the business procedures. For the above example, the function RECEIVE RETURNS will probably belong to a business procedure that involves undamaged returned items, as well. The two functions IDENTIFY RETURNS and EXAMINE RETURNS might also be shared in such a procedure.

Now suppose that, without giving consideration to business procedures, the first stage of our data base system project elects to consider the functions ISSUE DAMAGE SLIP, IDENTIFY RETURNS, and no others in the above procedure, based on the dictates of the data resource matrix that we have developed as a result of our analysis. The result will be services delivered to the associated organizational units which will support these selected business functions, with costs accrued in their development and delivery. However, because the delivered set of services does not support the complete procedure, in all probability the services that are delivered will be of little use to the organizational groups responsible as a whole for the overall function of the business procedure. This means that these services will not be used, and the accrued costs will therefore not be offset by any accruing benefits since these can result only from the use of services delivered as products from the data base system project. The conclusion to be drawn, then, is that once the data resource matrix has been determined, the next step is to structure the required business procedures from its functions. Each of these will then represent a minimum data base system project stage in the sense that delivery of services to support all of the functions of a given procedure will be complete for the overall business function that the procedure represents, and therefore can be employed by its users so that benefits can be accrued. Once the procedures have been identified, those procedures whose member functions are highest in the data resource matrix should be preferred as candidates for the early stages of the project, while those lower down in the matrix should be considered for the project's later stages.

In general, we can expect to find a number of such data base system project stage candidates. Because individual functions of the decomposition may belong to a number of these procedures, we will find that there are in all probability several first stage candidates, second stage candidates, etc. In the following sections of this chapter, therefore, we will examine further criteria for selecting the initial stage for the data base system project.

Before closing it should be pointed out that the decomposition functions of a business procedure map into the organization chart. For any given procedure, this mapping can be determined from the function-organization sharing matrix. Therefore, a business procedure corresponds to a set of organizational units, and it follows that this set of organizational units make up what has been referred to in the earlier chapters as a complete benefit group. In the final chapter of this book, we will look into implementation staging and cost/benefit analysis. This concept of the complete benefit group, which, as described above is based on the concept of business procedures and functional decomposition, is the essential ingredient in the structuring of both an implementation staging plan and a cost/benefit model.

Current Data Processing Quality

It should be clear that the effect of a data base survey is to produce indications, if not explicit information, on the nature of data processing in the organization as it stands now. Of course, the DP products currently produced and their inventory represents information concerning the current systems, and in a certain sense are characteristic of the current nature of data processing. This characteristic quality derives from the fact that DP products are the external representation of the results of computation. To put this in a different way, we may say that we employ resources at the computer center to prepare and introduce data, to update systems and manage them, to operate those systems, and finally to produce results for end users. Systems, of course, may do many other things, but DP products are overt evidence of systems having done something.

Similarly, data processing is observed outside of the computing room and outside of the data processing department itself by the ultimate end users in terms of data processing's ability to plan, design, and develop new system products. Clearly, any product that is consuming extreme data processing resources for its development, is delivered with a lot of fanfare, and then is totally ignored by users, is signatory of a certain characteristic, and as a consequence, a quality of data processing.

It is important to understand the quality of data processing in an organization, both in its production aspects and in its development aspects, in order to get some feel for the likelihood of success of a data base system project. It has been pointed out earlier that data base projects depend on users for their definition of requirements in the form of services. The service analysis is itself an exercise in coordination with the user in the planning of the data base system. Raw information therefore lies with the user, and as a consequence that user must be able to have faith in the ability of data processing to carry off the project.

One does not want to deal in pure opinion in such areas, however. A user may be offended by the nature of his data processing support, but indeed there may be very good reasons in both the problem, and in the method chosen for its solution in the computing system to, in fact, justify the kind of support he is getting, with "justify" used in the sense of "the best that could be done under the given circumstances."

Thus, it is necessary to examine the quality of the current data processing activities in the organization so that we may ascertain the degree of positive support we can expect from the users and to learn more about the data processing organization itself. It should be remembered that data processing has status within the organization it supports. We must determine if that status is high or low in order to properly evaluate the risks being taken with data base.

User Satisfaction

Is the user satisfied with the results he gets from data processing? In large degree, of course, the answer to such a question depends on who asks it and, furthermore, the answer might be seriously influenced by internal politics. But the inventory of DP products which the information gathering has developed does indeed offer us a significant opportunity for getting a clear picture of the user's feelings about data processing support. We can therefore list a collection of qualities these products might have which a user can be asked to rate. These would be, in no particular order of importance:

TIMELINESS
COMPLETENESS
ACCURACY
APPLICABILITY
ARRANGEMENT

The timeliness of a system, particularly with respect to support of a crucial business function of the organization cannot be overplayed. There is nothing more frustrating than being forced to use the information from a prior report simply because the current information is not available, even though due some while ago. Furthermore, if information in a report that is late is available by some means of derivation from systems and their products, then the temptation to do this may become institutionalized in a set of manual procedures. Before we know it, these manual procedures have become not only part of the organization's operations, but we will probably come to depend on them to deliver the information that should have come from the report in a timely fashion. If the report supported a crucial function, then this part of the crucial function becomes institutionalized as crucial itself.

DP products are complete if they have in them everything that is needed. They are incomplete if the information found in one must be employed with information found in another to adduce conclusions on some specific subject. That is, many organizations find their employees expending significant hours of effort drawing information out of report sets and putting them into other reports in summary or graphical fashion in order to satisfy the final reporting needs of someone to whom they themselves report. This again will very likely become an institutionalized manual procedure that may very well be obviated by making the DP products complete in the first place.

A system's usefulness verges on nil if its results are inaccurate. It is bad enough if a report or screen is consistently inaccurate, but much worse if it is only inaccurate on occasion. Under the former circumstance we may learn the bias that is in the product, or the dangerous areas that should be stayed away from, or a means for correcting the errors that are always present. In the latter case, however, the user will never know when the DP product has failed, and if it is only an occasional failure, he may rely on it at just the wrong moment to make the major or crucial decision. It is at this point that the DP product lets its user down. In this case the system has let him down and the repercussions may be enormous. Hence the accuracy of a DP product must be unquestionable, with that accuracy measured not only in the information values that appear, but by the currency or up-to-date quality that these values have as well.

Many DP products are received and put in the "circular file." A recommended activity in the execution of a data base survey is to make up an inventory of these products and then to review them with their recipients. There is no doubt that at some point it will be discovered that the received product is being neatly filed in shoulder to shoulder cabinets already filled with its earlier brothers. The paper is barely wrinkled and on inquiry it is found that the report was designed and developed by a Mr. Hopper who has long since departed the company. Nobody else even knows it is there.

There is also the situation in which the DP product is received but hardly used at all. Take the case of a report providing detail on the day's orders. This report might consist of 1600 printout pages and be literally loaded with the total information on all orders taken in the previous 24 hour period. Someone has decided, however, to arrange the information by alphabetical sequence based on the street address in the ship-to field. The report comes this way because it also goes to distribution and that is the subject in which they are mostly interested. However, the report as it turns up on the sales analyst's desk has little applicability in this arrangement, and as such we may well wonder why the report is there at all.

Finally, the subject of DP product arrangement is in itself obvious. Some products are easy to read and provide the reader with virtually all of the information that he needs or desires. Other products contain all of that information and yet are totally impossible to read. Any report or screen that is unreadable is unusable, therefore inapplicable, and might just as well not be delivered. As in the last paragraph, what is good for distribution might be useless for sales. Furthermore, the same report might not be userful to both of them even though the information content in the report is essentially the same. Consider a distribution report organized in ship-to address sequence and a sales report organized in item order. The information might be largely the same, but the use, application, and meaning of the report is very much different, and as a consequence, very much dependent on its arrangement.

All of these foregoing points are descriptive of the user's satisfaction with the results he gets from data processing. The user has other results to be gotten from data processing, however. On-line users entering data, answering questions, inquiring into inventory, and so on, surely make up a non-report using community that must be considered.

All that this is saying, then, in condensed and possibly oversimplified terms, is that the data base survey brings with it a necessity to understand the degree to which the current DP products work either well or poorly. Functions for which the products work well, which involve major and/or crucial business functions, and which are expensive to replace and are completely satisfactory to all involved, may indeed be the only candidates for data base. In such a case, if there are no better choices for early candidates, data base should perhaps be deferred until some degree of dissatisfaction has set in.

Upper Management's View

It is not unreasonable to say that upper management's view of data processing, and all of the things that it supports, is rather narrow; upper management is interested in bottom lines. It is perhaps unfortunate, however, that so many diverse events contribute to any particular bottom line that the responsibility for lack of performance may not, in the view of upper management, be at all clear. It is often the basis for a lot of finger pointing, with data processing blaming the equipment, the users blaming data processing, and the customers going to the competition. But upper management does indeed have opinions or perceptions of the quality of data processing, and it is these which must be heard. Very frequently a manager is willing to compare his data processing group's performance to what he understands is the performance of data processing groups in other, similar industries and organizations. After all, this manager probably belongs to a professional association or two. He meets with his peers and they discuss business. These days a large part of that business is certainly data processing and, as a consequence, he will have formed some idea of who is doing what, and ultimately some idea of what he thinks data processing is doing in his own organization.

The difficulty here in eliciting a management view of the quality of data processing lies in the fact that from data processing and its technologies, and perhaps even its products, do not have any solid basis on which to develop an opinion from inside the organization itself. The best that such management can do is, again, in terms of a bottom line, an attempt to isolate the sources of the difficulties perceived. Thus, a carefully attentive manager may discover that telephone sales performance is off significantly. He may then question those who should know why this is the case and ultimately learn that data processing has unilaterally decided to deliver a complete pricing catalog for each telephone sales category, with the net result so bulky that in a particular telephone sales session within a given category, the turnaround time on the telephone simply precludes any improvement in volume and, in fact, has caused the decrease.

This is not so subtle a reason that an interested manager could not unearth it by a moderate amount of sleuthing. What he has discovered is a data processing created situation, one that probably has a number of resolutions. It is not up to this manager to determine what the best solution is, but rather to see that the problem has been illuminated and solutions offered. For these solutions he must rely on his technical support to provide him with choices among alternatives. In this context then, such a manager may have entirely valid opinions about the quality of data processing, opinions which may carry significant weight in making data base decisions.

Data Collection: Data Processing Quality

In order to make an overall evaluation of data processing quality we use the form shown in Figure 6.1. This form is distributed to both upper management and the user community. It should be treated as a rating form and a scale of zero through ten established, with zero the worst score and ten the best. This evaluation should be applied to all of the DP products identified in the inventory. Ratings should be made here by the respondents for the particular details of the product's quality as they perceive them.

Before leaving the subject of data processing quality, it is worthwhile to point out that each of the DP products rated are in fact DP service sources. This suggests that the session in which these service sources are collected is an ideal time for receiving their individual quality and filling out the form. Then, when the service analysis interviews are conducted to develop the in-depth requirement, the interviewing team will have not only service sources as a springboard for discussion, but user opinion regarding their problems as well.

Resource Assessment

We have characterized the overall data base system project as being long term, high risk and expensive. Any data processing effort uses resources of diverse types of achieve its goal, but in view of the above it is clear that the data base system project is going to soak up the required resources over a considerably longer period of time. This is due mostly to the fact that a data base system and the data resource are not accomplished by the implementation of one organizational function under data base, but rather, by achieving some degree of data based data processing, or as we have characterized it earlier, the 80% objective. Thus, the data base system project is a complex of systems pyramided toward this goal, and as a consequence, we have on our hands what may very well turn out to be the largest consumption of various data processing resources that the organization has ever experienced.

(Rate on scale of 0-10)

DP Product	Time-liness	Com-plete-ness	Accu-racy	Applica-bility	Arrange-ment	Comments

Figure 6.1/DATA PROCESSING QUALITY FORM

Furthermore it must be pointed out that the data base system project is not executed in a vacuum, but rather must carry on in parallel with the current data processing activities, in both production and development, which provide the organization with its day to day computing support. Virtually the same resources that are required for data base are necessary for these more general data processing purposes and, as a consequence, a successful data base system project will have to find its resources as an augmentation of the organization's current data processing capacity. Experience has proven that these resources do not magically appear simply because the organization has willed a data base system project; therefore, it is properly a part of the data base survey and the overall investigation of the feasibility of a data base system project to examine what resources are available in the context of the demands that such a project is likely to make.

Available Manpower and Skill Levels

Let us suppose that our manufacturing organization has a production track record brimming with success, with management achievements to match. They have been selected as the business area to be treated first. Let us further suppose that we manufacture dashboard components for automobiles and that the period December - June is the zenith of our development and production activities. It is now mid-January and in the midst of all of the crucial activities of the business itself, data processing and manufacturing services grandly announce the advent of their data base system project.

At best, data base will not begin until July 1 and, at worst, data base will not begin at all because of the egg-on-the-face factor. It is clearly a compromising situation that easily could have been avoided by the simple expedient of assessing the resources available for the planned data base system project. In particular, the manpower resources in both the data base system client group manufacturing service and in data processing needed to be reviewed.

The personnel in manufacturing services are responsible

for formally defining the data base requirements in terms of services, and to do this they must be available for interview with the data base project team. This is not a trivial expenditure of time for manufacturing services by any means, if the subject is to be treated at any more than a casual level. It furthermore needs the time of a data base project team, but to a larger degree than that simply required to conduct interviews, take notes, and assemble results. This project team must, in fact, understand what data base means well enough to answer the client's questions on the subject that will naturally arise during the service analysis interviews.

The team must understand the need for and the context of a data base requirement, the meaning of services and the role they play in the data base system's technical development, the methods of carrying out a service analysis, and, in particular, a service analysis interview and the techniques for organizing the service analysis information into a meaningful whole that will support the data base design effort. All of which is to say that data processing manpower must be available not only to carry out the service analysis itself, but to learn how to carry out that effort as well. That is, skill levels must be raised, and very likely in an area that is essentially non-technical in the sense of data processing, but fundamentally important to the success of the data processing project.

But the service analysis is only one portion of the data base system project effort. It will be recalled that in Chapter 1 many different project activities were described in project chart form, and relative to these various project activities a number of project roles were formulated. Each of these activities require personnel for support, and the roles require training. Taken overall then, we may say that any data base system project will demand an early rough assessment of these manpower and skill requirements in order to ascertain to what degree they are available within the organization and how far it is willing to extend itself to acquire the necessary manpower increments.

Training History and Attitude

One aspect of the resource availability issue with respect to personnel is the question of raw numbers. Are people available for the numbers of man hours estimated to be required for the initial stages of the data base system project, and if not, how can these man hours be provided? Given that a solution exists in terms of personnel quantity, we must then consider the question of personnel quality.

The data base system project clearly demands skills that are generally not immediately available in most organizations. Data base is a relatively new technology in the first place and the whole concept of a data based data processing objective, as well as the data base system project, is essentially new to computing. The project encompasses many diverse roles, crosses organizational boundaries both horizontally and vertically on the organization chart, and involves a spectrum of organizational levels from upper management down to programmers and operations personnel. This breadth of jobs, the scope of the data base system project's activities, and the roles which must be played in the project's activities, and the roles which must be played in the project all imply a rather broad spectrum of skill requirements. And in one way or another the organization itself will have to provide the necessary training.

In many organizations training is institutionalized. This means that there is a training department whose sole purpose and function is to provide skill level enhancement in all functional aspects of the organization. In any firm this may stretch from assembly line training for new employees, through internal management practices for middle management personnel, to career development programs offered as a fringe benefit and further inducement for employment. Such training organizations provide the necessary instruction by a combination of professional education offered by commercial groups and training developed in-house and presented by members of the training staff. Any legitimate assessment of the available resources in the personnel area for the inauguration of a data base system project must therefore take into account the skill levels and manpower availability that exist within the training organization.

It is just as frequently the case that organizations have no formal mechanism for the upgrading of skills and rely on a hit or miss approach, with the aiming left largely up to local managers. In such cases, budgetary considerations severely impact such training decisions and one often finds skill level improvement at the bottom of the heap, if it is in the heap at all. The data base survey must ascertain if this is the case, particularly with regard to individual departments and the attitudes of their management toward training. If the training budget in the data processing department has traditionally been approximately $100 per employee per year, the training habit is not at all serious. If it is more in the region of $1500 per person per year, then it is serious indeed and the swerving of some portion of that budget in the direction of data base system training should present virtually no difficulties.

Thus, it is safe to say that an essential ingredient in this first assessment of the feasibility of a data base system project must be the nature and characteristics of the training offered by the organization and the attitude of the organization and its functional elements toward training and its support. Without training, a data base system project has little chance of success unless the organization is willing to provide most of the required resources in the form of outside consulting services. This may be suitable for the beginnings of such a project, but at some point the consultants must be replaced with in-house talent, and the training demands remain the same.

Data Collection: Current Skills Inventory

The purpose of the form shown in Figure 6.2 is to aid in the collection of information relating to the current skills available in the data processing organization. The skill areas shown in the form are associated with requirements for the design and implementation of data base systems.

- For each area, include total training separately from experience

Name	Data Base Concepts	Data Communi-cations concepts	Data Base Design	Data Communi-cation Design	Query Languages	Direct Access Methods	Higher Level Language Prog.	Data Base Language Programming

Figure 6.2/CURRENT SKILLS INVENTORY FORM

All members of the data processing organization should be included in the skills survey. For each individual and for each area on the forms two entries should be made. The first entry should be training in the area and the second, experience. A common time unit for noting training and experience is useful. The one week time period is usually most convenient so that an individual will mark a certain number of man-weeks of experience in the area.

The first four columns of the form are concerned with both data base and data communications at each of two levels. The first is the conceptual level and the second the design level. The final column of the form is concerned with programming training and experience using a data base language. This is a package language which is generally embedded in a higher level programming language, and therefore training and/or experience here implies such experience in both data base and data communications implementation.

Many people have dealt with data base systems without being aware of it. This happens when using a query language on an available data set to make reference to that data. There is no issue of the architecture of the data raised, but rather only that of the programming requirements dictated by the query language itself. This implies at least a first exposure to the notion of execution. However, because report generator systems are in fact not query language systems, and generally do not operate on data base, but rather on file oriented structures, it would be misleading to include such training or experience under this heading.

Training and experience with direct access methods is indicative of at least an initial familiarity with the concepts of keys, physical distribution, data independence (or dependence, depending on the access method employed) and some of the characteristics of design and programming entailed by direct access executions.

Finally, training and experience in the application of a higher level language is important in a data base system project since many organizations take the opportunity offered by the project to introduce not only a language standardization, but a program structure standardization as well.

Computing Resources

In the early stages of the industry's interest in commercial data base systems, it probably was true that the first users -- or perhaps experimenters -- with data base techniques were very large organizations with extremely extensive data processing capabilities. Large scale computers -- plural -- were available, and extensive external storage and associated data transfer capacities already existed. There were large operations staffs and data processing was supported by an equally large systems staff. As a consequence, one of the last concerns in considering whether or not to enter a data base system project was the availability of computing resources. Upper management naively assumed that data base was just another programming system effort, and the data processing people, ever optimistic, did not let the issues of computing resources unsettle their enthusiasms for this new and most fascinating thing called data base. But reality, of course, has a way of asserting itself, and many of these organizations soon learned that not only does a computing resource have a real capacity, but furthermore that data base and the data base system project can use it up at a great pace. Planning is demanded, and without it a computing room disaster is almost guaranteed.

As the technology developed, organizations with lesser data processing power wanted to get into data base projects as well. Here the computing resource issue is obviously far more severe, and in the initial stages many organizations merely took the attitude that, as a foregone conlcusion, data base would demand an upgrade to the next level of system size. Indeed, it is true that with an unlimited budget, the degree of planning and innovative project problem solving required is significantly reduced. If, however, funds are not available as a general solution to the computing resource questions, then intelligence must substitute, and in this regard, making some estimate of the computing resource demands of the data base system project relative to the capacity that remains to fill those demands is essential.

CPU and Disk Capacity

The CPU capacity of a given computing system is the number of time units of computation it makes available in a given period of time. If we measure the time unit in seconds and observe the system for one hour, then 3600 CPU-seconds are available. This is the CPU capacity of the system and is distributed for the execution of either applications programs, or programs of the operating system (including the communications system and any other general processing activity that cannot be classed as an application). There are also points where jobs are present in the computer but no job is able to use the CPU. Such a circumstance occurs when all jobs are awaiting the termination of their respective I/O activities. This is a condition under which we say that the CPU is cycling. Finally, when no jobs are present in the system at all, the CPU is idling.

Thus, the CPU capacity, measured in, say, CPU seconds, is distributed into four mutually exclusive, all-inclusive categories. But it is particularly important to note that the operating system load is created because of the application program load. This is also true for the cycled load. That is, without applications to execute, neither operating system nor cycle loads would have been created. Therefore, if we add any new jobs to the system, we will increase at least the operating system load, and may increase the cycle load. Since the capacity is fixed, this increase in total load due to, first, the application programs and, then, the consequent operating system and cycle loads, which must come from somewhere. Because the four categories are all inclusive and mutually exclusive, this "somewhere" is idle CPU load. In effect then, we are saying that the computing configuration, in order to support data based data processing, will have to get any incremental CPU load demanded from the currently available idle CPU load.

Of course, it is usually the case that much of our data based data processing will replace a good deal of our current non data based data processing, and therefore the incremental difference between the old loads and the new loads should be used in the estimate. At a more practical level, however, it must be recognized that old loads do not get replaced by the new data base loads simply because we have started a data base system project. Rather, the old loads remain for a substantial period of time while the data base system is designed, implemented, tested, field tested, and finally turned over. Thus, at any stage of the data base system project the current development of that stage will be imposing a positive incremental load on the computing system. This total load may then drop significantly when finally the old system is replaced by completed data base stages. Meanwhile, we had best be aware that these data base loads cause us to use up more of the available CPU capacity.

The easiest and most straightforward way to estimate the available capacity for supporting the first stages of a data base system project is to use the average idle capacity in periods of the computing day when it is expected that development, and later on data base execution for production systems, will be carried out. This represents the current remainder CPU capacity of the system, and the next step is designed to estimate the amount of that remainder capacity that might be required by the data base system project.

For this purpose, it is necessary to get a rough estimate of the amount of CPU load that is employed by the systems producing the current DP products. Then assume that the data base system that replaces it will make the same CPU computations, once the data is found. It is in this second area that the potential for CPU load savings can be provided by data base, since it is likely that the data base system will not require the formal passing of all records in the file, but rather will make a more direct access to the records that are necessary for supporting the data processing activity. Therefore, make a guess at the expected number of "hits" to satisfy the data needs of the application program. The average CPU time per record in the old system is then multiplied by this number of "hits" estimated for the new system to arrive at an order of magnitude figure for the data base programs.

As an example, let us suppose that our inventory update system in the management services group modifies about two hundred inventory items per day. We can then assume that the largest part of the CPU activity for execution of this program in a data base system context will be due to operations on these two hundred records alone, rather than on all records of the inventory file as part of the process of finding the two hundred of interest.

The issues concerning external storage, i.e., disk, are largely the same. Although the subject is somewhat more subtle, we can indeed formally define capacity characteristics for external storage which almost exactly parallel those described above for the CPU. In simplified terms, however, what it adds up to is the amount of available storage space on the disk devices.

A first reaction to the external storage space problem might be that since we use removable disks, we have only to put a blank pack on an available drive, and the problem is solved. Obviously, however, if data base operations occur when other non data base activities have used all of the disk drives for their respective storage, then this expedient will not quite work. At the very minimum, some degree of file migration is required to consolidate enough current data for these non data base systems onto a smaller number of packs so that drives are available to mount new packs devoted to data base. This consolidation might have a significant impact on the execution of the current system, and should not only be planned carefully, but certainly should be monitored after any such consolidation plan is carried out.

In looking at the data base requirements for external storage we can make some rough guesses by assuming that the total number of bytes employed will about equal those that are in the files which the data base will replace. Commonality of data should be taken into account where possible in making these estimates. The information-organization sharing matrix of Chapter 3, along with the inventory of DP products will be invaluable for this.

The process of developing a data base system project, particularly in its implementation stages, will demand that we build test data bases, and in many cases we will simultaneously build our production data bases as well. Both of these will exist in parallel with the data of the current systems that new data base system stages will replace. Hence we will have a clear need for an incremental storage capacity, at least during the development of our initial data base system stage.

Memory Capacity

In the system performance measurement field there are also well-established formal measures of memory load and memory capacity. In much the same way that we can discuss and deal with estimates for external storage capacity, we are able to look at the main frame memory capability of our system. It should be noted that the application systems we run now use memory in concert with the operating system and the other system software constituents, such as communications, that may be present. If we intend running application programs for a data base system then we must have memory available for them as well. Again, the data base system stages may not immediately replace their non data base counterparts, but will have to coexist with them through development and testing, and in fact will probably go through a parallel testing stage during which both the old and the new systems are actually co-resident within the computer. If we have a non-VS system, then the best we can do is to look at the total memory minus the requirements of the operating system and general system software and ask how much of that memory is available on the average throughout the time period of computer utilization that will be of interest to us in our initial development stages. What memory is available can then be applied to the data base system effort.

It should also be pointed out here that while the data base effort is in the development and testing stage it increases the development and testing load generally imposed on the computing system. This is possibly a special category in computing operations, but in general that load in all dimensions -- CPU, external storage, and main memory -- can be significantly higher than the loads observed on the system before the development portions of the data base system project make their impact felt.

And, finally, we must note that the data base system project is supported in its computing effort by a DBMS, or data base management system package. The purpose of the DBMS is, as described earlier in Chapter 1, to provide a basic tool for both describing and manipulating the data bases of the data base system. This package is represented by a set of programs, usually rather hefty, which reside in main memory during the execution time of the data base system. Space must therefore be made available for the DBMS, and there can be no greater embarrassment to the project than to discover that with the first stage of the data base system design and implementation well under way, installation of the selected DBMS failed simply because there was no room in the main memory for anything over 10K.

Data Collection: CPU Resource Evaluation

The previous sections have discussed several aspects of the computing resource problem which should be reviewed in the data base survey. Of these, the most important are probably CPU and memory availability. Figure 6.3 shows a data collection form which is useful for gathering information in these areas.

Each system that might be replaced by data base is named and an estimate of the CPU loads it currently imposes is made. In the third column an estimate of the CPU load created by the replacement data base system is entered, using the simple method described earlier, or by using any

System Name	Estimated Current CPU Load	Estimated Data Base CPU Load	Current Memory Req.	Estimated Memory —DB	Net CPU Load Change	Net Memory Change	Comments

Figure 6.3/CPU RESOURCE EVALUATION FORM

other valid estimate sources. The next two columns are for similar estimates of memory loads imposed. In the data base case, however, do not include the DBMS package, as that will make a single contribution to memory requirements for all data base programs. The final two columns are used to record net estimated change in both CPU and memory loads. Note that one data base function, or system of programs, may replace several current systems. In this case each of the current systems and their estimated loads should be recorded relative to the replacement data base system.

Staging Plan

Our first effort in the analysis of the information we have gathered will result in a list of candidates for data base treatment, identified as business functions aggregated into procedures.

The DP products that currently support them are reflective of the kind of support they are now getting and, with the non-DP service sources, should serve as a springboard from which to develop the formal requirements necessary for a data base system effort. However, it has to be recognized as well that in all probability the scope of the organizational area that we have covered thus far is much too broad for a single data base system stage. As a consequence it may very well be necessary to look among these several candidates in order to choose a first, and then order the rest in terms of a potential sequence of stages for data base development. The question, then, is what are our criteria for choosing our first data base stage, and then ordering the remaining candidates?

The prime consideration at the outset of our data base system project has to be the selection of an initial stage in which we minimize risk. This is important since the data base system project team must establish a track record quickly and successfully in order to maintain upper management support, user interest, and a development momentum. Therefore, minimum risk must be the primary initial criterion. It is certainly a mistake to take on some function that is crucial to the well-being of the organization, where the data base project involves massive data files and huge design and development efforts, or where application programming systems require large computing resources. In such a case, the first stage will take an inordinately long period of time to develop; whether or not it will work when the development effort is complete will be an open question until the last drop of testing has satisfied everybody in sight — and then it must perform successfully almost immediately since the function it replaces is crucial to the organization. This suggests, therefore, that our minimum risk choice is best related to small problems that do not support necessarily crucial functions. Since we have concentrated on major and crucial functions for the most part in our analyses, we are recommending the choice of a smaller major function as the best initial data base stage.

A second criterion is minimum cost. This is associated with minimum risk, but if there is a choice between two projects whose risk of success seems to be about equal, the nod should go to that one which minimizes the development dollars, and the system and personnel resources required. This will take some of the pressure off the project team to perform with speed and to perfection, since there is less risk in dollar terms.

A third criterion should be to maximize the benefit. Benefits must ultimately be discussed in terms of dollar value to the organization as a whole, and to the entities supported by data base in particular. At this point it may be difficult to find a first data base system stage with which we can identify serious benefits that allow us to say data base is therefore worthwhile. That will come as we accumulate benefits from our series of developed stages. Benefit in this context then, may mainly be related to implementing data base stages which develop a growing data resource and move toward our 80% objective for data based data processing.

These are the primary issues in making our choices for the first and subsequent stages of the data base system project. Minimum risk, minimum cost, and maximum benefit, in that order, although conservative, account for realities in most organizational circumstances. We can, however, add to this list two more general criteria which certainly can be given some thought in laying out a staging plan. The first of these is consideration of undertaking a specific data base system stage for which we expect a large return in terms of relief of current system resource utilization. This suggests that among our data base candidates we have some members which impose tremendous resource loads on our computing environment. These may be old systems using outmoded techniques, systems in emulation, or simply poor approaches to the problem in the first place. We, therefore, may have determined that data base offers an opportunity to provide extensive savings in terms of the computing resource, and this may be a very powerful motive for considering a particular functional area as a first stage. A second consideration parallels this in terms of the relief of large personnel loads to support current efforts. Here we may find that the personnel load imposed by current DP systems now supporting the business functions of a candidate area in terms of maintenance, data gathering, data preparation, and so on is excessive, and that data base offers us an opportunity to moderate these personnel loads extensively. This therefore, may become a strong factor in considering such business functions for the initial stage.

Some Additional Criteria

There are three other criteria that may be of significance in evaluating the project stage candidates. These involve investment in current systems that may be impacted by the selection, data assurance issues, and problem environments that demand a certain type of data processing.

Large Investment in Current Systems

It goes without saying that our capital investment in data processing must consistently show some return on investment. This does not necessarily mean that data processing must make a profit, but rather must have a payoff. In many organizations it is not possible to measure that payoff in monetary terms, or even in quantitative terms based on other dimensions. But service is supplied, major and crucial functions are supported, and as a consequence we can say that our investment in data processing has both point and purpose, justifying its presence in the overall organizational structure. As a consequence, it follows that we cannot casually build systems and throw them away. Such systems expend resources in terms of money, manpower, machine time, supplies, and depreciated value of plant and equipment. Therefore, to build a data processing system, put it in the field, test it, and have it accepted by our end users, and then to announce almost immediately that it will be replaced by a magical item called data base would be not only economically foolish, but politically unwise for data processing as well. Thus, if we have determined that we have large investments in systems that have just been developed, or whose development is nearing completion, and that it is these systems which indeed support areas that would otherwise be our best candidates for data base, then it is clear that data base at this time would be inopportune and all of the technical enthusiasm in the world should not override the weight of this argument.

Two Other Areas

In the course of the data base survey it may develop that there are certain areas of the organization which are involved in activities that necessarily demand degrees of data security and the maintenance of significant data privacy. These two subjects were discussed in earlier chapters. They are described briefly by saying that security has to do with the safety of the data base environment, and any user identification technique is part of the privacy environment. There are very elaborate methodologies available in both areas and in many respects they have much in common. The point here is that security and privacy are expensive to achieve in data processing terms, and particularly in data base.

If an organization does not have a security and privacy habit in its data processing — that is, if this has not been a severe requirement in any area of the organization treated with data processing thus far — then introducing these conditions as an early problem in data base presents a new set of difficulties. Security and privacy techniques require not only good data processing methodologies, but experience and management discipline within the organization using these data processing methodologies. In this sense then, we might say that if our first projects make severe security and privacy demands, then our first projects may very well run a high risk of failure.

Another point which has not been dealt with in any detail, although it has significant technical overtones, has to do with requirements for sequential processing. When we speak of sequential processing in this context we mean the passing of records of data in files, usually large, in physical sequence. The process is required to look at all records of the file, and as a consequence turns out to be an extremely expensive one in terms of the overall resources of the system. If this physically sequential processing is to work as a data processing mechanism, it is generally necessary to seize that file for this process alone. This means that the file cannot be shared with other application programs in the computing system, and as a consequence the use of the data is severely restricted. In a data base system environment sequential processing, particularly on a large scale, can be disastrous since the file is seized, the device on which the file resides is seized, extremely large channel loads are incurred, and in order to produce any kind of throughput efficiency the application program will need a high priority. In effect then, a significant segment of the entire computing system is tied up by one user and locked out to all other users. We, therefore, take the general position that sequential processing is to be avoided to the largest extent possible in the data base system environment. If we have problems whose formulations cannot be restated to avoid sequential processing, so that this data processing methodology will have to be used for the selected data base system project stage, we must raise serious questions as to the viability of data base for the associated collection of business functions. By the same token, if it turns out that our prime candidate areas depend on physically sequential processing, we may well discover that on delivery of data base systems for these areas their performance is so poor, or their impact on the performance of other systems so profound, that results will be unsatisfactory for all concerned.

Detailed Considerations

Up to this point we have used information that is directly associated with various major and/or crucial business functions of our organization. We have determined the function-organization-information relationships, and from this have developed a data resource view of the potential project stages. All of this is related to issues concerning the directions in which the data base system project should proceed, stage by stage, and has as one major objective the achievement of an overall data base system project plan.

It is one thing of course to have a plan for the data base system project and yet another to know that the general resources for that plan are available. Therefore, a second part of the analysis is to develop some idea of the skills that are available, the availability of CPU resources, and, on a large scale, some sense of the solidity of the management commitment.

Skills

A data processing organization has in it a number of diverse data processing skills. At the outset of the data base system project these skills are in all probability not well suited to the requirements of a data base effort. Therefore, we have conducted an inventory of current skills to get some feeling for the kind of experience and training that we may rely on for staffing the necessary project roles that must be played. Our skills inventory has featured those areas that are deemed to be important in the data base system proejct. Of interest are experience and training, and we are looking for the amount of experienced effort that we can bring to bear in the project relative to the amount of training that will have to be accomplished in order to bring the various stages of that project to successful conclusion. This presumes that we have some idea of the manpower required in the various skill categories to suit the needs of each of the projects stages in our project plan.

The best guideline that can be provided in this regard is to state simply that at the outset expect to use the same level of both design and implementation effort for a data base project as would be required if the development were to proceed along more traditional lines. This will be a conservative estimate to be sure, and in later stages of the data base effort as we get closer to the 80% objective, would be completely misleading. At the outset, however, it is sufficiently accurate to use in our initial estimations. As experience with data base system development is acquired in the organization, these estimates can be made accurately.

At the starting point of a data base system project it is extremely difficult to make accurate estimates of not only the manpower by skill type that will be required to complete the first several stages, but it is also difficult to make a good estimate of the calendar time to completion. But some estimate is better than no estimate at all, and such figures are necessary if we are going to give any meaning to skill requirements.

With manpower estimates in hand, we can compare the skills required to the gross skills available. This availability estimate is made from the information collected in the skills inventory. Then we must determine the availability of those individuals with the skills that we expect to use in the data base system project. This, of course, can only be determined from the supervisors in the organizations in which they work, and in this regard some negotiation may be necessary in order to free up at least a part of an individual's time for the data base effort.

Where the final computations indicate that sufficient manpower for the first stages of the data base system project will not be available, it will be necessary to either hire that talent or to train it. Given the general unavailability of data base talent in the manpower market place, it is expected that training will have to be considered. The skills inventory will, therefore, indicate where the training must be concentrated in order to satisfy the data base system project's requirements.

CPU Resources

At the 80% objective it is generally true that the imposed data processing loads on our computing system will be significantly less in total than those loads that would apply were we using nondata base methods. Reaching that point, however, may generally impose somewhat larger loads than the system is already observing. This occurs because we must design, implement, test, and install our data base system stages while nondata based data processing continues. Not only does this apply to new systems which augment our data processing capability in general, but to systems which replace current data processing capabilities. As a consequence, we need additional external storage for both testing and installed data bases, internal storage for the DBMS, and as stages are developed, for data base executions. Of course there will be additional CPU loads to accomplish those executions.

It is, therefore, the purpose of the CPU resource evaluation form to give us some basis for making estimates of the availability of our computing resource for a data base system project stage. As can be seen in that form, we are mostly interested in the net CPU load change for each of the systems that we are considering. If the data base system replaces a current nondata base counterpart, then we must consider loads imposed during the development stage as augmenting loads imposed by the systems to be replaced. Thus, the estimated current load and the estimated data base load must be added together to produce the total load on the computer. In our form, this means that the net CPU change will be positive and due entirely to the estimated data base load. At a later point where the replacement data base system is ready to cut over to production, we will then impose the net difference between the two CPU loads. If we are designing and implementing a data base system which does not replace any current data processing function, the load impact both in development and in execution is positive and is not offset by any loads being replaced. Similar guidelines for measuring the impact of the memory requirements on the data processing facility are employed as well. It must be remembered that whenever data base testing is underway, the DBMS package is present in the memory, and, as a consequence, represents a basic memory expense which must be accounted for. The application programs and their associated working storage buffers will require memory space and, as above, this may be in addition to that required by the system being replaced, ultimately providing for a net change at the cutover date.

The total CPU load change and memory load change during various periods of the staged development of the data base system project can therefore be computed. If the change is positive, then the additional CPU resource requirements must be drawn from available idle capacity. Suppose our CPU requirements are expected to go up by five hours per month for the next three months during implementation and testing of these systems. Then in each of those three months we must find sufficient idle capacity to accomodate these five hours of CPU requirement. If this time is not available in the first shift, then some shift extensions may be needed. Another alternative is to use an external data processing service for the development of portions of the system so as not to impose any new loads on the computer until final installation and testing. This raises some configuration difficulties that should be closely investigated since quite often package operations and performance are very closely linked to the specific details of a system's configuration.

Management Commitment

The final resource of interest is the commitment of upper management to the data base system project. Presumably the project has received official management blessing in the form of a funds authorization to proceed. On the other hand, management has to have a reasonable degree of understanding of what the data base commitment implies and what payoffs are to be expected. Without that, the fact that the data base system project takes a significant period to provide a visible payoff may lead to management disappointment with the project, and a less than enthusiastic support for supplying it with its necessary manpower and system resources.

The problem of educating management as to the meaning of the commitment is not an easy one and should be thought through carefully. Perhaps it is best left to outside organizations who can come in with no chips to play as a non-vested interest third party. However it is accomplished, management must understand that the data base system project is long term, high risk, and of significant expense. They must plan to see it through its first several stages to the point where the cost/benefit analysis predicts an expectation of project success in cost/benefit terms.

As to selling the data base approach and the recommended first stage project, the best route is via the current data processing experience. This is usually depicted rather vividly in terms of the data processing quality information that has been gathered in our investigation along with the data resource matrix. The first provides a manager with an opportunity to get the user's view of the quality of data processing supporting his major and/or crucial functions, and to compare their own opinions of data processing as well. It is, in fact, this comparison that will provide upper management with the special motivation needed to get involved in more direct management responsibilities relative to the data base system effort. If the message about risk and expense is clear, and an alert and interested management realizes by means of the DP quality responses that they have lost contact in this prime area of the organization, then support of the data base commitment will most surely be forthcoming. Thus, one purpose of the data processing quality form is to inform management about the data base system project and its potential for providing satisfactory and accessible data processing support to those in the organization whose functional activities are or will become dependent on data processing, and ultimately data based data processing.

The second product of the analysis effort, the data resource matrix, usually stands on its own as an inarguable component of the recommendation. In combination with the personnel and resource assessments, and the candidate selection criterion, there should be little difficulty in getting the plan accepted.

One Final Point

All of the foregoing have been intended as a general guideline to understanding the meaning of the information collected. Our overall objective is to come up with a plan for the data base system project in terms of best candidates organized in a staged development sequence. This sequence is not sacred, but should rather be reviewed as each stage is developed so that we are assured that the information that pertained when the plan was laid down is indeed valid at the current time. It also should be remembered in establishing the criteria for laying out a staging plan that weights will vary as the stages of the overall data base system effort are developed and we approach our 80% objective. At this point, remember that we expect to find a significant portion of the data, both in type and in volume, in our data base for the new stages that we take up. This may indeed alter the priority we give to the various candidates. Minimum risk may no longer be the overriding concern once we have developed a relative expertise in our organization with the structuring and building of data base system stages. Minimum cost may cease to be a serious issue since we have deferred all of the maximum cost systems because of minimum risk considerations, and at this point we may have only maximum cost crucial functions left to undertake.

CHAPTER 7
IMPLEMENTATION STAGING AND COST/BENEFIT REALITIES

Many of the organizations in our data processing community are faced with the need to make data base decisions. But these are not issues to be settled casually, no matter how compelling the technical arguments. The simple fact to be dealt with is that here, more so than in most other aspects of data processing, costs are high and must be reconciled by benefits. Furthermore, these costs are heavily loaded at the front end, with the benefits only potential until a later date that is probably well beyond successful data base system project stage testing. Three basic issues are involved:

1. There are the costs for design, development and ongoing operation.

2. Much more difficult and far less tangible are the questions concerning the benefits that can be expected.

3. Overall, there is the issue of feasible time.

As to the final point above, there is no doubt that given enough time and enough money virtually any data base system objectives can be achieved. In actuality, however, projects are not supported forever solely on the high hopes of their developers. This leads to cost/benefit reality #1:

To be successful a data base system must achieve a favorable cost/benefit ratio within a reasonable amount of time.

That there must, at some time, be a favorable cost/benefit ratio is simple common sense. Anything else is tantamount to an act of charity on the part of management. This means, then, that the time within which the project is completed should not exceed the reasonable life of the system if it were completed today. That is, if a new technology will replace our entire hardware environment in ten years, the idea of building a product on today's equipment that will be finished in twelve years makes little sense.

Thus, time is a necessary item in the cost/benefit equation. Before we can say anything definitive about it, however, we must have a more solid definition of the term "cost/benefit ratio." For this discussion we will take it to mean the ratio of the sum of all costs accrued to a certain point in time, to the total of all benefits accrued to that time. The ratio is favorable when it is less than unity.

Costs and Benefits

The costs of a data base system fall into two large categories: the costs to produce and the costs to operate. The production costs can be broken down into initial costs, implementation costs, and the finishing costs for the system at delivery. The costs to operate, are the day-to-day operating costs of the data base system once completed.

The benefits consist of two large categories as well. In the first of these are benefits from systems replaced by data base systems. In the second category are the ultimate benefits of a new system introduced into the organization's operations.

In general, we can say that a firmer grip is available for the costs than the benefits, particularly in the case of new systems. This is because the benefits of a new system are generally uncertain with regard to exactly what gains will be made, and it takes the finished product and some careful measurement to place a value on such benefits after the fact. However, in replaced systems, opportunities should exist for making reasonable benefit estimates. We will investigate the elements of making such evaluations in a later section of this chapter. For the moment we will concern ourselves with the beginnings of a data base system project implementation stage and the collection of sufficient information to make whatever cost and benefit estimates are possible. This demands a solid understanding of the data base problem so that we can determine stages for the overall implementation and then evaluate costs and benefits for each of these stages. That is, the development of a project stage begins with requirement definition.

THE SERVICE ANALYSIS

In its simplest description, a data base system is merely a mechanism for managing a collection of data that some community of users treats as a utility. The development of a data base system therefore must deal with a definition of who this community of users will be and to what purposes they will apply this data base. The objective is to gather certain information of a detailed nature that in its entirety creates a formal specification of the data base system problem. The entire procedure is referred to as a "service analysis."

Data Base System Clients

The first step of a service analysis is to identify the users, or clients of the data base system. These can be classified in two main categories: the customers of the firm and management of the firm. Each of the users in these classifications will impose distinctive requirements on the data base, and these requirements can be looked upon as services. Let us suppose, for example, that our business is warehousing, and we act as a distribution center against customer orders. Then customer inquiry about any inventory item represents one of the services that our data base system will have to perform. The acceptance of a new order from a customer is a second example of a data base system service, while a management inquiry into the dollar volume status of all orders shipped west of the Mississippi is a management service that involves data largely different from that associated with customer services. Overall, the purpose of these service descriptions is to establish user functions in relation to data requirements in the data base. To put this another way, if we are able to delineate the collection of services for a particular class of user, and the information requirements for each service, then clearly we have described in some fashion the set of data types that must be present in the data base system if the service is to be available.

Service Specification

The basic motivating forces behind the service analysis approach are the delineation of classes of clients for a data base system, the collection of services that they will individually demand of it, and for each of these services the identification of the information that must be represented in the data base by data elements if these service requirements are to be satisfied. We refer to these information requirements for satisfying services as "information elements." These information elements will map into data elements in the data base system as discussed in the opening sections of Chapter 3.

Thus, a service for a particular client class will correspond to some set of "information elements" with suitable data in the data base if the service is to be supplied. However, we can go further in our service-information elements description by setting out a specification of the frequency with which a particular service is called for. Since each service corresponds to a set of data elements of the data base, frequency information about our services, therefore, tells us something about the frequency of reference to data elements.

We can add two more specification details to our service analysis description. The first of these is referred to as "information availability" and the second as "function."

Information availability in its roughest description is

merely the turnaround or response time requirement for a particular service. However, the meaning implicit in the term is contained in the word "information." That is, the data base deals in data, while information is some form of synthesized structural relationship among data that has meaning to its user. To put this differently, for data to become information in the eyes of the beholder, some mechanism in the data base system must not only collect all the necessary data, but convert and arrange it into forms suitable for use as information by its recipient. Thus the data in the data base is signatory of information, and the services that are involved in our data base system are, from the user's point of view, related to information and not data. Therefore, the notion of information availability is that of the response time to receive the "information" of a request, translate it into machineable form, act on the parameters of that form in the context of the data base system, retrieve all data necessary to the satisfaction of the request, and finally to formulate and deliver the results as information to the user. The notion of information availability, therefore, relates to the idea of how available to a user of the data base system is the information that its data holdings represent.

The function description of a service represents a specification of the required operations on the several information elements in order to deliver that service. That is, we have a set of information elements associated with a particular service, and the function portion of the description is an informal specification of the way in which those information elements are to be employed in order to bring them together in the required form and format for the user. Out of a collection of information elements for a service, some of these may be specified as inputs (keys) and others as output. Furthermore, these inputs and outputs may then be sorted on certain criteria and placed in specific positions on the output page. In essence then, the functional portion of the service description may be thought of as a programmer's "process chart" specification for producing the particular service.

In summary, we see that the data base will have a collection of clients, and each client can be associated with a collection of services. Each service has four specification dimensions: frequency, information availability, information elements, and function.

The Service Analysis Book

Each major client classification of a service analysis can generally be broken down into finer subcategories that imply, individually, a collection of services that have properties or qualities in common. For example, our warehouse inventory may contain items that are categorized by type, such as electronic, industrial, household, and so on. Customers for these various types of inventory items may, therefore, have very different inquiry requirements depending on the type of item involved. For instance, let us consider a service that we might refer to as "delivery data." If the reference is to heavy machinery, delivery data must involve the method of delivery, physical dimensions for determining point of delivery, loading requirements and restrictions, and so on. This, of course, is a different set of delivery data than that required for a stereo amplifier. If such distinctions can be made in terms of customer categories, it is useful to segregate such customers, and to associate with these subcategories the set of services that are germane. There is in fact nothing lost if services are duplicated for customers of differing categories, and as will be pointed out later, the more categories the better.

In the management service area, the distinctions are more straightforward. In an organization there will be many interests in the data base on the part of financial management, marketing, sales, customer relations, personnel, payroll, etc. Each of these has a set of particular services to apply to the data base and its system, and therefore lend themselves to segregation into such groups. In fact, recalling the description of the functional decomposition, it will be recognized that its results, when mapped into the organization chart via the function-organization sharing matrix, do indeed create this segregation. And at this point, it should be evident that the distinction between customer and managerial services is equivalent to the distinction between the source and derived data types of Chapter 2.

A completed service analysis is represented by a book of services that defines the clients of the data base system, and for each of these clients the set of services that the system is to supply. For each service appearing in the service analysis book, we furthermore have gathered information concerning the frequency with which the service is called for, the information availability requirement for the service, the set of information elements that must be represented somewhere in the data base as data elements if the service is to be supplied completely, and finally the functions to be executed on these information elements in order to deliver the service. The complete service analysis book then represents a central compendium of all information about the data base system project stage development. In fact, it is a complete specification of user requirements for the project stage.

Service Analysis Fallout

It should be noted again that the information elements listed for services will ultimately appear in the data base system as data elements. Of course, there will be some degree of usage redundancy in these data elements; i.e., individual data elements will be referenced by a number of different services. This corresponds directly to the earlier relationship described in Chapter 3, of information elements to organizational units and service sources. Once information elements in services have been identified with data elements, individual services are identified with these data elements, and the process described in Chapter 3 can be applied. To review this process for data elements, suppose that we write the alphabetic string, or descriptor of the data element on a three-by-five card along with the service to which it refers. Then every service will have one card present for each of its associated data elements. Now sort all of these three-by-five cards alphabetically by data element descriptor. The result will be that all data elements that are common throughout the service analysis description will appear in a group within the sorted result. As an example, let us suppose that equipment number is the descriptor of one of our data elements and that this data element appears in five different services of our service analysis. In the sorting we will discover five cards for equipment number, with each of these cards referring back to their respective services.

It should be immediately evident that one fallout from the service analysis is information regarding the degree of usage redundancy implied by the services to be supplied by the data base system. Furthermore, the sorting process has indicated the degree of usage redundancy with respect to each of the data elements that will appear in the data base system. Now we can say that if there is no usage redundancy in any of these data elements, it is clear that there is no need for a data base system. That is, there is virtually no community of users of the data since each service requires its own unique set of data elements. This, of course, should have been evident at the information-organization level of the earlier data resource investigation.

More generally of course, there will be redundancy to a greater or lesser degree, depending on the particular set of services to be supplied. This degree of redundancy can be noted on one of the cards in a redundant data element set along with the set of services to which it refers. The remaining redundant cards can then be set aside. The result of this operation is a unique set of data elements with notations giving the degree of redundancy and the set of services with which each is associated.

The development of a data base system is a long term affair. It is undoubtedly the case that over this period of development the respective clients of the data base system will begin to consider other approaches to their own individual operations that take into account the imminent availability of the data base facilities. This in turn may lead these clients to consider modifications to their requirements as originally stated. Thus the service analysis book, as a central source for these requirements, offers the data base system development team a unique opportunity to negotiate and record all such changes. More importantly, the negotiation of such changes can be made in a context well beyond that of an isolated service, for it can take into account overall system requirements, other similar services, and perhaps even variations in the particular service in question. That is, the service analysis book provides an excellent opportunity to create and maintain an ongoing rapport with the clients of the data base system. This is an essential element for success in such a project and represents a truly valuable fallout from the service analysis procedure.

It follows that if all modifications negotiated into the service analysis book are recorded in that book as of the date of change, then in the development of the data base system project the book is at every stage of the development current and up to date, and serves as a user requirement specification. As a consequence, at the conclusion of the project development the service analysis book serves as the necessary beginnings for user documentation. It furthermore provides the basis for acceptance testing for the user community.

Implementation Project Stages

The service analysis also provides information that is valuable in initiating the design for the data base system project stage. An example of one design approach is based on the frequency information gathered as part of the service analysis. To see this, go back to the three-by-five cards sorted together into common data element groups. It will be recalled that each service is associated with a frequency, and therefore each data element can be associated with that frequency as well. For example, let us suppose that the equipment number data element appears in several services. In one of these suppose that the frequency is 600 times per day. Then for this service we may associate equipment number data element with this frequency of reference. That is, in order to supply the particular service 600 times a day it will be necessary to refer to this data element, among others, that many times as well. Thus each card in the equipment number group will give its respective frequency of reference. We can, therefore, add all of these frequencies together and record this on the one unique equipment number card. We then retain this as the total frequency of reference to this data element for all services to be supplied by the data base system project stages. Let us suppose that this has been carried out for each of the unique data elements and that we now sort all of these three-by-five data element cards by frequency. The result will be all of our data elements in frequency of reference order, and we can now turn our attention to possibilities for association of the data elements into groups that might then be considered as potential files of our data base system.

The Implementation Staging Process

The criteria for this first analysis of data elements into files is based on approximate common frequency of reference. That is, if some data element A in our data base is going to be referred to 2,000 times per day, we must seriously question the placement of that data element in the same record with data element B that is referred to only 10 times per day. In this case we would find that 1990 times per day we have read data element B for no good purpose. This will require additional main memory, additional data transfer time between the devices and the main memory, and additional time to traverse a larger record on the storage device during searching operations. To elaborate this final point, suppose that with a certain set of frequently used data elements requiring 50 bytes we have associated a second set of data elements of very low frequency of utilization requiring 20 bytes. Then the total record size will be 70 bytes. Now suppose that we have 100,000 such records. Then we will require 7 million bytes to store these records, and to find any one of them we would require searching across the span of cylinders on the disk that would be to hold it. If, on the other hand, we restrict our records to only those data elements of a relatively common high frequency, then we have clearly shortened the size of the file that must be searched 2,000 times per day to supply us with our records, and as a consequence the amount of search time required should be significantly reduced.

Actually, this type of frequency analysis is more often used as a refinement or optimization technique for a given data base design. Other methods, known as "entity/attribute" and "normal form" analysis are usually employed at the outset. The technologies of these methods, however, put them beyond the scope of this book. But whatever approach is employed, the service analysis provides a first cut at the distribution of data elements into data base files. After this first distribution there are other criteria that have to be accounted for. Let us conceive of the distribution of the data elements into files as being equivalent to the separation of the three-by-five data element cards into individual piles representing data elements that we expect will go together. Our first approximation for this distribution might be on the basis of a relatively common frequency of access, or any of the other procedures available. Thus we divide our complete set of data element cards into a collection of subsets. Now place these piles of data element cards on a large table and write one three-by-five card for each service that appears in the service analysis book and put them around the edge of the table in groups by client category. The next step is to relate the data elements in the files to the services they support. The objective is to determine a group of files whose data elements are sufficient to satisfy all of the needs of the complete set of services for one or more client categories. Such a group of files should not, and probably will not, include all files. But the file group will be determined by the set of services that we are seeking to satisfy.

To illustrate this procedure, the circles in Figure 7.1 each represent a proposed file, and the boxes each represent a set of services for a client category. For the client category A involving services S1, S2, S3, the solid lines in

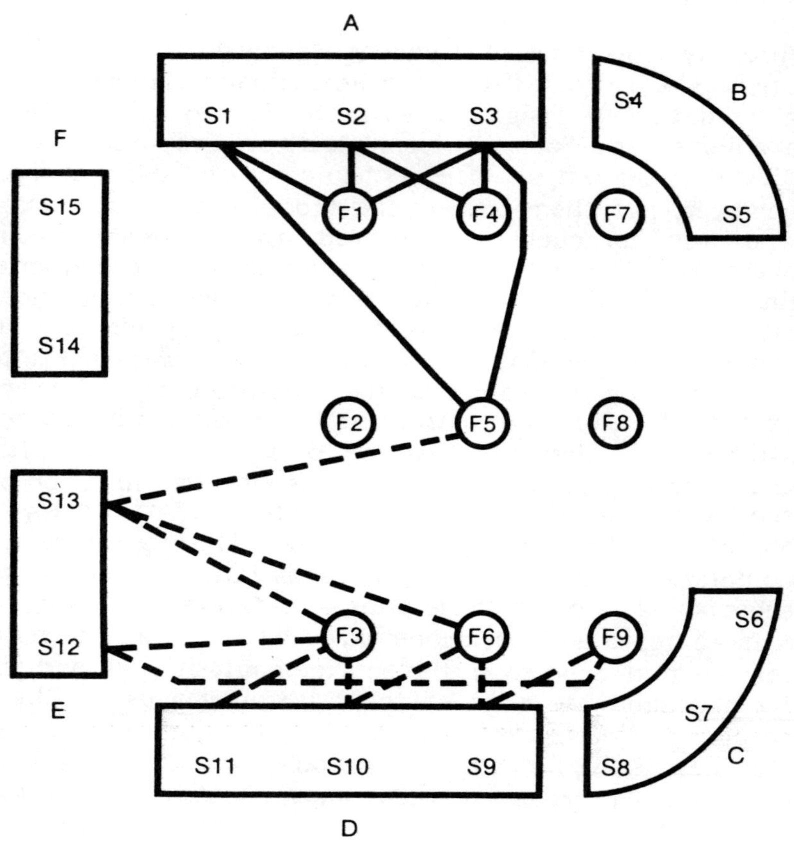

Figure 7.1/PROJECT ARCHITECTURE

the figure lead to files in which the required data elements are to be found. For example, to satisfy service S3, references will have to be made to files F1, F4 and F5. Furthermore, these three files jointly satisfy all of the requirements for the remaining services of this category. We therefore could consider these three files for implementation as one stage of the project. The completion of this stage would then satisfy client category A, so that on delivery, benefits from this stage could be derived.

The broken lines in this figure show that client categories D and E relate to data elements F3, F6, F9 and F5. Let us suppose that sufficient benefits can be realized only if both of these categories are implemented jointly in a common stage. Now assume that client category A was to be done first. Then we must develop an implementation for files F3, F6, F9 followed by an integration with this first stage through file F5 which is common to both. This is the general pattern for a staged development: implementation followed by integration.

Suppose now that in order to meet the information availability requirements for services S9 and S10 it is determined that a certain file organization for file F6 is required. Suppose further that service S13 cannot reference its data elements in file F6 under this organization at a rate that is suited to its own information availability requirements. Then the corresponding data element cards can be moved from file F6 to some other file, or they can be used to form a new file. If the service has data elements in common with services S9 and S10, these data element cards can be reproduced and then placed in other files. In this case we are creating a degree of redundancy, but to an explicit purpose.

In the opening sections of Chapter 6 it was pointed out that individual functions of the functional decomposition have natural groupings into business procedures. In Chapter 1 we introduced the idea of complete benefit groups, and in the above discussions have developed client groups around service sets that correspond to file sets that have been structured by the data base design. It should be evident on reflection that these client groups are best defined as the set of users participating in a specified business procedure, and that they then will form a complete benefit group.

The above described procedure is thus a simulation of sorts, representing the effect of our distribution of data elements, and possibly redundant data elements, into files. When this operation has been carried out to a stage of completion that satisfies the designer, he should then find that there are groups of files. Obviously these data elements, their files, and the associated services can be considered as a stand alone element in the staged implementation of the data base system. More specifically, we may remove such service pages from the service analysis book and form a service analysis "sub-book" which will then provide precisely the fallout items described earlier, and that will further stand as a service analysis book for a particular implementation stage of the data base system project development.

Thus an additional fallout from the service analysis procedure is information for distributing data elements into files, associating these files with complete benefit groups and constructing sub-books of the service analysis that can then be considered as independent development stages in the overall data base system product. We now have to determine an overall plan for the staged design and implementation of each of these data base system "pieces." All of these points, however, lead us to reality #2:

A service analysis is the preliminary step in any data base development project.

An Implementation Staging Example

Let us suppose that we have completed a service analysis for a certain area of our organization and have determined that there are very distinct stages in which the implementation development can be accomplished. We will refer to these as stages A, B, and C. Then the division of the service analysis book into three sub-books, each of which corresponds to the set of services to be supplied by the particular implementation stage, and represents our basic document for the work on each of these stages. The accomplishment of all three stages will then correspond to the implementation of the entire data base system project stage.

Let us suppose that for our stages we have determined the following individual requirements:

STAGE A - Data conversion is required.
- Current manpower is sufficient.
- Current hardware is sufficient.

STAGE B - Data must be originated.
- Data conversion is required.
- New implementation manpower is required.
- Current hardware is sufficient.

STAGE C - Data conversion is required.
- Current manpower is sufficient.
- New hardware is required.

In this example we have presumably accomplished a complete service analysis and distributed the data elements into files for stages to be carried out in the sequence given above, and therefore our next problem is to estimate the required development time for each of these stages. From the example, however, we can express reality #3:

A data base system project has to be staged according to manpower, resource, and data criteria.

That is, in our consideration of which of several available stages to put next in the sequence we must consider these three fundamental aspects of any development stage of the data base system. Overall, however, it is safe to say that we should attempt to minimize the risk that a next stage represents. Therefore we would like to minimize the additional manpower required, the number of computing resources to be utilized, and the amount of data to be originated or converted. For our example, let us suppose that we are able to make the scheduling estimate shown in Figure 7.2. The figures above each end point of the line segments indicate the months at which the particular stage is completed, and the figures below the end points of the line segments indicate the starting point for the next stage.

Costs and Benefits

The staging of a data base system project to arrive at a representation as shown in the example of Figure 7.2 is no easy task and generally requires a basic knowledge of the amount of time that will be required to accomplish each of the elements of the particular stage. We will elaborate many of the areas in which costs are involved and these can be taken as areas for time expense as well. That is, these are points at which development time will be expended. Included in this as a set of general categories is the manpower time to design and implement, data origination, data conversion and/or installation time, and finally the lead time necessary to acquire any additional system resources that may be required to complete the development of a particular stage. For the moment, however, it is assumed that sufficient information is at hand so that we are able to complete a staged implementation plan for each of the service analysis stages that represent milestones in our total project development. Therefore we are able to say that through the development period of the given stage we will create the cost of that development, and with the completion of this stage we may then consider that we begin to derive benefits from the completion of that stage. This is also indicated in Figure 7.2 for each of the stages.

The Development Cost Elements

In concert with the effort to establish an implementation staging for the development of the data base project, we must also make an attempt to identify the several cost

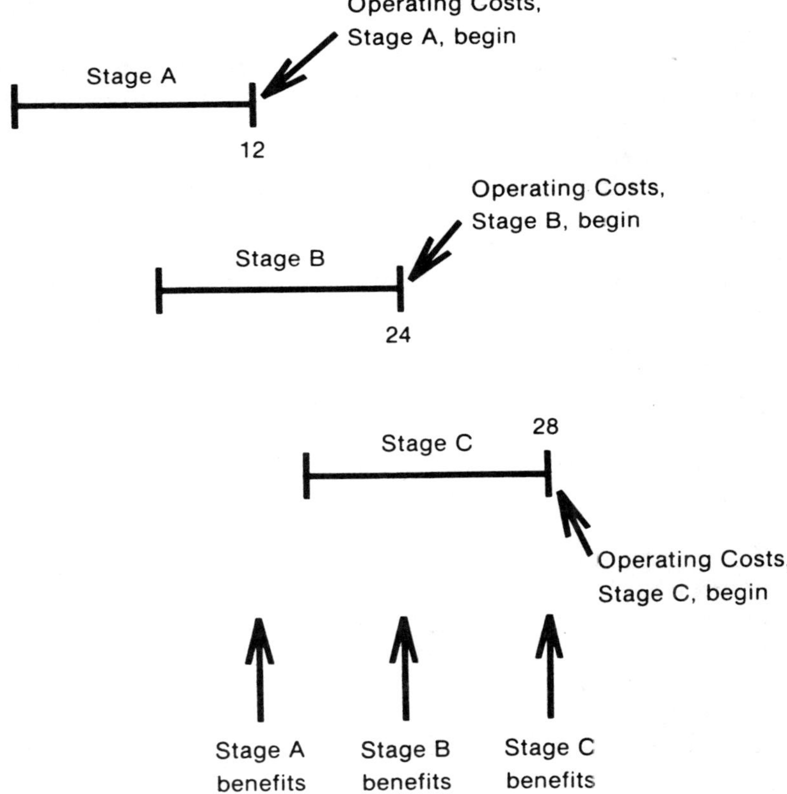

Figure 7.2/BENEFIT SCHEDULE

details that the development will entail. These can be discussed in three major categories. These are initial costs, front end costs, and finishing costs.

The initial costs are one time only and involve data base survey, the completion of the service analysis, and the development of a package evaluation and final selection. None of these is trivial, and all are necessary in any carefully developed data base system project. This is particularly true with respect to the service analysis, which is perhaps the one area in which over emphasis is not possible. In fact, it can safely be stated that a successful service analysis carried through to completion, probably implies an ultimately successful data base system.

The choice of DBMS must be made with the business functions in mind to which the package will be applied. This implies that criteria for selection have been developed, and evaluation procedures applied to each of the packages under consideration. In all of these areas, care must be taken, and therefore the careful attention of personnel is required. This in turn implies areas of initial costs for the data base system project.

The front end costs involved in the development of a particular implementation stage of the data base system must involve design, data origination, data conversion, data verification, implementation and module testing. The cost impact of most of these should be evident. But particular emphasis must be placed on costs that will be associated with data. When we speak of data origination, we mean the creating of data in machineable forms and formats from broad data sources. Such sources may be handwritten or typewritten material, carried in paper files, or in other media such as microfilm. The effort and consequent cost involved to realize such data in machineable form can be extreme and must definitely be accounted for.

Data conversion involves the reformatting of data in one machineable media to satisfy the purposes in a second machineable media. Thus, tape files must be converted to data base files in the sense that the data in tape files must be changed to the required formats and then the data of these records must be distributed over the several files of the data base. And finally, with respect to data and its costs, it is necessary to include the effort required to verify that the data is correct and correctly placed, and that its format and general syntax is proper. This is especially true if the data has been originated from a noncomputing source.

The remaining front end costs involve implementation of the data base system and the testing of the individual modules to bring the whole to the state of tested completion.

Finally, there are the finishing costs. These are costs that are too easily neglected, or disregarded as negligible in a computing system project and may assume significant proportions in a data base system context. The finishing costs involve system testing, parallel operations, and the documentation of the finished project.

When we test the data base system, it is necessary to insure that actions in one portion of the system have precisely understood effects in other portions. In particular, we are concerned with knowing that satisfaction of services, particularly those which in some way modify the data base, is carried off successfully and to completion. Furthermore, we must be certain that such services are satisfied in accordance with the service analysis conditions laid down as a user specification of requirements for the system as a whole.

Parallel operation refers to the process of turning the system over to the users, particularly in that context in which the current system is being replaced by the data base system. Here we seek to operate with the same set of inputs and to produce comparable outputs using the replacement data base system. To operate in parallel means that we must be able to operate both systems "concurrently," at least to a sufficient degree to determine that the replacement results measure up to those which they replace, and at the same time completely satisfy user requirements. The documentation of the data base system is of course an absolute necessity. In particular, as a finishing cost effort we must remember to document the data base system for its users. The service analysis stands as an initial effort in this direction insofar as it specifies services by benefit group (and business procedure), and the conditions under which the services will be delivered.

Operating Cost Elements

Once a stage of the data base system has been delivered we can, as pointed out earlier, expect to accrue benefits. However, there are additional ongoing or operating costs to be associated with each delivered stage that go beyond the personnel to operate the equipment. It requires personnel to maintain the data base system and to provide for reorganization, reloading and recovery when necessary. All these operations, or course, will employ the computer, and therefore we must associate with the data base system certain ongoing operating costs for machine usage.

The data base administration function not only requires personnel, but will in addition require the use of the computer for maintenance of the data dictionary, collection of operational statistics, and so on. The data base administrator must publish his conclusions regarding the usage and operations of the system. This usually takes the form of policies, and these policies must be enforced. These are only a few of the many operating costs areas that may be associated with the data base administration function.

Finally, an ongoing cost for a developed stage of this system will be the cost of the data base management package that is employed in its implementation. These packages may be purchased outright, in which case the ongoing cost is reflective of the depreciation rate for the package, or it may be leased. In either event, the package has a cost, and that cost may relate to maintenance of the package as well as to maintenance of the system, and will surely involve machine utilization. Certainly the package imposes a number of decisions on the data base administrator regarding its utilization, and thus indirectly creates operating costs in the data base system.

Some General Costs

The foregoing discussions have been related to costs directly associated with the delivery and operation of a stage of a data base system. However, there are some lifecycle costs which will continue throughout the existence of the system and they should be identified and recognized. These costs are for staffing, education and documentation.

Staffing requires the location and employment of sufficient talent at a suitable level to satisfy the needs of an expanding and developing data base system project. It is clear that data base systems which are successful tend to suggest their own additions and extensions. Furthermore, data base system projects extend over a number of years and involve relatively large numbers of technical people. For both of these reasons, then, staffing must be a definite concern in the planning of the data base system.

Education, particularly at the present stage of the industry's development of data base systems, must also be considered as a necessity. To date there is a relatively small number of professional talent with sufficient experience in the development of data base systems. This suggests that staffing alone will probably not be sufficient to bring a project up to suitable development levels. Organizations must therefore concern themselves with educational plans for raising the talent level of individuals already in the company so as to fill out these staffing requirements. This is a good idea in metropolitan areas where there is generally a large pool of professional talent and a relatively high turnover. In such an environment, educational opportunities offered by an organization may serve as additional fringe benefits for attracting individuals of interest to the organization.

Finally, documentation must be stressed. A data base system is a complex and dynamic entity. It represents a utility that stands as a community of data for a community of users. The successful data base system is one in which this means that documentation must be developed to keep pace with such growth, and such documentation must be of a quality and nature to in fact pace that growth. Furthermore, documentation must now relate to data, and in such a way that it is both readily understandable and immediately usable to those who are involved with data. This means that documentation must be designed not only for the technical users of the data base system, i.e., the application program and system maintenance people, but for the end users as well in terms of their information needs as reflected by services. Keeping such documentation up to date and effective is no mean task, and must be reckoned with in the planning.

Benefits

The identification of costs in the data base system is a relatively easy task to accomplish. If there is a plan for system development which is reasonably well understood, then the technical analysis of the approach to achieving that plan will, as a byproduct, produce several areas where costing has to be accounted for, and as a result we can develop an overall estimate of the cost in each of our stages in the process. Benefits, however, are generally more difficult to come by. Here it is only possible to identify some areas that can be conceived of as being applicable to benefit analysis. The general benefit areas that can be identified are listed below:

Personnel Savings
Improved Services
Resource Utilization Improvement
New Functional Capabilities
Expansion Capabilities
Standardization
Organizational Efficiencies

This list is intended only as a suggestion of the areas from which benefits of a data base system may be derived. A particular organization must look into each of these with respect to its current data base system project plans to determine whether such benefits are indeed applicable, and if so, to what degree such benefits might be realized in dollar terms.

A COST BENEFIT MODEL

An Example

In earlier sections we discussed the service analysis procedure and then assumed that the service analysis technique had been employed to develop an implementation staging for a particular project. The result was identified as stages A, B, and C. The next task was to develop an estimate of the scheduling for these stages, which for this example was illustrated in Figure 7.2. Then we went on to discuss in general terms the several elements of costs and benefits that must enter into our calculations. We now consider stage A and look at some details of cost development for this particular stage. These costs are shown in Figure 7.3.

In this example, the costs for data conversion, manpower and finishing have been computed, and the total cost for the development of this stage is shown at $226,950.00. Referring to Figure 7.2, we see that the development period is twelve months, at the end of which time operating costs for the stage will begin as well as benefits to be derived. It is assumed that we are able to make a similar calculation for stages B and C as well. Figure 7.4 shows the development costs for the stages. In Figure 7.4 we have also included the completion dates, the operating costs estimated for each stage, development costs depreciated over a 36 month period, and finally an estimate of benefits. We have not gone into the details of the cost of development for the last two stages, but have instead presented only the resulting figures.

Stage A

Data Conversion

Transcription 5 people, 2 months, @ 2.50 hr.	$ 4,000
Keypunching 45K cards @ $ .10	4,500
Programming 3 mm @ $2,500	7,500
Machine time 15 hrs. @ $175	2,625
Clerical time 1 person, 3 mos., @ $650	1,950
Management time 1 person, 3 mos., (¼ time) @ $3000	6,750
	$27,325

Manpower

Design 2 people, 3 mos., @ $3000	$ 18,000
Programming 4 people, 9 mos., @ $2500	90,000
Clerical 1 person, 10 mos., @ $650	6,500
Machine Time 50 hrs., @ $175	8,750
Management 1 person, 9 mos., @ $3000	27,000
	$150,250

Finishing Costs

System testing 3 people, 2 mos., @ $2500	$15,000
Parallel operation 25 hrs. @ $175	4,375
Documentation 3 people, 3 mos., @ $2000	18,000
Delivery 2 people, 3 mos., @ $2000	12,000
	$49,375

Stage A total = $226,950

Figure 7.3/STAGE COSTS

Stage	Development Cost	Completion Date (mos.)	Operating Cost ($/mos.)	Amortized Development 36 mos. ($/mos.)	Benefits ($/mos.)
A	226,950	12	1850	6300	12,550
B	306,825	14	1490	8520	9,800
C	182,100	8	1720	5060	11,050

Figure 7.4/COST/BENEFIT SCHEDULE

Figure 7.4 shows that the development cost for stage B is $306,825.00, and that it will require 14 months to complete. From Figure 7.2 we also see that we are able to initiate stage B at approximately the tenth month in the development of stage A. This implies that the necessary design talent from stage A becomes available at this time for application to stage B. It also has been determine in Figure 7.4 that the operating cost for stage B, once completed, is $1,490.00 per month, and that amortization of the total cost over a 36 month period creates a continuing monthly cost of $8,520.00. The estimated benefits from the completion of stage B amounts to $9,800.00 per month.

Using the figures shown for all three stages we can now approach the development of a cost/benefit model that accounts for feasible time.

Cost/Benefit

Figure 7.5 is a reproduction of Figure 7.2 in which the initiation and termination points of each stage are shown by month and by quarter. To develop a cost/benefit model, therefore, we must at each month add up the accumulated depreciated costs and operating costs, if any. In addition, any accrued benefits are accumulated as well. Referring to Figure 7.5, at the end of the first quarter of the implementation efforts stage A has been initiated and has accrued three times its monthly depreciation cost. This is shown in Figure 7.4 to be $6,300.00 per month, so that the total accrued cost at the end of the first quarter will be $18,900.00. By the end of the third quarter of the project's implementation a total of $56,700.00 has been accrued, all of which is due to the monthly depreciation figure charged against stage A. In the fourth quarter, starting at month 10, however, stage B has been initiated. From this point on, depreciation charges for this stage will be accrued in addition to the depreciating development charges for stage A. This continues up to month 12, after which the operating costs for stage A begin to accrue as well.

Figure 7.5/DEVELOPMENT SCHEDULE

Figure 7.6 is a tabulated summary of all of these costs and the associated accrued benefits. The figure has comments on the left and the tabulation is carried out by quarter. For example, in the fifth quarter the total costs are $50,010.00. This represents three months of operating costs for stage A and three months of development costs for stage B. The total accumulated costs to the end of this quarter are $142,650.00 representing accrued development costs charged to stage A thus far over the 15 month period, the three months of operating costs charged to stage A, and the five months of accrued development costs for stage B. It will also be noted in this table that a total benefit has been accrued in this quarter for the three months of operation of stage A. This amounts to $37,650.00. Taking the ratio of the accumulated costs ($142,650.00) to the accumulated benefits ($37,650.00) we get a cost/benefit ratio at the fifth quarter of 3.8.

In the 20th month, which falls within the seventh quarter, stage C is initiated. Up to this point eight months of benefits have been accrued from the completion, delivery and subsequent operation of stage A, while 20 months of development costs for stage A have been accrued. Ten months of development costs for stage B have been accrued to this point as well. The table also shows that at the end of the seventh quarter $247,730.00 of total cost has accumulated while $112,950.00 of total benefit has accumulated. Therefore, the cost/benefit ratio at this point of the project development is 2.2.

The table indicates a progressive reduction of the cost/benefit ratio up to the 13th quarter. At this point, the complete development cost for stage A has been amortized, while its operating costs and its benefits continue. Furthermore, stage B and stage C have been completed, and therefore their respective operating costs and benefits are also accumulating. However, both of these stages have yet to amortize their respective development costs, so that these continue to be added into the total accumulated cost figures. By this time, however, sufficient benefit has accumulated so that the cost/benefit

Comment	Quarter	Cost/Q	Accum. Cost	Benefit	Accum. Benefit	Ratio
Start Stage A	1	$18,900	18,900	—	—	—
	2	18,900	37,800	—	—	—
	3	18,900	56,700	—	—	—
Stage B Started	4	35,940	92,640	—	—	—
Stage A Operating Costs and benefits started	5	50,010	142,650	37,650	37,650	3.8
	6	50,010	192,660	37,650	75,300	2.6
Stage C Started	7	55,070	247,730	37,650	112,950	2.2
	8	65,190	312,650	37,650	150,600	2.1
Stage B Operating Costs & benefits started	9	69,660	382,580	67,050	217,650	1.8
Stage C Operating Costs & benefits started	10	73,100	455,680	89,150	306,800	1.5
	11	74,820	530,500	100,200	407,000	1.3
	12	74,820	605,320	100,200	507,200	1.2
Stage A Amortized	13	50,370	655,690	100,200	607,400	1.1
	14	50,370	706,060	100,200	707,600	.99

Figure 7.6/COST/BENEFIT MODEL

ratio has been reduced to 1.1. We then see that at the end of the 14th quarter the cost/benefit ratio becomes favorable at .99.

Accommodating Feasible Time

In the foregoing example, the favorable cost/benefit ratio occurs at the close of the 14th quarter. Let us assume for the purpose of example that the feasible time period for this project is 36 months, so that the cost/benefit ratio must be favorable by the close of the 12th quarter. The question is, what can be done to modify the point at which the cost/benefit ratio becomes favorable so that it occurs within this required feasible time?

Returning to the table of Figure 7.4, we see that by initiating the project with stage A, we selected a relatively high development cost over a relatively long period for completion, and the highest of the three operating costs. This stage also has the highest of the benefits. However, stage C not only has the smallest development costs, but also the shortest period to complete. Therefore, we might consider initiating our development with stage C, followed by stage A and finally by stage B. In these circumstances stage C will begin accruing benefits after the eighth month, rather than after the 12th. This rearrangement of the schedule might then make a significant difference in the time at which the cost/benefit ratio becomes favorable. The final result, of course, is dependent on the rest of the scheduling. The point here is that by trying out various scheduling plans we can then determine the particular schedule that provides the earliest occurrence of a favorable cost/benefit ratio.

A second approach to modifying the time of occurrence of a favorable ratio so as to accommodate a specified feasible time is to rearrange the planning for particular stages so as to cut costs or to improve benefits. As an ancilliary approach, we might consider raising the development costs of a stage by increasing the personnel assigned. This makes sense if the increase in effort results in a significant foreshortening of the development period. In this case the stage is delivered at an earlier point and therefore benefits will begin to accrue at an earlier time.

Remark on the Service Analysis

It was said at the outset of the service analysis discussion that our interest centered on client classes that could be identified with complete benefit groups, and that for each we would establish a chapter of the service analysis book. Furthermore, it was suggested that the number of groups be kept large. As a consequence, the set of services for each class would therefore be reduced. Later on in the development of the service analysis technique it was pointed out that in order for a particular stage to be established as a stand alone unit of the overall development, it is necessary that the set of all services provided by that stage's development and delivery be complete. That is, if the set of services were complete for a given benefit group or set of groups, then on delivery, clients could use the system and therefore benefits would be accrued. With respect to these benefit groups, then, the minimum stage would have to encompass all services of the category. Clearly, if we have broken down the set of all clients into a large number of categories, then each of our stages can be relatively smaller. This leads us to expect that each development period would be relatively smaller as well, so that benefits from the particular development for a given client category, or group of them, would occur early in the development cycle. This suggests that the general approach to the service analysis should seek to provide a large number of smaller, lower cost, more quickly completed, data base system stages. The result would then be benefits that begin at earlier points in the overall development cycle.